# THE ICONIC OBAMA, 2007–2009

# The Iconic Obama, 2007–2009

*Essays on Media Representations of the Candidate and New President*

*Edited by*
NICHOLAS A. YANES *and*
DERRAIS CARTER

McFarland & Company, Inc., Publishers
*Jefferson, North Carolina, and London*

LIBRARY OF CONGRESS CATALOGUING-IN-PUBLICATION DATA

The iconic Obama, 2007–2009 : essays on media representations of the candidate and new president / edited by Nicholas A. Yanes and Derrais Carter.
    p.    cm.

Includes bibliographical references and index.

**ISBN 978-0-7864-4602-5**
softcover : acid free paper ∞

    1. Obama, Barack — In mass media.  2. Presidents — United States — Press coverage.  3. Political campaigns — United States — Press coverage.  4. Presidents — United States — Election — 2008.  5. Mass media — Political aspects — United States.  6. Press and politics — History — 21st century. 7. Social networks.  I. Yanes, Nicholas A., 1982–  II. Carter, Derrais.
E908.3.I36 2012
973.932092 — dc23        2012014908

BRITISH LIBRARY CATALOGUING DATA ARE AVAILABLE

© 2012 Nicholas A. Yanes and Derrais Carter. All rights reserved

*No part of this book may be reproduced or transmitted in any form or by any means, electronic or mechanical, including photocopying or recording, or by any information storage and retrieval system, without permission in writing from the publisher.*

On the cover: President Barack Obama, November 23, 2009 (Photograph by Chuck Kennedy)

Manufactured in the United States of America

*McFarland & Company, Inc., Publishers*
  *Box 611, Jefferson, North Carolina 28640*
    *www.mcfarlandpub.com*

For my friends, family,
mentors, teachers and professors
— *Nicholas A. Yanes*

\* \* \*

To Rosie L. Carter,
Dolly Young and Elois Miller
— *Derrais Carter*

# Table of Contents

*Acknowledgments* . . . . . . . . . . . . . . . . . . . . . . . . . . . . . . . . . . . xi
*Introduction*
    DERRAIS CARTER . . . . . . . . . . . . . . . . . . . . . . . . . . . . . . . . 1

### ONE— Forging a Brand: Introducing Obama-Mania

Popular Culture in the Age of Obama
    ANGELA NELSON . . . . . . . . . . . . . . . . . . . . . . . . . . . . . . . 9
The Modern *E Pluribus Unum* Man: How Obama Constructed His American Identity from His Global Background
    ETSE SIKANKU AND NICHOLAS A. YANES . . . . . . . . . . . . . . 16
Myth, Symbol, and the Branding of an American Presidency
    PATRICK B. ORAY . . . . . . . . . . . . . . . . . . . . . . . . . . . . . . . 28

### TWO— Film and Television: Change Televised

Character-in-Chief: Barack Obama and His Pop Culture Predecessors
    JUSTIN S. VAUGHN . . . . . . . . . . . . . . . . . . . . . . . . . . . . . . 45
Barack Obama or *B. Hussein*? The Post-Racial Debate in *Boston Legal*
    JENNY BANH . . . . . . . . . . . . . . . . . . . . . . . . . . . . . . . . . . 63

### THREE— Hip-Hop Culture: Remixed Response to Obama's Popularity

"The Audacity of Dope": Rap Music, Race, and the Obama Presidency
    TRAVIS L. GOSA . . . . . . . . . . . . . . . . . . . . . . . . . . . . . . . . 85
The Politics of Tagging: Shepard Fairey's Obama
    ERIKA SCHNEIDER . . . . . . . . . . . . . . . . . . . . . . . . . . . . . . 97

### Four — Comic Books: Obama's Popularity and the Original Superhero Medium

Obama and Spider-Man: A Meta-Data Media Analysis of an Unlikely Pairing
ROBERT G. WEINER AND SHELLEY E. BARBA.................... 113

Comics and Politics: An Interview with Larry Hama, Creator of *Barack the Barbarian*
NICHOLAS A. YANES........................................ 128

### Five — News Media and New Media: The Impact of Presidential News Politics and Digital Social Networks

Change That Couldn't Happen: News Media's Commitment to Hegemonic Masculinity through Collective Memory in the 2008 Presidential Election
ROBERT E. GUTSCHE, JR., JAMES CARVIOU, AND RAUF ARIF ....... 133

The President Speaks to America's Schoolchildren: Outline of a Brouhaha
JOHN T. "JACK" BECKER..................................... 151

Obama Jungle Fever: Interracial Desire on the Campaign Trail
CAROLINE A. STREETER ..................................... 167

How to Understand Obama's Election News Coverage: An Interview with Daniel Berkowitz
NICHOLAS A. YANES, WITH DERRAIS CARTER AND ROBERT E. GUTSCHE, JR. .................................. 184

New Media's Impact on Elections: An Interview with Obama Girl Creator Ben Relles
JAMES CARVIOU ........................................... 189

### Six — International Responses: Obama's Popularity Goes Global

Obama for Obama: Barack Obama in Japanese Popular Culture
YUYA KIUCHI.............................................. 197

Obama-Mania in Turkey: Popular Culture and the Forty-Fourth President of the United States in a Secular Muslim Nation
ZAFER PARLAK AND TANFER EMIN TUNC .................... 213

France's News Media and Obama's French Popularity: Interview with Sébastian Compagnon
NICHOLAS A. YANES........................................ 231

Conclusion: What Happened to Obama-Mania?
  NICHOLAS A. YANES.................................236

*Appendix: A Bibliography of Obama in Comics*
  NICHOLAS A. YANES.................................245
*About the Contributors*...............................251
*Index* ...............................................255

# Acknowledgments

NICHOLAS YANES: Like all people who have written an acknowledgments section for a book, I have to take a moment to shine a spotlight on those who have greatly helped me on this project. I'm perpetually thankful to my family and friends (both real and imaginary) for providing moral support for this endeavor. In particular, I'd like to thank my niece whose freakish knowledge of the 2008 campaign — occurring when she was six — made me realize just how much of an impact Obama was having on popular culture.

Since I've taken on this project I've been fortunate enough to have several friends continue to encourage me. Of significance is my friend Derrais Carter. When I initially pitched this idea to Carter we had only just finished our first semester as Ph.D. students in the University of Iowa's Department of American Studies. Carter was thrilled by the idea and agreed to become this collection's co-editor. In addition to being another pair of eyes, he consistently encouraged this project's development when I considered simply walking away as I slowly realized just how big a task this book was. He has proven himself to be a great friend and brilliant professional.

Every academic stands on the shoulders of the fantastic mentors that they've had along the way. From the undergraduate time at Florida Atlantic University's Harriet L. Wilkes Honors College to the now gone but not forgotten American Studies Program at Florida State University, I have been fortunate to have had phenomenal professors who invested greatly in my future. I need to take a moment to give thanks to the University of Iowa's Dr. Laura Rigal, Dr. Corey Creekmur, and Dr. Deborah Whaley. They are the three faculty members that gave me excellent feedback about the initial proposal Carter and I put together, and consistently offered us words of encouragement.

Finally, I have to thank Dr. Robert Weiner. Not only was he the editor behind my first two publications and a contributor to this project, but his experience putting together collections proved to be invaluable. In terms that only us comic book fans would understand, Weiner is the ideal Professor X–like mentor that all new academics need.

DERRAIS CARTER: There are many people whose continued support allows me to thrive in work, art, and life. I would like to thank Barbara Carter, Roy Carter, and Sheryl Carter for being loving and giving parents. Their extraordinary wisdom and faith continues to inspire me. My siblings Steve, Derrick, Takayla, Watts, Darion, Cam, and Dom keep me grounded and motivated. They truly are a rare breed.

Mentors and colleagues at the University of Iowa have supported this project in various ways. Particularly, American studies and African American studies faculty have fueled my growing interest in cultural production and intellectual dexterity. I would like to extend a special thanks to Bridget Harris Tsemo, Deborah Whaley, and Vershawn Young who provided key insights during the early stages of this project. The participants of the 2009 National Council for Black Studies Summer Institute keep activism, education, and rigorous debate at the forefront of my scholarly pursuits. Thanks for good times, 2 A.M. horoscopes, and knowledge of self. The participants of the 2010 Clinton Institute for American Studies at University College Dublin offered friendship, academic support, and laughs. Thanks to Donald Pease for being a passionate and open-minded workshop leader. Jenny Kelly, Marisol Lebron, and Jennifer Harford Vargas gave me strength in ways I still cannot fully articulate. Thank you.

I am in debt to the mentors, colleagues, and friends who remind me that it is okay to let my guard down and enjoy life (while there's not enough space to name everyone, please know that I appreciate your work on and off paper): Chico Herbison, Shawn Leigh Alexander, Dorothy Pennington, Robert Rodriguez, Allyson Flaster, Krissy Gordon, Angela Watkins, Marc and Lisa Carlton, Christina Myers, Chris De La Cruz, Robert Page, Ajani Jackson, Andrew Plisner, Robin Ann Lewis, Kasey Cullors, Chris Reine, Mo Mack, Terrell Matthews, Mutsa Kajese, Shona Johnson, Berneta Haynes, Billy Drew, Naqeeb Stevens, Seashia Vang, Zardon Richardson, Jenny Oh, Malynn Rattana, Bryan Murray, Helen Achanzar, and Jamie James.

Finally, I thank my co-editor Nick Yanes for adding me to this project. He trusted me with sharing the responsibility for this collection and I greatly appreciate his friendship.

# Introduction
## DERRAIS CARTER

This book presents a series of arguments regarding Barack Obama's presence and appropriation within popular culture from 2007 to 2009. It explores the widespread enthusiasm associated with Obama and its implications for the study of popular culture. The project's overarching argument is that Barack Obama's campaign and transition into the American presidency created a space in which activists, politicians, fans, and artists converged, using Obama's image to represent their respective ideologies. In pursuing this claim, the volume's contributors use representations of Obama to map the influence of popular culture around the world. Popular culture warrants attention for it depicts the superficial and subconscious aims of citizens throughout the globe.

Focusing on pop culture representation, this book works against affirming or denying Obama's political agenda. Instead, it emphasizes the possibilities his campaign created both in the United States and abroad. These representations are fluid, vacillating through newspapers, television, and the Internet; yet they also have implications for the study of music, film, and comic books. Though some of the essays address race as it is constructed within the United States, this collection also contains essays whose approaches to Obama do not rest primarily on his blackness.

This book has six divisions, each of which works through a set of representational mediums. The first section includes essays by Angela Nelson, Etse Sikanku and Nicholas A. Yanes, and Patrick B. Oray, each of which examines the development of Obama's pop culture representations. These essays set the project's tone, for they explore Obama's seemingly symbiotic relationship to popular culture. Nelson's piece demonstrates the efficacy of exploring Obama *as* popular culture. In doing so, she outlines the ways in which Obama's presence has already created touchstones for exploring race, gender, and globalization in popular culture. Sikanku and Yanes' essay complements Oray's work insofar as they take up "Obama the man" and "Obama the brand." Through close readings of Obama's memoirs and speeches, Sikanku and Yanes examine how Obama forged his American identity by negotiating his multiracial, ethnic, and national background. If, as Sikanku and Yanes argue, Obama's negotiation of identity reflects his American experience, Oray's piece elevates Obama's identity into the realm of myth. Oray argues that Obama's brand reflects the development of a new national U.S. myth that restructures the disjuncture between race and nation. In doing so, Oray examines the Obama brand as a reflection of this new national myth. Oray asks readers to consider the Obama brand as a promulgation of the media landscape, creating a network of associations that reshape our understanding of U.S. national identity.

The second section examines representations of Obama in television and film. Justin S. Vaughn reads Barack Obama in relation to filmic depictions of black presidents. Offering a corrective to journalistic portraits of positive black presidencies in film, Vaughn argues that a critical light must be shown with respect to these representations. Considering actors like James Earl Jones, Morgan Freeman, and Dennis Haysbert, Vaughn examines the legacy of the filmic black presidency. He discusses the oscillation of these representations, addressing their positive and negative implications. If, as journalists suggest, Barack Obama's victory was positively influenced by these representations, Vaughn's essay posits a more contentious relationship. Jenny Banh takes on the series *Boston Legal* examining how Obama is discussed in relation to white liberal ideology. Banh argues that although the election of Obama is no indication of post-racialism, he does represent a turning point in American racial discourse. The characters in *Boston Legal* take this conversation head-on over Thanksgiving dinner. This essay uses Obama as a warrant, asking readers to reorient themselves in the ever-evolving discussion of race in America.

The third section examines Obama in relation to hip hop culture. Travis L. Gosa's "The Audacity of Dope" brings rappers to the fore of the post-racial debate. Similar to Banh's contribution, Gosa uses Obama as an entry into post-racialism via rap lyrics. Gosa's essay proposes that debates on post-racialism take place within hip hop culture. This is particularly evinced in endorsements from artists like Will-I-Am to the activist-oriented group Dead Prez. Hip hop, then, evinces the multiple investments rappers have in Obama's presidency while shedding light on scholarly and artistic claims to Obama's racial authenticity. Erika Schneider's piece argues that Obama was a conduit through which artist Shepard Fairey could interweave fine art with politics. Using graffiti as his primary medium, Fairey's Obama-inspired art became synonymous with Obama's official campaign and its grassroots following.

The fourth section continues the previous section's engagement with visual culture with a critical eye on comic books. Robert G. Weiner, Shelley E. Barba, and Nicholas A. Yanes, through an interview with Larry Hama, focus on Obama's presence in comic books. Weiner and Barba use meta-data analysis to explore why the press found the pairing of Obama and Spider-Man so engaging. Citing the special case of Marvel Comics, Weiner and Barba discuss the import of the Obama-Spider-Man pairing, for it was the first time a president-elect formed an equal partnership with a comic book hero. Offering the perspective of a comic book artist, Nicholas A. Yanes interviews *Barack the Barbarian* creator Larry Hama. Through the interview, Hama briefly discusses the story behind the creation of the comic, but what's more evocative about the interview is the post-racial world imagined within the book.

Though digital technology has dominated much of the media landscape, print media still has a strong influence in shaping representation. Consider, for instance, the many empty newspaper stands following election night. Many people kept papers celebrating the election of the United States' first black president. This in mind, the fifth section turns to news media and new media to examine the circulation of Obama's image within popular culture.

The section opens with Robert E. Gutsche, Jr., James Carviou, and Rauf Arif's essay on hegemonic masculinity and collective memory in the 2008 presidential election. They argue that news media depictions of Obama during the 2008 primary locate him within a political narrative that frames presidential candidates as powerful, masculine, and sex symbols. Addressing Obama's place within this narrative provides an entry-point for assessing and redefining the contours of masculinity within political and media discourse.

John T. "Jack" Becker analyzes media attention surrounding President Obama's televised message to schoolchildren. In "The President Speaks to America's Schoolchildren" Becker takes an expository look at the event, chronicling the standpoints represented before and after the speech. Becker's essay is followed by Caroline A. Streeter's essay titled "Obama Jungle Fever." Streeter meditates on two interracial narratives depicted during Obama's campaign. The first narrative centers on the historical and symbolic relationship between white women and black men. The second narrative also looks to white women and black men, yet does so through a mother-son dynamic. For Streeter, these narratives come to a head in Obama's campaign.

The section concludes with interviews by Nicholas A. Yanes (with Derrais Carter and Robert E. Gutsche, Jr.) and James Carviou. Yanes interviews journalism scholar Daniel Berkowitz. Looking specifically at uses of narrative and technology throughout the presidential race, Berkowitz and Yanes map the Obama campaign's impact on televised campaign ads and election news discourse. Carviou interviews Ben Relles, the creator of *Obama Girl*, a YouTube video in which a young woman sings about having a crush on Barack Obama. Relles' motives behind creating the piece seem less politically charged than

Larry Hama's comments in Yanes' interview, but Carviou's inquiry reveals much about the connections scholars make between cultural production and social values.

Obama's international presence cannot be discounted. Since his election, the world has watched him receive the Nobel Peace Prize and visit the Cape Coast Castle in Ghana. Newspapers around the world have cited stories of children being named "Obama" in tribute to the U.S. president. This final section examines these international investments in Barack Obama. The essays range in scope and content, yet each reveals how Obama was appropriated to articulate cultural identity in an international context.

Yuya Kuichi's essay "Obama for Obama: Barack Obama in Japanese Popular Culture" revisits the notion of the Obama brand while keeping an international focus. His essay explores how Obama — the brand — circulates in Japanese popular culture via commodification. In demonstrating how this process unfolds, Kuichi also takes into consideration how Obama is appropriated when a distinctly U.S. political agenda is not at stake.

The next essay, "Obama-Mania in Turkey" by Zafer Parlak and Tanfer Emin Tunc, views the election of Barack Obama as a turning point in U.S. international relations. Under the Bush regime, they argue, Turkish media saw the United States as the force behind global strife. Obama, however, was a symbol of hope and transformation, leading Turkish media outlets to associate him with peace and possibility.

Nicholas A. Yanes concludes the section with an interview with French journalist Sébastian Compagnon in which he asks how Obama's presidential victory was received by French citizens. Obama, in this context, represents the flow of U.S. news in an international context. Compagnon's responses regarding the Bush administration are similar to Parlak and Tunc's, showing that Obama symbolized seemingly common themes across national boundaries.

Representations of Barack Obama continue to pervade contemporary popular culture. A brief foray into cyberspace alone yields a number of examples. A hip hop inspired parody "Head of the State" by Baraka Flocka Flame plays on southern rapper Waka Flocka Flame's song "Hard in da Paint." In other instances, Obama is Photoshopped to appear to look like Abraham Lincoln, George W. Bush, and in one extreme case a zombie. This even extends to clothing. One T-shirt represents Obama as a direct beneficiary of Martin Luther King, Jr., and the Civil Rights Movement. Another T-shirt, inspired by pioneering rap group Run DMC, features Obama adorned with a black fedora tilted forward, gazelle glasses, and a thick gold rope chain. The caption below reads "Run DC." These examples stand alongside protest posters that critique the Obama administration. One example is the poster depicting Obama as the Joker from the film *Dark Knight* (2008). The poster appeared at a 2009 Tea Party rally in Washington, D.C. This short list of examples shows that representations of Barack Obama are still up for grabs. As a new election year arises, more representations will proliferate. More commentators will weigh-in on the political climate. Candidates will attempt to increase their visibility in preparation of the election. All the while, Obama's official and unofficial campaign supporters will remix and re-imagine the image of the United States' first black president.

SECTION ONE

FORGING A BRAND:
INTRODUCING
OBAMA-MANIA

# Popular Culture in the Age of Obama
## Angela Nelson

## *Introduction — New World Pop and Obama*

The scholarly study of popular culture has multiplied greatly in the last forty years. This is due in part to the increase in information technologies, the availability of online primary sources, and the emergence of new media technologies and social networking services which have opened doors for new areas of study and that have created new access points for scholars from different disciplines (traditional and new) in different parts of the world to collaborate. The boundaries between disciplines are shifting, converging, and synergizing, and many diverse areas and subjects are being examined. Another recent shifting event that signifies racial and generational change and is indirectly connected to this change in the academy is the election of Barack Obama as the forty-fourth president of the United States in November 2008. As the first African American president of the United States, Obama's election and current office brings into focus change and boundary shifts in the political landscape of the United States and the world and brings into focus race and ethnicity, religion and spirituality, land and territory, popular culture, and globalization.

## *Obama's Popularity and Popular Culture*

The fact that Barack Obama is the first president of color in the United States, is one of the youngest and has such a multi-cultural background raises the issue of his popularity, the reality of blackness, and their connections to popular culture. Philosopher Douglas Kellner shows in his essay, "Barack Obama and Celebrity Spectacle," that Obama's use of the logic of the "media spectacle" promoted his candidacy and that now he is a "master of the spectacle and global celebrity of the top rank" (716–717). Through his background in community organizing in Chicago, Obama's implementation of his grassroots philosophy during his presidential campaign exploded into an Internet spectacle that consisted of new media and social networking sites. Obama raised an unprecedented amount of money on the Internet, generated more than 2 million friends on Facebook and 866,887 friends on MySpace, and, reportedly, had a campaign listserv of over 10 million e-mail addresses, enabling his campaign to mobilize youth and others through text messaging and e-mails. In addition, videos compiled on Obama's official campaign YouTube site were accessed over 11.5 million times (Kellner, 718–719).

Obama's use of new media and social networking sites seemed to attract and draw young people to him and to his message of hope and change (Millward). The involvement of young people in Obama's campaign is unprecedented compared to presidential campaigns of the last sixteen years and represents a shift in the boundaries between generations of people because both the young *and* old supported Obama. However, Ronald Williams, in his essay "Barack Obama and the Complicated Boundaries of Blackness," attempts to understand the unprecedented popularity that Barack Obama — an identifiable African American — enjoyed with American whites as a candidate for the Democratic Party's nomination for president from another angle — that of race. It is significant to note and demystify this moment in American political history because Kellner reminds the reader that the celebrity spectacle of a major U.S. party primary is largely reserved for white males (717). For the Democratic Party in 2008, the top candidates for the Democratic nomination were not white males, but a white female (Senator Hillary Clinton) and a black male (Senator Barack Obama).

So why was Obama so popular with American whites? Williams believes the answer rests in the complexities of African American identities. He describes two groups of Americans with the claim to "African American" as a racial designation: the indigenous African American and the non-indigenous African American (55). The indigenous African American is one who was born in the United States and whose identity has been forged in the face of the institutions of slavery, Jim Crow, and other forms of state-sanctioned racism (Williams, 56). Non-indigenous African Americans are those who were born in another nation or country and who have voluntarily immigrated to the United States for various reasons (Williams, 55–56). Along with these designations exist differences and divergences in social psyches, social statuses, and social capital. That is, various studies have shown that indigenous and non-indigenous African Americans differ in terms of household income, employment, education attainment and achievement, socialization, group dynamics, collective behavior, and race consciousness, with non-indigenous African Americans faring better in virtually all categories (Williams, 56).

Obama complicates the boundary of "African Americanness" because many of the characteristics found to be central to indigenous and non-indigenous African Americans are not central to his origins and background. In short, Obama is an anomaly, being that he is the son of a father from Kenya, Africa, and a mother from Kansas; that he was raised in Hawaii, then Indonesia, then Hawaii again; and that he was educated in the United States at Columbia University and Harvard Law School (Johnson, 174). Williams asserts that during Obama's presidential campaign, American whites saw him as "different" from normative representations of African Americans, which in part accounts for his popularity (58). Expanding upon this "difference," Williams summarizes the reasons for the popularity of Obama among American whites:

Because he is not a descendant of American slavery and its legacy, Obama is able to genuinely present himself not only as an example of what African Americans "are" and more of an example what they "should be" or "could be." Representing himself as an African American without a sentiment of anger or bitterness toward the United States because of its wrongdoings or toward American whites because of the transgressions of their primogenitors; an African American who has bought into the idea that America and its proverbial dream can materialize for all of its citizens — including those who were once slaves — enables (American) whites to connect with a possibility that American racism is a thing of the past (58).

## *Popular Culture and Boundary Shifts in the Age of Obama*

America has not had such a popular presidential candidate and president since John F. Kennedy. With that popularity and with the knowledge that popular culture and media culture were important to his campaign, we can now ask: What effect will Barack Obama's presidency have on the popular culture of the average person in the United States and in the world? I believe one significant thing that Obama's presidency will demonstrate is that race *still* matters in the United States and that shifts can occur and are occurring in traditional, boundary-laden areas such as American politics. It is not that the United States has entered an age of post-racialization, but that the nation was introduced to a candidate and now president who spoke about hope and change with vision and purpose. Obama did not ignore race; he simply looked beyond it. Critic and essayist Charles Johnson describes the significance and success of Obama's presidential campaign in this way:

[A] black presidential hopeful could only become the leader of the most powerful nation in human history if he rose above the racially provincial and parochial. That is one enduring lesson of Obama's dramatic, historically unprecedented campaign. The truth that real excellence is color-blind, and that broad service to others has no tribal affiliation... [175].

Obama's presidency directly and indirectly affects the popular culture of the average person in two ways, one minor and one major. On a minor and more superficial level, Obama is connected to the average person's popular culture because his image is everywhere. During his campaign, Obama's image and the word "HOPE" were captured on T-shirts and on art posters and stickers that were posted on stop signs, underpasses, buildings and billboards in major cities like Los Angeles. In addition, street artists created Obama graffiti and urban art (Kellner, 719). Also, during his campaign, Obama staged daily stump speeches, and these appeared on national news programs, the Internet, and political talk shows. Today, as president, Obama is seen on television and in the print news, giving news conferences, meeting with other heads of states, meeting with Senate and House committees when introducing new bills such as the Health Care Reform Bill of March 2010, and boarding an airplane when his family goes on vacation. Obama, an identifiable African American, makes the social construct of race a daily news item. Many Americans may see African American males in their local television news and newspapers and on television and film, but with a black president, at the very least, a black man (their president) is seen or discussed on television and in print. It is impossible to assume that Americans are not on some level reflecting regularly on their beliefs and values about race or about what they believe about black people.

Along with the leader of the United States on television, other African American men appear too, but in the world of television cooking shows. Although the programming landscape of TV cooking shows is heavily white and non–Hispanic (Collins, 249), five current weekly series feature African American males: Chef Gerry Garvin in *Turn Up the Heat with G. Garvin* (TVOne, October 2004–present); Pat Neely in *Down Home with the Neelys* (Food Network, February 2, 2008–present); Aaron McCargo, Jr., in *Big Daddy's House* (Food Network, August 3, 2008–present); Darryl Robinson in *Drink Up* (Cooking Channel, May 31, 2010–present); and Roger Mooking in *Everyday Exotic* (Cooking Channel, May 31, 2010–present) (Johnson, 175). Each series is sophisticated, fun, and lively. With the exception of *Down Home with the Neelys*, the series are urban and clearly focus on the role of the host as the star of the show, although guests sometimes appear with them. *Down Home* features a husband-and-wife (Gina Neely) team who already own successful barbeque restaurants in Memphis, Tennessee. The importance and significance of marriage and family permeates the show and the couple, with appearances from their daughters, mothers, Pat's brothers, and friends allowing

America to see a *functional* (rather than dysfunctional) black family relating well with each other as they cook and enjoy fellowship. *Down Home with the Neelys* reinforces a positive image of a black family that we are also reminded of when President Obama is boarding a plane for a vacation with First Lady Michelle and daughters Sasha and Malia.

On a more abstract level and one that is more significant and profound is the fact that Obama's campaign and presidency, which broke racial and generational boundaries, demonstrates what popular culture has been able to do for a long time, and that is to engage with other cultures, crossing cultural boundaries (Hall, 290). Historically, popular culture has become the dominant form of global culture, but at the same time it has been the scene of commodification and of the industries that manufacture this commodification: television, print, Internet, music, and film (Hall, 289). The prominence of popular culture today is aided by globalization. In fact, today, globalization is perhaps the single most influential process and force behind boundary shifts in popular culture (although boundary shifts have existed in popular culture long before industrialization, urbanization, and commercialization).

One popular icon often at the center of several cultural practices and that particularly has opened access to boundary shifts in society is food. A simple, biological necessity, food has crossed cultural boundaries in several ways. In the daily lives of Americans, many of the common foods that they eat today are a direct product of globalization and the crossing of cultural boundaries. These foods include spices, tea, coffee, the potato, the tomato, and the chili pepper ("Globalization"). When Americans eat a fast-food product such as a taco, it reveals the crossing of cultural boundaries but also the complexities of globalization and how food production works in America. For example, a group of architecture students in a class at the California College of the Arts deconstructed a taco to establish the geographical boundaries of its ingredients. What they found was surprising: the ingredients of a taco from Juan's Taco Truck in San Francisco had traveled a total of 64,000 miles, some of the ingredients were made locally, and many of the ingredients were made globally ("Your Taco").

Another example of food crossing cultural boundaries is the integration of whole food products in American popular culture. A case in point is Mexican and Chinese foods and, more recently, foods from Indian and Japanese cultures. Mexican and Chinese foods have been a part of American popular culture for many years, which should not be surprising considering the relationship of the U.S. with Mexico and China. Mexican and Chinese foods and ingredients appear in restaurants, grocery stores, and food warehouses. American foods have been exported to other countries as well, particularly as "fast food." In fact, a person would be hard pressed to *not* find at least one McDonald's restaurant in every major city in the world. However, this process is not a one-way transaction. There has been reciprocity in this area as well. As U.S. companies have opened fast-food restaurants in other countries, these countries have also opened competitors — local fast-food restaurants that produce and sell burgers, fries, donuts, and chicken wings. A very interesting aspect about this process is that now these competitors are opening their own franchises in the United States. Examples of franchises in major U.S. cities include Jollibee from the Philippines, FamilyMart from Japan, Pollo Campero from Guatemala, and Beard Papa's also of Japan ("New Fast-Food").

Another popular text that crosses cultural boundaries just as fluidly as does food is hip hop culture and rap music. Hip-hop culture is decidedly global, urban and connected to youth culture according to Halifu Osumare (2, 69–72). It brings together some of the most complex social, cultural, and political issues in contemporary American society and is the epitome of black popular culture today because of its involvement in black cultural trafficking. Hip-hop culture and rap music, through globalization and the transnationalization of U.S. popular culture, is circulated internationally, giving birth to other hip-hop forms and genres in such disparate regions as Colombia (South America), France, Poland, Bosnia and Croatia, Japan, Brazil, South Africa, Jamaica, Cuba, and native Hawaii.

## Conclusion: What You Need to Know

Popular cultures cross cultural boundaries in much the way that President Obama's presidential campaign crossed racial and generational boundaries. The result is that there are no pure, authentic cultural experiences but ones that are infused with elements from parts of the global society in which we live in the twenty-first century. The life, presidential campaign, and presidency of Barack Obama is an example of how influential popular culture has become in our society, how globalization has helped to facilitate the movement of peoples and their popular cultures, and how boundary shifts are (and have been) occurring for many years in many different places. Obama has made peace with popular culture and as a result has used it to his advantage. The study of popular culture in the age of Obama will continue to grow and thrive because of globalization and information technologies.

## REFERENCES

Collins, Kathleen. *Watching What We Eat: The Evolution of Television Cooking Shows*. New York: Continuum, 2009.

Dudziak, Mary L., and Leti Volpp. "Introduction — Legal Borderlands: Law and the Construction of American Borders." *American Quarterly* 57, no. 3 (September 2005): 593–610.
Elam, Harry J., Jr., and Kennell Jackson. *Black Cultural Traffic: Crossroads in Global Performance and Popular Culture.* Ann Arbor: University of Michigan Press, 2005.
"The Globalization of Food and Plants." Yale Global Online. http://yaleglobal.yale.edu/about/food.jsp (accessed March 27, 2010).
Hall, Stuart. "What Is This 'Black' in Black Popular Culture?" 1992. In *Popular Culture: A Reader*, ed. Raiford Guins and Omayra ZaraGosa Cruz, 285–293. London: Sage, 2005.
Johnson, Charles. "The Cultural Challenge of Barack Obama." In *The American Journey of Barack Obama*, editors of *Life* magazine, 174–175. New York: Little, Brown, 2008.
Kellner, Douglas. "Barack Obama and Celebrity Spectacle." *International Journal of Communication* 3 (2009): 715–741.
Millward, Jessica. "Teaching African-American History in the Age of Obama." *Chronicle Review.* chroniclereview.com (accessed March 27, 2009).
"A New Fast-Food Invasion." *Time*, March 29, 2007. http://www.time.com/time/magazine/article/0,9171,1604946,00.html (accessed March 27, 2010).
Osumare, Halifu. *The Africanist Aesthetic in Global Hip-Hop: Power Moves.* New York: Palgrave Macmillan, 2007.
"What Is Globalization?" Levin Institute. http://www.globalization101.org/What_is_Globalization.html (accessed March 24, 2010).
Williams, Ronald, II. "Barack Obama and the Complicated Boundaries of Blackness." *Black Scholar* 38, no. 1 (Spring 2008): 55–61.
"Your Taco, Deconstructed." *GOOD Blog.* http://www.good.is/post/your-taco-deconstructed (accessed March 27, 2010).

# The Modern *E Pluribus Unum* Man
## How Obama Constructed His American Identity from His Global Background

ETSE SIKANKU *AND* NICHOLAS A. YANES

The phrase *E pluribus unum*—Latin for "Out of many, one"—is foundational to understanding America's creation and continual cultural development. While the meaning of *E pluribus unum* has evolved over time, it still represents the multi-racial, ethnic, and national identities of U.S. citizens. With the widespread acceptance of people having multiple racial backgrounds (evidence for the acceptance of multi-faceted identity being the 2000 Census, which allowed people to check multiple races for the first time in U.S. history), it is clear that the definitions layered onto *E pluribus unum* will include the belief that a true American can come from several different backgrounds, a reality that few people represent better than President Barack Obama.

Referring to Obama as America's first African American president pays tribute to the ongoing civil rights struggle in this country, with cognizance of the role of identity politics in America's democracy. However, referring to him as the United States' first African American president creates a view of Obama that minimizes his rich and atypical cultural and racial backgrounds. After all, he is the son of a white woman from Kansas and a Luo-Kenyan man, while also being the stepson of the Indonesian, Lolo Soetoro. As a result of his immediate family's international makeup, Obama has half siblings and family members all over the world. One result of his global heritage was that Obama's election victory inspired scenes of jubilation not just in the United States but in many places around the world. The atmosphere was particularly celebratory in Kenya where Obama wields a direct paternal connection. On the morning of his election, the *East African Times* wrote that "Kenya is ecstatic at the news of Barack Obama's historic election as president of the United States." The newspaper also reported that "upon hearing news of their beloved 'son's' win Wednesday morning residents of Kogelo village burst into song and cheers of joy" (*East African Times*, 1). Libyan leader Muammar Gadaffi, who historically had a frosty relationship with the U.S., called Obama's electoral triumph a "beginning of victory for black people" (Dalje.com). Back in Kenya, a former European colony, President Mwai Kibaki went on to declare a national holiday in honor of their "son." Clearly Africans felt a strong connection to Obama due to his immediate paternal connection to the continent.

The son of a Kenyan man who grew up under British colonial rule with a Swahili first name and a Luo surname, Obama's identity and ethnic makeup was a significant issue of conversation throughout the election cycle. Viewed as outside the white mainstream, and reluctantly accepted as a "true" African American by the black community, Obama has been referred to sometimes as a "half–African." Former House speaker Newt Gingrich and conservative writer Dinesh D'Souza have both called him a "Kenyan anti-colonial" (D'Souza, 2; *National Review*, 1). Responding to politicians and media commentators' statements on Obama's racial identity, this essay treats Barack Obama's two autobiographies, *Dreams from My Father* and *The Audacity of Hope*, along with his speeches as primary artifacts to understand how he constructs his ethnic identity. In particular, this essay will focus on how Obama grew to understand his unique African heritage; how he began to build his own African American identity; and finally, how he negotiated between his global background — having a Kenyan background and spending a portion of his childhood in Indonesia — and the United States.

This study examines Obama's framing of his biracial identity by using data from *Dreams from My Father* and *The Audacity of Hope*, along with other related speeches and based within the theoretical framework of post-colonialism and globalization. The analysis uses the methodological approach of framing. Framing refers to the process of "interpretation, and presentation, of selection, emphasis, and exclusion, by which symbol-handlers routinely organize discourse, whether verbal or visual" (Gitlin, 7). In short it refers to the process and manner in which issues are portrayed. While framing has been a flourishing and long-studied technique in journalism and mass communication, a major contribution of this study is its extension to identity construction, thereby deepening our understanding of the concept in this area.

## Learning What It Means to Be African

No one is born with a conscious understanding of their heritage. Like most forms of knowledge, people learn what it means to be of American,

Cuban, Ghanaian, Irish or Kenyan descent. Since Obama was primarily raised by his mother, he was not acculturated into Kenyan culture throughout his childhood. However Obama's "Africanness" can be explained through the concept of Afrocentricity where Africanity of the African heritage is seen as a key prism to understand phenomena or explain one's persona. Obama's repeated references to his father and his African or immigrant background indicates his acceptance of his Africanness, thus foregrounding rather than backgrounding this aspect of his identity.

However, he did not come to such a stage easily, as he had constantly struggled to reconnect with his Africanity while growing up. Obama's own reflections on such contestations offer some insights. For instance, Obama was engaged in a constant dilemma with how to perceive his connection to his remote father and his distant connection to the Luo tribe to which his father belonged. Exacerbating this emotional disconnection with his African heritage was an experience on his first day of class back in Hawaii in which his class "giggled" and made fun of his African ancestry. As Obama states, "When I finally said Luo, a sandy-haired boy behind me repeated the word in a loud hoot, like the sound of a monkey. The children could no longer contain themselves," and later "a redheaded girl asked to touch my hair and ... a ruddy faced boy asked me if my father ate people" (Obama, *Dreams from My Father*, 55). This experience illustrates how at a young age Obama was confronted with the reality that he has a cultural background most Americans only know of through false racist stereotypes. And, made worse through the absence of his father, he lacked the support system which would properly educate himself about his heritage and give him the tools needed to confront and counteract the pain caused by these moments.

Though young Obama had a loving white family, there is sufficient evidence in his writings to suggest that he felt out of place in the largely white community he lived in. These experiences not only marginalized Obama's African identity as a Luo and a Kenyan, but made it clear that his physical characteristics marked him as an outsider. This is visible through the use of what Gitlin refers to as "trivialization," which explains the marginalization of Obama's African identity as a Luo.

However, Obama's initial perception of his Africanness can be further gleaned from a conscious but honest assessment of his struggle to find a permanent identity when he laments that, "whatever my father might say, I knew that it was too late to ever truly claim Africa as my home" (Obama, *Dreams from My Father*, 106). But no event marked this confusion more than his realization in midair aboard a flight to Kenya that he was "a westerner not entirely at home in the West, an African on his way to a land full of strangers" (Obama, *Dreams from My Father*, 275). This was after a conversation with a Brit who had expected him as an American to share in his view of Africans as "poor buggers" from "Godforsaken countries," a view which Obama perceived as "dim" (Obama *Dreams from My Father*, 274–275). This encounter confirms Achille Mbembe's assertion that "the African human experience constantly appears ... as an experience that can only be understood through negative interpretation" (Mbembe, 1). All this made Obama look within, and he found a "great emptiness there" (Obama, *Dreams from My Father*, 275).

## *Reclaiming Blackness and the African American Community*

In general this theme of "reclaiming" blackness refers to Obama's serious attempts to connect with the African American community in the United States — a population he was not connected to in the same way that other African Americans were. The analysis of this aspect of Obama's identity is once again drawn from both of Obama's books and a newspaper interview.

Specifically, even as Obama sought to reconnect to his African roots, he never forgot that he was the son of a white American as well, and as such, he would have to discover what being an African American meant specifically for him. In America, Obama reclaimed his identity within the black community as he sought to clarify the abstractions imposed by his mixed race. In July 2004, he asserted his African American identity when he told the *New York Times* in no uncertain terms that he considered himself an African American. He stressed that African Americans are a "hybrid people" whose culture is a mixture of African, Native American and European peoples. He reasoned, "If I was arrested for armed robbery and my mug shot was on the television screen, people wouldn't be debating if I was African American or not.... There's no reason why I shouldn't be proud of being a black man when good things are happening" (Davey, 1). In most literature he's hailed as the first black president of the *Harvard Law Review* and one of the few African Americans in the country's history to enter the Senate. This demonstrates an understanding of race which reflects how much the civil rights movement has accomplished while simultaneously minimizing Obama's mixed-race background — the biological equivalent of *E pluribus unum*. It is also an understanding of race Obama would have to struggle with as an African American.

Yet this characterization has not been without problems. During the earlier stages of the Democratic primaries, Joe Biden said of Obama, "I mean, you got the first mainstream African American who is articulate and bright and clean and a nice-looking guy" (CNN, 1). Biden's controlled praise was anchored by the broader stereotypical image of African Americans, which only served to reinforce such racial binaries. By saying Obama was the exception, he admitted to the larger national racial imagery of African Americans. Obama's response was to remain a centrist, admitting that "our nation is not immune to stereotypes that our culture continues to feed us" (Obama, *Audacity of Hope*, 235) but he conceded at the same time that "I have witnessed a profound shift in race relations in my lifetime" (Obama, *Audacity of Hope*, 233).

Still on his African American identity, reclaiming his blackness had not come easy as he struggled to endear himself to the African American population who questioned his blackness, which is something that other African Americans did not face. In his article for the *New York Daily News*, Crouch writes, "After all, Obama's mother is of white U.S. stock. His father is a black Kenyan. Other than color, Obama did not — does not — share a heritage with the majority of black Americans, who are descendants of plantation slaves. So when black Americans refer to Obama as 'one of us,' I do not know what they are talking about" (Crouch, 1). Obama's black identity is therefore complicated by the differences in his experience as a black person in America. He himself writes, "My own upbringing hardly typifies the African American experience" (Obama, *Audacity of Hope*, 233). Perhaps one of the most vivid results from Obama's complicated racial identification is the absence of legitimacy for mixed racial categories of Americans, thereby forcing such people to place themselves within a distinctly categorical construct.

What is also instructive here is the fact that in doing so Obama carefully navigated such tropes by presenting himself as a unifier. Within his writings and speeches, Obama employs the *emphasis* device by harping on his "multi-cultural identity," preferring to appeal to the "better history of Americans" (Obama, *Audacity of Hope*, 400) as the son of a black man and white woman born in the "racial melting pot" that is America. During his pivotal "race" speech in response to his pastor the Rev. Jeremiah Wright's comments, Obama stated, "I can no more disown him than I can disown the black community. I can no more disown him than I can my white grandmother — a woman who helped raise me" (Obama, "A More Perfect Union"). In short, Obama is reiterating a major narrative from his book when he rejects any form of sharp categorization of his identity by stating that first and foremost "I am an individual" (Obama, *Audacity of Hope*, 92). It formed the basis for his life as a community organizer in Chicago, which he used as his political launchpad with civil representation of racial and ethnic minorities, especially African Americans. It was the basis of his universalist frame when he posits that "what would help minority workers are the same things that would help white workers: the opportunity to earn a living wage, the education and training that leads to such jobs, labor laws, tax laws" (Obama, *Audac-*

*ity of Hope*, 246). Here we get an insight into the foundations of another emergent theme in Obama's identitarian framing, his cross-national or global appeal as he declared, "My identity might begin with the fact of my race but it didn't, couldn't end there" (Obama, *Audacity of Hope*, 103). In sum, Obama's decision to embrace his African American self by becoming a community organizer in Chicago established his self-empowering understanding of blackness.

## Obama the Global Citizen

The third dominant frame in Obama's construction of his identity is one that recognizes his international appeal as a "global citizen." *Global citizen* is used in this article to refer to Obama's internationalist background and perspectives, which also played a role in the way Obama constructed his personality. From an identity perspective, global citizen as explicated in this paper denotes the current spate of globalization and cross-cultural connections which seeks to perceive the peoples of the world as a common humanity, thereby fostering the idea of a "common citizenship." Within the framing paradigm, we perceive frames as either tools for reasoning or centralization by organizing their component parts into a meaningful theme (Gamson and Modigliani, 157; Entman, 52). Here again, narratives from Obama's books and related speeches are used to address this aspect of Obama's identity.

Obama, in making meaning or organizing his different identitarian components, casts himself as a global citizen when he refers to himself as a "citizen of the world," declaring to his audience that "the burdens of global citizenship continue to bind us together. A change of leadership in Washington will not lift this burden. In this new century, Americans and Europeans alike will be required to do more — not less." For Obama, "partnership and cooperation among nations is not a choice; it is the one way, the only way, to protect our common security and advance our common humanity" (Obama, "A More Perfect Union"). Barack Obama did not come to such a philosophy by chance.

To give this global depiction some perspective, it's clear that Obama's cross-national connections occurred on a personal level. He had family relations that included siblings from Indonesia and Kenya and other blood relatives of Chinese and American descent, so that "family get-togethers over Christmas take on the appearance of UN General Assembly meetings" (Obama, *Audacity of Hope*, 231), causing him to declare that "I've never had the option of restricting my loyalties on the basis of race or measuring my worth on the basis of tribe" (Obama, *Audacity of Hope*, 231). This accounts for his reluctance to dabble in American exceptionalism, which had been a feature of the Bush government that was before him. It also formed the basis of his worldview, which was that "no one nation, no matter how large or powerful, can defeat such challenges alone" (Obama, "A More Perfect Union").

Another major pointer to his global citizen frame is in the "World beyond Our Borders" chapter of his book *The Audacity of Hope*, when he states, "Our challenge then is to make sure that US policies move the international system in the direction of greater equity, justice and prosperity—that the rules we promote serve both our interests and the interests of a struggling world" (316). The majority of Obama's foreign policy positions are therefore mediated through both personal and intellectual philosophies of inter-relationships which reject absolutes. When, in *Dreams from My Father*, his Auntie Auma makes racist statements about Asians and foreigners, he immediately springs to their defense, saying that he has friends from India and Pakistan back in the United States, "friends who had supported black causes, friends who had lent me money when I was tight and then taken me into their homes when I'd had no place to stay" (Obama, *Dreams from My Father*, 317). His Auntie was however unconvinced and reprimanded him for his naïveté.

The reason for her insistence may be difficult to untangle, but two explanations could be assigned here. Conceptually, it might refer to the situation where nativist and indigenous groups tend to blame societal troubles on foreigners by problematizing them as the "other" or "outsider" group. Like Obama's Auntie Auma, foreigners were "ostracized" for causing societal problems and, as "A More Perfect Union" notes, are given derogatory names such as "*Makwerekwere*," a word referring to the unintelligibility of foreign languages. Clearly, Obama is closer to Mbembe's assertion that "the theoretical and practical recognition of the body and flesh of the stranger as flesh and body just like mine, the idea of a common human nature, a humanity shared with others" than his Auntie Auma (Mbembe, 2).

Secondly, to a broader extent, Simon Gikandi argues in his "Globalization and the Claims of Postcolonialty" that the post-colonial theory of globalization involves a reconsideration of the temporality of location and space since certain functions—such as the role of the outsider—seem to permeate national boundaries. Auntie Auma depended on "the authority of the nation-state as the central institution in the management of social relationships ... and as the embodiment of symbolic hierarchies such as patriotism and citizenship (Gikandi, 634). Obama departs from Gikandi here by focusing on his biracial elements and the law (Obama, *Audacity of Hope*, 399) to call on "people of the world" to build a "common history, and seize our common destiny, and once again engage in that noble struggle to bring justice and peace to our world" (Obama, "A More Perfect Union").

## *Conclusion*

Obama relied on his personal experiences and not just biological factors to feature in the construction of a complex but all-inclusive identity. In other words, Obama was always a firm believer that his present identity was mediated or shaped as much by genetics as by social and cultural factors. Even though he formally identifies himself as an African American, his identity is linked with all aspects of his multi-racial, ethnic, and national heritage. When placed within the context of news framing techniques, it is evident that in the case of Obama's identitarian framing, the cultural resonance component of frame determinants stands out most (Gamson and Modigliani, 157).

Consequently the analysis shows that the three dominant themes in Obama's framing of his identity include (1) Africa/"Africanness" and the search for identity, (2) reclaiming blackness and the African American community and (3) Obama the global citizen. The African component of his identity can be gleaned from his father, but Obama himself made conscious attempts to embrace this aspect after struggling with it in the early stages of his life. The ridicule he faced from his classmates when they learned he came from the Luo tribe of Kenya is consistent with the often negative representation of Africa in the West. Obama himself counteracts this image by narrating experiences of warmth which he experienced on his trip to Kenya to the extent that it influenced his definition of family based on Africa's communal systems when he states that in Africa, family "seemed to be everywhere" (Obama, *Dreams from My Father*, 299). From then on, Africa is depicted by Obama as part of the world and not as an outsider group, leading him to proclaim in his visit to Accra, Ghana, that "I do not see the countries and people of Africa as worlds apart; I see Africa as a fundamental part of the world" (Obama, "Ghana Speech"). This depiction of Africa is fundamentally different from what scholars have referred to as the "absolute otherness," where Africa "constitutes one of the metaphors through which the West ... assert[s] its difference from the rest of the world" (Mbembe, 2).

The second theme that comes up is the African American component of his identity. This was more of an outgrowth of social impositions on him by American race categorizations which he did not denounce. Yet he also embraces this part of himself by proclaiming that "there is no reason why I shouldn't be proud of being a black man when good things are happening too." Coupled with his marriage to Michelle and his work with the black community in Chicago, he maintains that "these people are a part of me. And they are a part of America" (Obama, "A More Perfect Union") as much as his white grandparents are. From a practical point of view, however, the African American frame was a hotly contested one as Obama struggled to assert his centrist cultural identity without renouncing his blackness. This is evidenced by his persistent referral to his reason for running for president by saying time and time again that "I chose to run for the presidency at this moment in history because I believe deeply that we cannot solve the challenges of our time unless we solve them together — unless we perfect our union by understanding that we may have different stories, but we hold common hopes; that we may not look the same and we may not have come from the same place, but we all want to move in the same direction — towards a better future for our children and our grandchildren."

The global citizen theme comprised the last of Obama's multiple identities. Again this is a complex frame, but three factors are suggested here: biological permutations, his lived experiences in Indonesia and Africa, and his intellectual disposition with the law. After all it was his central thesis that the basic reality of our human nature should bind us together despite our differences. In Berlin he called on the world to accept that "the burdens of global citizenship continue to bind us together." He further comments that "this is the moment when we must come together to save this planet." This is similar to Posel's argument that "the right to life is considered to be a basic human right, which means that it is allocated to all human beings on the basis of their shared humanity" (Posel, 312).

In sum, identity studies remains an intricate issue mired in several theoretical possibilities. The limitations of this study include the fact that it might not have provided sufficient conceptual explanations to justify a particular claim or category for Obama's identity construction. Future studies might take a more in-depth analysis of his speeches by using textual analysis techniques. As stated earlier, it is clear that other theoretical formulations may also provide further insights into this issue. Obama himself has pointed out during discussions on race in America that we shouldn't "expect the debate to be settled anytime soon" (Obama, *Audacity of Hope*, 244). Moreover, it is important to note that one of the major goals of political campaigns is to win elections. While not detracting from the problems Obama has faced with his identity while growing up, it is helpful to view his racial constructions within this context as well. Admittedly his was a complex and somewhat complicated case that naturally urged a fusion between two races and different worlds without the privileging of either component frame. In the end it might be fair to say that while Obama's polity was America, his crosscutting identitarian makeup granted him an audience beyond physical boundaries.

## Post-Script

Obama's trip to Africa had been framed by many around him as a "pilgrimage" or return to his "roots." He summarized his feelings and those of his friends prior to his going to Africa during his going-away party when he said that "Africa had become an idea more than an actual place, a new promised land, full of ancient traditions and sweeping vistas, noble struggles and talking drums. With the benefit of distance, we engaged Africa in a selective embrace — the same sort of embrace I'd once offered the Old Man" (Obama, *Audacity of Hope*, 276). Simply put, he felt detached from his "Africanity." This framing narrative gains further conceptual strength through Mbembe's characterization of the continent as "constantly eluding and escaping us" (Mbembe, 1) or one that belongs to a "world we cannot penetrate" (Mbembe, 2), thereby grounding the problematic endeavor involved in perceiving the "other." Obama hoped his trip would fill his emptiness and "relinquish the distance" that had grown between him and has father's homeland (Obama, *Audacity of Hope*, 276). He was therefore elated when someone at the airport on arrival recognized his name and his family. This moment brought a great sense of belonging to Obama. "For the first time in my life, I felt the comfort, the firmness of identity that a name might provide, how I could carry an entire history in other people's memories, so that they might nod and say knowingly, 'Oh, you are so and so's son.' ... My name belonged and so I belonged, drawn into the web of relationships, alliances and grudges that I did not yet understand" (Obama, *Audacity of Hope*, 279).

The foregoing discussion comprised of phrases and themes shows the various frames involved with Obama's African identity. However, if we combine this with his declaration during his first trip to sub–Saharan Africa that "I have the blood of Africa within me" (Obama, "Ghana Speech"), we realize that Obama eventually accepts his "Africanness." This will come in handy as he seeks to strike a global appeal and assert American policy in Africa.

## REFERENCES

Abrahamsen, R. (2003). Africa studies & the post-colonial challenge. *African Affairs, 1*(2), 189–210.
Africanpolicy.org. (2008). Talking about "tribe." Retrieved November 2008 from www.africapolicy.org/bp/ethnicl.htm.
Allen, A. (2008). Power and the politics of difference: Oppression, empowerment, and transnational justice. *Hypatia, 23*(3), 156–171.
Appadurai, Arjun. (1996). *Modernity at large: Cultural dimensions of globalization*. Minneapolis: University of Minnesota Press.
Ball, J. A. (2008). Barack Obama, "connected distance," Race and 21st Century Neo-Colonialism. *Black Scholar, 38*(4).

CNN. (2007). Biden's description of Obama draws scrutiny. Retrieved November 15, 2009, from http://edition.cnn.com/2007/POLITICS/01/31/biden.obama.

Crouch, S. (2006, November 2). What Obama isn't: Black like me on race. *New York Daily News.* Available at http://articles.nydailynews.com/2006-11-02/news/18339455_1_black-world-alan-keyes-people-of-african-descent.

Dalje.com. (2008). Gaddafi says Obama election is victory for blacks. Retrieved November 2010 from http://dalje.com/en-world/gaddafi-says-obama-election-is-victory-for-blacks/200882.

D'Angelo, P. (2002). News framing as multiparadigmatic research program: A response to Entmann. *Journal of Communication, 52,* 870–888.

Davey, M. (2004). The speaker; a surprise Senate contender reaches his biggest stage yet. Retrieved October 20, 2010, from http://www.nytimes.com/2004/07/26/us/the-speaker-a-surprise-senate-contender-reaches-his-biggest-stage-yet.html?sec=&spon=&pagewanted=all.

D'Souza, Dinesh. (2010). How Obama thinks. Retrieved November 2010 from http://www.forbes.com/forbes/2010/0927/politics-socialism-capitalism-private-enterprises-obama-business-problem.html.

*East African Times.* (2008, November 5). Nation erupts in ecstasy at Obama election.

Entmann, R. (1993). Framing: Toward clarification of a fractured paradigm. *Journal of Communication, 43*(4), 51–58.

Gamson, W., and A. Modigliani. (1989). Media discourse and public opinion on nuclear power: A constructionist approach. *American Journal of Sociology, 95,* 1–37.

Gikandi, S. (1996). Colonial culture and the question of identity. In *Maps of Englishness: Writing Identity in the Culture of Colonialism* (pp. 1–49). New York: Columbia University Press, 1996.

Gikandi, S. (2001, Summer). Globalization and the claims of postcoloniality. *South Atlantic Quarterly, 100*(3): 627–658.

Gitlin, T. (1980). The whole world is watching: Mass media in the making and unmaking of the new left. Berkeley: University of California Press.

Hall, S. (1997). The local and the global: Globalization and ethnicity. In Anthony King (Ed.), *Culture, Globalization, and the World System* (pp. 19–40). Minneapolis: University of Minnesota Press, 1997.

Kaplan, C. (1994). Questions of travel: An introduction; Traveling theorists: Cosmopolitan diasporas. In *Questions of Travel* (pp. 1–26, 101–142). Durham: Duke University Press.

Loomba, A. (1998). *Colonialism/postcolonialism.* New York: Routledge.

Mbembe, A. (2001). *On the postcolony.* Berkeley: University of California Press, 2001.

Mendell, D. (2007). *Obama: From promise to power.* New York: Amistad, imprint of HarperCollins.

Mpe, P. (2001). *Welcome to Our Hillbrow.* Pietermaritzburg.

Nagourney, A. (2008, November 5). Obama wins election; McCain loses as Bush legacy is rejected. *New York Times.* Retrieved November 22, 2009, from http://www.nytimes.com/2008/11/05/us/politics/05campaign.html.

*National Review.* (2010). Obama's Kenyan's anti-colonial worldview. Retrieved November 2010 from http://dalje.com/en-world/gaddafi-says-obama-election-is-victory-for-blacks/200882.

Nkrumah, K. (1973). Revolutionary path. New York: International publishers.

Nyong'o, T. (2009). Barack Hussein Obama, or, the name of the father. *Scholar and Feminist Online, 7*(2). Retrieved November 15, 2009, from http://www.barnard.columbia.edu/sfonline/africana/nyongo_01.htm.

Obama, B. H. (1995). *Dreams from my father: A story of race and inheritance.* New York: Times Books.

Obama, B. H. (2004). *2004 Democratic National Convention keynote address.* Retrieved November 22, 2009, from http://www.americanrhetoric.com/speeches/convention2004/barackobama2004dnc.htm.

Obama, B. H. (2006). *The audacity of hope: Thoughts of reclaiming the American Dream.* New York: Crown.
Obama, B. H. (2008a). Speech delivered in Berlin in commemoration of the fall of the Berlin Wall. Retrieved November 22, 2009, from http://edition.cnn.com/2008/POLITICS/07/24/obama.words.
Obama, B. H. (2008b). "A more perfect union," National Constitution Center, Philadelphia, 18 March 2008. Retrieved November 19, 2009, from http://www.npr.org/templates/story/story.php?storyId=88478467.
Obama, B. H. (2009). Obama Ghana speech. Retrieved November 5, 2009, from http://www.huffingtonpost.com/2009/07/11/obama-ghana-speech-full-t_n_230009.html.
Obeng, S. (1997). *Selected speeches of Kwame Nkrumah* (Vols. 4–5). Accra, Ghana: Afram Publication.
Posel, D. (2003, February 6–7). A matter of life and death: Revisiting "modernity" from the vantage point of the "new" South Africa. Paper presented to the workshop "Bio-Politics, States of Exception and the Politics of Sovereignty," Wits Institute for Social and Economic Research, University of Witwatersrand, Johannesburg.
Posel, D. (2005). "Democracy in a time of AIDS." *Interventions* 7(3), 310–315.
Sceufele, D., and Tewksbury, D. (2007). Framing, agenda setting, and priming: The evolution of three media effects models. *Journal of Communications, 57*(1), 9–20.
Shohat, E. (1993/1998). Notes on the post-colonial. In A. Loomba (Ed.), *Colonialism/postcolonialism.* New York: Routledge.
*Time.* (2007). The identity card. Retrieved November 22, 2009, from http://www.time.com/time/magazine/article/0,9171,1689619,00.html.
Uduku, O., and Zack-Williams, A. (2004). *Africa beyond the post colonial: political and social cultural identities.* Hampshire, England: Ashgate Press.
Walters, R. (2007). Barack Obama and the politics of blackness. *Journal of Black Studies, 38*(7), 7–29.

# Myth, Symbol, and the Branding of an American Presidency

PATRICK B. ORAY

Presidential campaigns have traditionally employed slogans and other mass media conduits to persuade the American electorate. Barack Obama's historic run for the presidency, however, has inspired an unprecedented wave of interest in the study of political campaigning. Obama's electoral success was a masterstroke of politicking and public relations that made him more than just a presidential candidate and popular culture icon. As *No Logo* author Naomi Klein avers, Obama is the "first U.S. president who is also a superbrand." The political persona Obama and his campaign surrogates created during the 2008 presidential election is symbolized by an icon that, according to Klein, "creates an appealing canvas on which all are invited to project their deepest desires ... big enough to be anything to anyone yet [has] an intimate enough feel to inspire advocacy."

Thanks to the work of scholars and professionals from fields such as political science, marketing, and communication studies, there is no shortage of insightful commentary on the effect of "Brand Obama" on U.S. popular culture. However, as valuable as these analyses are, I find that much of their focus centers on how the Obama campaign succeeded in parlaying the candidate's mass appeal into fund-raising dollars and votes. This essay takes a deeper look into the symbolic processes that explain the cultural significance of "Obama-mania." Surely, the skillful combination of traditional and new media has been the engine driving the Obama brand, and I will pay some attention to their use in this work. The bulk of this piece explores how the appeal and durability of this brand lies in its strength as a symbol that reorients America's civic identity and contextualizes it within a new national myth. At the center of this myth is a reframing of the United States's historic identity crisis — the rift between the concepts of *race* and *nation*.

In my analysis I describe two social constructions or *architectures* at play in the construction of the Obama brand. First, I explain the significance of myth and symbolic imagery in Obama's presidential campaign by illustrating how he and his surrogates used these tools to negotiate racial tensions during his candidacy. While mass media research on political campaigns offers a useful starting point for this discussion, the theoretical grounding for this essay is the body of cultural studies scholarship on *semiology*—the study of signs and how they take on their meaning. I then segue into how another type of architecture also empowers the Obama brand. My focus in this part of the essay is on the concept of the *network society*, which, according to social theorist Manuel Castells, "is a society where the key social structures and activities are organized around electronically processed information networks" (Castells and Ince, 26). These theories help me illustrate how two social processes work in tandem in the creation of America's first political superbrand—an important marker for the symbolic terrain on which politics and popular culture meet.

## On Myth, Semiology, and National Identity

*Myth* is a concept that has taken on varied meanings over time. Cultural critic Raymond Williams describes myth as a form of narrative that emerges from "a particular imaginative construction" and finds its "cause in the circumstances of [a] fabulous history" (Williams, 211–12). In this sense, myths are fantastical, often used as an origin story to explain natural phenomena or human nature. Alternatively, myths can have value beyond mere legend. With the rise of anthropology as a social science in the nineteenth and twentieth centuries, myths took on a more utilitarian function as a site for understanding the social organization of cultural practices, how people understand the world around them, and the rituals constructed around that understanding (ibid.). In this sense, myths are more than just fables; they are a way of constructing meaning.

For the purposes of this piece, I borrow from Roland Barthes' seminal work *Mythologies*, in which he identifies myth as a type of speech, "a system of communication ... a message" that is laden with meaning (109). Like language, myths are shaped by the cultural contexts in which they appear. As Barthes elucidates further, myths are "a type of speech chosen by history: [they do not simply] evolve from the 'nature' of things" (110). We can find elements of myth everywhere, which is to say that they "speak" to us through many different kinds of communication such as language or art. Barthes points out that "[m]ythical speech is made of material which has *already* been worked on so as to make it suitable for communication: it is because all of the materials of myth ... presuppose a signifying consciousness, that one can reason about them while discounting their substance" (ibid.).

It is here that we can locate the theoretical grounding for semiology and its use in the analysis of symbols and the myths that give them meaning. Semiology is a "science of forms" that "studies significations apart from their content" (Barthes, 112–13). In other words, semiology decodes modes of expression; it is not so much concerned with the mode itself as it is with how that expression gets its meaning. It is a dialectical process that looks at the relationship between two basic elements, a *signifier* (a medium of expression) and the *signified* (the idea being expressed). Together, the signifier and the signified make up the *sign*, "the associative total" of the signifier and the signified (ibid.). Barthes uses the example of a bunch of roses to make his point. The roses themselves are signifiers used to convey, or *signify*, the idea "passion." Together, the roses and the notion of passion blend, or "decompose," into a unit of symbolic meaning in which roses come to represent passion (Barthes, 113).

Although we often use the concepts *signifier* and *sign* interchangeably, in Barthes' theoretical framework they are distinct. Let's say, for instance, I make a gesture holding up two fingers. This gesture can express any number of ideas depending on the context. For example, it could be a peace sign. Alternatively, it could express "V" as in "victory." Or it could just simply convey the number two. In and of itself, the gesture I make with my two fingers means nothing — to use Claude Lévi-Strauss' term, it is a "floating" or "empty" signifier (63–64). It only becomes a sign when I "weight" this gesture with meaning.

The relationship I have just outlined constitutes the first order or "linguistic" plane of semiology that describes how a sign conveys its message. The second order, the "mythological" plane of Barthes' framework, interrogates the underlying logic of signs. While the goal of semiology's linguistic plane is to discover the message conveyed by a particular sign ("x" means "y"), the mythological plane reveal the processes through which signs are infused with meaning (how has "x" come to mean "y"?). Alternatively, if a sign in the first order of semiological analysis is a linguistic expression, in the second order, the sign is a starting point for deciphering the metalanguage of which it is a part (Barthes, 115).

The mythical component of Barthes' semiological system is an extension of its linguistic roots, with the sign as its starting point. In the second order of semiological analysis, the sign becomes a *mythic signifier* or *form*. As a sign, the mythic signifier has meaning; as a form, however, that meaning is shallow until we understand the process behind its creation (Barthes, 119). As a signifier of the second order, the mythic form is dependent upon a *signified* for its interpretive value. This accomplice is found in a *concept* that conveys a "certain knowledge of reality" that is expressed through the mythic form (ibid.). To put it another way, the concept gives the mythic form a history and provides the context through which that history is understood. *Signification* is the final product of semiological analysis, the logic that unites the mythic form and concept. Like the linguistic sign, signification names the correlative process that culminates in the ordering of myth through formal analogy. As Barthes states, "Signification is the myth itself... the relation which unites the concept of myth to its meaning" (121–22).

Barthes' semiological model offers a theoretical grounding for the "myth and symbol" strain of American culture studies. Exemplified in works such as Henry Nash Smith's *Virgin Land: The American West as Symbol and Myth* (1950) and Leo Marx's *Machine in the Garden: Technology and the Pastoral Ideal in America* (1964), the union between myth and symbol is "an intellectual construction that fuses concept and emotion into an image" that constitutes "a product of imaginative perception, of the analogy-perceiving, metaphor-making, mytho-poetic power of the human mind" (Kuklick).

The model I have outlined provides a scheme with which we can unpack myths, symbols, and their use in the construction of national identities. Before I apply this construct to my analysis of the Obama brand, however, consider this example taken from Barthes' discussion of race and French national identity. In one section of *Mythologies*, Barthes directs his attention to a 1955 *Paris Match* magazine cover photo depicting a black youth in military-type garb, hand raised in a salute and eyes fixed on an object in the distance. In Barthes' estimation, that object is the *tricoulour*, the French national flag. This photograph documents a series of semiological processes. The photo itself is the linguistic signifier; the signified is the combined representation of "Frenchness" and "militariness." Together, the signifier and signified become a sign for "French imperiality" (Barthes, 118).

At the level of myth, this symbol becomes the form for a larger concept — the French Empire. From here, we can read various meanings into this particular signification of French colonialism and the history that informs it. One interpretation Barthes offers implies the beneficence of France's colonial exploits and an expression of the enthusiasm with which its subjects serve under the nation's flag. Alternatively, we can also read this photo as an alibi masking the oppressive practices of French colonialism (Barthes, 123).

Barthes' analysis of this *Paris Match* cover photo demonstrates how semiology can uncover symbolically coded constructions of race and national belonging. In the next section, I apply this method to unmask the cultural work done by the Obama brand to rework the idea of "progress"— a myth central to American national identity.

## Race, Nation, and Reframing the Myth of American Progress

In *Black Is a Country: Race and the Unfinished Struggle for Democracy*, Nikhil Singh makes use of African American painter Jacob Lawrence's 1950s series "Struggle ... from the History of the American People" to frame his discussion of race and its role in shaping U.S. national identity. The Struggle series depicts key events in the establishment of democratic rights in America. In it, Lawrence juxtaposes scenes from black history with seminal moments in the creation of the U.S. nation where African Americans are conspicuously absent. Two notable images in the series are *Struggle No. 2 (Massacre in Boston)* which portrays the infamous slaughter of Crispus Attucks, and *Struggle No. 5*, which depicts the resistance of slaves and free blacks to racial oppression in pre-revolutionary Boston. The program notes provided by the museum housing the Lawrence exhibit at the time praised the series for reaching past black history to represent the whole of the American experience (Singh, 15). As a historian, Singh brings a more critical reading to the Struggle series. For him, Lawrence's work highlights the general erasure of African Americans from much of U.S. history and critiques "the projection of images of black inclusion (often through the elevation of exemplary individuals) [that minimize] a contentious, unfinished history of collective struggles against white supremacist monopolies on nationalist ideals and practices" (Singh, 17).

How might we understand the symbolic images evoked by Obama's election victory in light of Singh's commentary? In one sense, Obama's achievement represents the ultimate transgression of America's "color line," the concept W.E.B. DuBois created to describe endemic racial divisions in U.S. society. Certainly, Obama's victory is an important symbolic intervention into America's struggle with race. In a statement that presages Obama's ascendancy to the presidency, Singh sums up his reading of Lawrence's Struggle series by averring that "there is no more powerful way to represent the political universality of the U.S. nation-state than to have black people stand in for the nation at large" (17). Critical race scholar Michael Eric Dyson applies this notion to Obama in his post-election commentary for *Ebony* magazine: "If Barack Obama's emergence as the most powerful man in the world has not relieved the pull between color and country, it has proved that the Black story *is* an American story" (90).

Of course, it would be naive to assert that Obama's achievement has effectively erased America's color line. In fact, I would argue that in many ways Obama's election actually brings America's color line into clearer focus. To borrow from Singh's critique, Obama's victory highlights the idea that "enlisting blacks in the story of the nation's transcendence of the racial past perpetuates the idea that the exemplary national subject is still somehow not black and that visible racial difference remains the real deficit and obstacle to be overcome" (17). Although Singh's analysis centers on Martin Luther King Jr., his commentary is especially compelling when we put Obama at the center of "[c]ivic myths about the triumph over racial injustice [that] have become central to the resuscitation of a vigorous and strident form of American exceptionalism — the idea of the United States as a unique and universal nation" (ibid.). The image of a black man as leader of the free world offers us the opportunity to revisit this concept and examine how Obama's symbolic power reworks the relationship between race and U.S. national identity.

"American exceptionalism" is a trope that originates in the Puritan belief that the U.S. holds a special place in the eyes of God, and that its "exceptional destiny ... is to transform itself into a model nation" (Madsen, 14). Poignant expressions of exceptionalism include John Winthrop's famous declaration in 1630 that the fledgling Massachusetts Bay Colony would be a "city upon a hill" that would stand as an example for the world to follow, and the concept of "Manifest Destiny" coined by John L. O'Sullivan in 1839 to justify nationalist expansion.

Exceptionalism's long history as part of America's origin myth has always carried with it an internal contradiction. While Winthrop cast himself and his followers as God's chosen people, he also characterized Native Americans as obstacles to the establishment of his imagined "city upon a hill." For O'Sullivan, the westward march of "Manifest Destiny" was an endeavor that he (and many others) envisioned would be carried out by the boots of white settlers, demonstrated by his fervent support for the annexation of Texas. Ultimately, the idea of universality that is purportedly at the core of American exceptionalism often manifests itself as a pretense for white superiority.

John Gast's 1872 allegorical painting *American Progress* and the narrative that often accompanies it by George Crofutt offer an instructive view into the United States' exceptionalist myth. According to Crofutt, America's westward movement is led by a "diaphanously and precariously clad" Caucasian female angel-like figure floating above the landscape, the "Star of Empire" on her forehead. In her right arm is a schoolbook, a symbol of American enlightenment; from her left hand trails a telegraph cable, a sign for the nation's technological prowess. An examination of the rest of this scene finds other images associated with the settlement of the American West. For example, underneath Gast's angel are the wagons, stagecoaches, railroads, and waterways that symbolize the advancements in transportation that helped spur Americans westward. In the foreground are the miners and pioneers whose settling of western lands represents the adaptability and industriousness that ultimately led to the conquest of the frontier. The Indians depicted in the lower left of

Gast's painting are forced to flee into the few vestiges of the Pacific Coast left to them. In Crofutt's estimation, they, along with other symbols of the wilderness (buffalo, horses, bears and other game), become overwhelmed by the divinely ordered march of progress or "Manifest Destiny."

The trope of the frontier offers a way of decoding conceptualizations of "progress" that have predominated for much of U.S. history. Although it appeared some twenty years after the work of Gast and Crofutt, Fredrick Jackson Turner's landmark essay "The Significance of the Frontier in American History" puts the images and ideas presented by these two men into an instructive mythological context. Presented at the 1893 World's Columbian Expedition in Chicago, Turner defined the frontier as the "outer edge of the wave [of Westward expansion] — the meeting point between savagery and civilization" (Turner, 85). Interestingly, Turner uses the concept of *hybridity* to define the nation's cultural identity, but only to highlight certain types of cultural mixing that keeps the idea of "progress" oriented around a narrative of white domination.

The cultural works I have just examined offer a set of tropes, images, and a metalanguage for understanding how "progress" has crystallized as an ideology in America's national consciousness. They also show how certain aspects of the nation's history can be repressed, pushed to the margins, and, at times, be completely written out of the American narrative. But the important lesson Barthes teaches us is that myth and the interpretation of history are contingent and can be refitted to present an alternative historical narrative, for "[m]yth is a pure ideographic system, where the forms are still motivated by the concept which they represent while not yet, by a long way, covering the sum if its possibilities for representation" (127).

To illustrate this, I point to how the now iconic image of Obama created by artist Shepard Fairey speaks to the concept "progress" very differently than Gast's scantily clad white-female-angel figure. Fairey's creative work is a compelling representation of how Obama's presidential campaign engaged the ideological "frontier" between race and U.S. national identity. The ubiquitous image of Obama, his visage awash in swatches of red, white, and blue in Fairey's signature agit-prop style, is based on a 2006 Associated Press photograph taken by Mannie Garcia and fashioned after Alberto Korda's famous picture of the revolutionary Ernesto "Che" Guevara. Like Gast's *American Progress*, Fairey's rendering of Obama-as-Progress is ripe for semiological analysis.

Juxtaposing this image, captioned with the single word "Progress," along with Gast's painting and Jacob Lawrence's Struggle series has the makings of a rich semiological project. Together, these works mark out a continuum of America's historic struggle with race. While Gast's rendering of the concept "progress" is little more than a thinly veiled whitewashing of the national imaginary, Lawrence's work subtly and subversively points out the stark contradiction between America's lofty national ideals and real social practices; his Struggle series depicts the plight of African Americans who may be *in* but are not fully part *of* mainstream U.S. society.

Fairey's work brings to mind a different conceptualization of "progress" in America. His use of Obama's image crosses the symbolic "frontier" between race and nation represented by DuBois' color line. Unlike Barthes' reading of the young black soldier who pledges his allegiance to a flag of French colonialism, Fairey's rendering of Obama does not signal racial oppression. The former captures the image of a young boy saluting the colors of a nation that keeps him and his blackness at a distance. The latter turns our understanding of the relationship between race and nation in U.S. society on its ear by depicting a black man who's image reflects the colors of the U.S. nation. One might even say that Fairey's work "empties" Obama of his blackness and replaces it with the colors of the nation he would soon represent as its president, deemphasizing the racial identity of the United States's first black chief executive while enhancing his national identity (recalling Singh's statement that "there is no more powerful way to represent the political universality of the U.S. nation-state than to have black people stand in for the nation at large"). Fairey's icon is a compelling representation of the significance of Obama's achievement — as a *black man*, he successfully presented himself before the American electorate as someone who could credibly represent *everyman*.

The image of Obama-as-Progress captures the essence of an alternative national origin myth — one repeatedly told by Obama himself. Billed as the first black candidate with a genuine chance to win the presidency, Obama and his surrogates carefully cultivated a campaign that aimed to deemphasize the significance of race — or at least neutralize the subject when it did not gain him an advantage. An important key to Obama's mainstream appeal as a candidate was that he served as the embodiment of racial progress. During Obama's campaign, *hybridity* became a trope that marked the candidate's coming-out party at the 2004 Democratic National Convention ("There is not a Black America and a White America and Latino America and Asian America — there's the United States of America") and his triumph in negating the threat posed to his campaign by the incendiary comments made by the Rev. Jeremiah Wright about the condition of black people in the United States. Consider this well-known excerpt from Obama's famous speech on race in America:

> I am the son of a black man from Kenya and a white woman from Kansas. I was raised with the help of a white grandfather who survived a Depression to serve in Patton's Army during World War II and a white grandmother who worked on a

bomber assembly line at Fort Leavenworth while he was overseas. I've gone to some of the best schools in America and lived in one of the world's poorest nations. I am married to a black American who carries within her the blood of slaves and slaveowners — an inheritance we pass on to our two precious daughters. I have brothers, sisters, nieces, nephews, uncles and cousins, of every race and every hue, scattered across three continents, and for as long as I live, I will never forget that in no other country on Earth is my story even possible [Obama, "A More Perfect Union"].

Obama's claim that his unique personal story is "quintessentially American" strikes a chord similar in tenor to African American literary and jazz critic Albert Murray's take on race and national identity in his acclaimed 1970 essay collection, *The Omni-Americans: New Perspectives on Black Experience and American Culture,* in which the author asserts:

American culture, even in its most rigidly segregated precincts, is patently and irrevocably composite. It is, regardless of all the hysterical protestations of those who would have it otherwise, incontestably mulatto. Indeed, for all their traditional antagonisms and obvious differences, the so-called black and so-called white people of the United States resemble nobody else in the world so much as they resemble each other. And what is more, even their most extreme and violent polarities represent nothing so much as the natural history of pluralism in an open society [22].

By rescripting America's narrative with regard to race, Obama and his surrogates were able to forge a powerful political persona that mitigated the tension between race and nation that became an indelible part of Campaign '08. In the next section of my essay, I examine how the Obama campaign used this persona to build a grassroots movement around a symbol that has become the most recognizable brand in American politics.

## *Deconstructing "Brand Obama"*

A key aspect in understanding Obama's electoral success involves an appreciation of the skill with which he and his surrogates not only managed his identity as a presidential candidate, but also the ability of his campaign to effectively project to the American voters a vision of the nation created in Obama's own cosmopolitan image. In his edited compilation examining the 2008 elections, political science scholar Robert E. Denton Jr. articulates the significance of symbolic imagery to presidential campaigns. He notes:

Presidential campaigns are our national conversations. They are highly complex and sophisticated communication events: communication of issues, images, social reality, and personas. They are essentially exercises in the creation, recreation, and transmission of "significant symbols" through human communication. As we attempt to make sense of our environment, "political bits' of communication comprise our voting choices, worldviews, and legislative desires [xiiii].

Additionally, Anne Morton instructively points out that "[t]he President's representative function is ... first semiotic, only secondarily executive. The President does not serve simply as the executive of the popular will expressed through legislation. Rather, the President serves first as a symbol and, secondly, as rhetorical strategy" (87). Obama's presidential campaign provides an instructive lesson in political communication; it involved a strategic rhetoric of motives and moves that advanced his candidacy while negating the influence that race would have on his run for the Oval Office.

Not only did Obama prove himself an apt orator, but he and his advisers also a showed their mastery of the "significant symbols" that represented his candidacy. An ironic twist to my deconstruction of the icon of Obama-as-Progress is that the candidate never officially sanctioned the rendering that brought Shepard Fairey so much acclaim. As Fairey points out, he got an "unofficial nod and wink" from the Obama campaign when he sought permission to produce the image. It was only after Fairey's initial printing with the caption "progress" proved so popular that the campaign commissioned an official version of the print. The only caveat was that Fairey change the caption underneath the image from "progress" to "hope." The switch was calculated; according the artist, Obama's surrogates thought "'progress' sounded too Marxist" (Worthman, "'Obey' Street Artist Churns Out 'Hope' for Obama").

Such attention to symbolic nuances shows the high level of marketing acumen that fueled Obama's political success. The campaign took full advantage of Fairey's pop-art remixing of Soviet-era-style authoritative propaganda while avoiding any adverse political associations. Just as Fairey's rendering of Obama deemphasizes race, the switch in captions from "progress" to the now iconic "hope" works to "empty" a graphic style associated with agitprop of its revolutionary overtones (Kennicott).

These examples of the strategic choices behind Obama iconography show the skill with which the campaign maximized the popularity of the candidate while suppressing any controversy he might draw. In terms of the realpolitik involved in a presidential campaign, these moves make sense. However, it is ironic that a candidacy like Obama's, laden with so much history and symbolic meaning, could be represented so effectively by a the now famous logo that does not overtly reference any of it.

So what was the thinking behind the "O" logo? According to Sol Sender, owner of the graphic design team that came up with the concept, "We were looking at the "O" of [Obama's] name and had the idea of a rising sun and a new day.... The sun rising over the horizon evoked a new sense of hope."

Advertising experts quickly took notice of the design, commenting that "[p]atriotism is the foundation [of the logo], but above that is hope, opportunity, newness," and that it had "a nice, contemporary, dynamic, youthful vibe about it" (Yue, "Chicago Designers Create Obama's Logo"). The campaign logo adheres to a traditional color scheme of red, white, and blue and at the same time represents the qualities that made Obama such a standout candidate. New. Different. Attractive. Three things that make Obama the perfect brand (McGirt, "The Brand Called Obama").

These are very inviting descriptions. However, they belie some very important aspects of the "O" logo that offer a deeper explanation of its power as a brand. First, I find it interesting that beyond the ideas of "hope," "change," and "progress," the "O" logo suggests little else. Dare I say nothing else? Zero? I do not mean this in a derogatory way; it is a shrewd marketing move that the messages associated with Obama's campaign logo are limited to simple ideas that most anyone can relate to. Like Nike's famous "Just Do It" campaign, the "O" logo suggests values that people want to identify with. No additives. No preservatives. And, most importantly, no drama. As a black man running for president of the United States, Obama had to walk a number of political tightropes to maintain the image of unity his candidacy depended on. The Reverend Wright controversy that precipitated Obama's speech on race and, soon after, the disavowal of his former pastor posed the most serious threat to the everyman image that became Obama's stock-in-trade. That imbroglio helped fuel further speculation about Obama's personal values. Does he have a secret black agenda? Is he a Muslim? Is he a socialist? Is he even really American?

The "O" logo works against many attempts to cast Obama in an unpatriotic light, demonstrating one way of interpreting its symbolic meaning. In one sense, the "O" can stand for "openness." While suppressing the racial drama that accompanied Obama's candidacy, the "O" logo stands as a floating signifier, consistent with the candidate's ability to represent almost anything to anyone. The facility with which Obama appealed to a number of different constituencies proved to be his greatest asset during Campaign '08. At once, Obama presents himself as professorial, cool, elitist, a hip-hop icon, a sex symbol, an inheritor of the civil rights movement, racial healer, black (to some, too much; for others, not enough), authentic, and an outsider. While some have accused Obama of being a political flip-flopper, it must be said that Obama embodies what any good brand should—flexibility. It is no coincidence that as a function of his own racial and cultural hybridity, Obama can credibly occupy a number of different subject positions comfortably. He can hold court among the nation's elite and remain credible among the masses. He points to both Abraham Lincoln and his grassroots organizing on the

South Side of Chicago as his political influences. He exudes the intelligence and youthful exuberance of JFK and speaks in cadences that recall the lofty speeches of MLK. In this way, the "O" acts as a mirror that reflects the inherent diversity of the nation. It is also a portal through which Americans can look back on the difficulty of the nation's racial past and still have an optimistic outlook on its future. One only needs to look at the many different ways the "O" logo has been appropriated across myriad demographics for proof of its appeal as a brand during Obama's campaign. "African-Americans for Obama." "Asian-Americans for Obama." "Native Americans for Obama." "¡Obamanos!" As a floating signifier, the "O" logo at once absorbs, reflects, and represents the diversity of those who seek to identify with it. Consider the many social and historical references Obama had at his disposal during Campaign '08. Remember that he was not the first black politician to use the key words "hope" and "change" as his political rally cry. It was Jesse Jackson who made them part of his presidential bids in 1984 and 1988. Obama's "Yes We Can" speech, given after his defeat to Hilary Clinton in the New Hampshire primary, was his take on Cesar Chavez's famous rallying cry "¡Si Se Puede!" Such is the flexibility of the Obama brand that as a candidate he could "remix" a number of diverse American cultural references that suited his purposes.

The "O" logo is a perfect storm of marketing and politics that aims at "projecting and selling an image, stoking aspirations, moving people to identify, evangelize, and consume" (McGirt). To understand the pop culture explosion that fueled Obama's bid for president, one has to understand how neatly he fit into the diverse demographics to which he appealed for votes. As one advertising executive lucidly points out,

> Obama has his greatest strength among the young, roughly 18 to 29 years old, that advertisers covet, the cohort known as millennials — who will outnumber the baby boomers by 2010. They are black, white, yellow, and various shades of brown, but what they share — new media, online social networks, a distaste for top-down sales pitches — connects them more than traditional barriers, such as ethnicity, divide them [McGirt].

Which brings us to my last point about what the "O" logo represents as a brand — "opportunity." With his intelligence, good looks, charisma, and gift for oratory, it is no surprise that Obama was able to take full advantage of traditional media such as radio, print, and television during his run for the presidency. It was his campaign's command of new media that vaulted Obama from political neophyte to big-name player. Howard Dean first showed us how the Internet could be harnessed to political advantage in his ill-fated presidential campaign of 2000. By the time Obama launched his bid, the social networks used by a new generation of voters had come to full maturity. Applications such as YouTube, Facebook, and MySpace, along with instantaneous messaging capabilities from a number of new media, provided Obama's campaign with the ability to reach large numbers of voters with a minimum of effort. The significance of Obama's use of new media is that it made his campaign the hub of an organized network of active supporters. Though his campaign incorporated elements of a top-down structure that relied on broadly disseminated messages, its essence was built from the grassroots, employing established social networks to spread its message. In this way the "O" logo acted as the central node of a networked society of citizens. In such a society, according to sociologist Manuel Castells, "communication technologies, such as the Internet, allow for decentralization of operations and focusing of control, increasing the effectiveness of networks relative to hierarchical structures" (176).

Many observers have commented on how the Obama campaign's use of new media has "revolutionized" politics. This is true to an extent. But what often gets missed in such analyses is that this phenomenon is based on what are ultimately organic forms of social organization that have rallied around the ethos projected by Obama. Instead of focusing our attention on the power of new media to abet Obama's popularity, I argue that observers of this phenomenon should pay more attention to the "networks of influence" the Obama campaign used to great effect. While some might be tempted to believe that new media is the "message" behind Obama's support, I submit that they only highlight what makes social organizations effective in real life — commitment to a common cause.

This is not to say that the manner in which the Obama campaign grafted itself onto the decentralized nature of online social networks is not worth some special attention. Chris Hughes, co-founder of Facebook and coordinator of MyBarackObama.com, points out that while the site was the official center of Obama's campaign operations, it was also the "connective tissue" that held the movement supporting his candidacy together. MyBarackObama.com provided supporters with resources to extend Obama's influence such as do-it-yourself blog rolls, access to video and print materials, and contact information for undecided voters in local areas. The site enabled the creation of myriad unofficial Obama surrogates and "made it possible for people to participate where they wanted, how they wanted, using the tools and friendships they wanted" (Anonymous, "Web 2.0 Case Study"). For example, "Yes We Can!," the song and video put together by the Black Eyed Peas' will.i.am, is the quintessential example of this process. Created with footage from Obama's New Hampshire primary loss, "Yes We Can!" became an unofficial campaign ad for Obama disseminated over YouTube to millions of viewers.

The Obama brand's "viral" quality allowed this historic campaign to efficiently and effectively reach a large number of supporters across categories of race, age, gender, and class and unite them with a common purpose. The most important lesson we can take away from this example is the simple notion that with the right idea and the appropriate tools, a movement can be built by forging a series of small spheres of influence into a broad-based movement for social change.

Brands, like myths, are built on ideas that resonate with us. They are an expression of our desires. They also exemplify how we understand ourselves and how we understand the world around us. The ideas I have presented in this essay attempt to illustrate how semiological analysis can help us better understand the foundations of "Obama-mania"—to date, the most poignant example of how the worlds of politics and popular culture meet on the same symbolic terrain. In the age of new media, the processes of meaning making are taking on a new shape and intensity that are having a profound effect on the creation and circulation of ideas — and more importantly, of ideology. To what degree will new media help us understand this blending of the worlds of politics and popular culture? To what degree will new media further blur the lines between the two? What I have offered in this essay is a framework for understanding the significance of these questions and a starting point from which we can engage them.

## REFERENCES

Anonymous. "Web 2.0 Case Study: Barack Obama's Use of Social Media." *Global Human Capital Journal*, December 29, 2008. http://globalhumancapital.org/?p=216 (accessed October 10, 2009).
Barthes, Roland. *Mythologies*. 36th ed. Trans. Annette Lavers. New York: Hill & Wang, 2000.
Castells, Manuel, and Martin Ince. *Conversations with Manuel Castells*. Malden, MA: Blackwell Publishing, 2003.
\_\_\_\_\_. *Rise of the Network of Society*. Malden, MA: Blackwell Press, 2000.
Denton, Robert E., Jr. Preface to *The 2008 Presidential Campaign: A Communication Perspective*, ed. Robert E. Denton Jr., ix–xvi (Lanham, MD: Rowman & Littlefield).
Dyson, Michael Eric. "An American Man, An American Moment." *Ebony*, January 2009, 90–91.
Kennicott, Phillip. "The Power of Brand-Old Message Art." *Washington Post*, January 12, 2009. http://www.washingtonpost.com/wp-dyn/content/article/2009/01/12/AR2009011203422.html?referrer=emailarticle (accessed December 20, 2009).
Klein, Naomi. "Naomi Klein on How Corporate Branding Is Taking over America." *The Guardian*, January 16, 2010. http://www.guardian.co.uk/books/2010/jan/16/naomi-klein-branding-obama-america (accessed March 5, 2010).
Kuklick, Bruce. "Myth and Symbol in American Studies." In *Locating American Studies: The Evolution of a Discipline*, ed. Lucy Maddox. Baltimore, MD: Johns Hopkins University Press, 1999.
Lévi-Strauss, Claude. *Introduction to Marcel Mauss*. London: Routledge, 1987.
Madsen, Deborah L. *American Exceptionalism*. Jackson: University of Mississippi Press, 1998.
McGirt, Ellen. "The Brand Called Obama." *Fast Company*, April 1, 2008. http://www.fastcompany.com/magazine/124/the-brand-called-obama.html (accessed March 5, 2009).

Murray, Albert. *The Omni Americans: New Perspectives on Black Experience and American Culture.* New York: Outerbridge and Dienstfrey, 1970.

Norton, Anne. *Republic of Signs.* Chicago: University of Chicago Press, 1993.

Obama, Barack. "A More Perfect Union." Keynote address given at the National Constitution Center, Philadelphia, PA, March 18, 2008. http://www.constitutioncenter.org/amoreperfectunion (accessed May 14, 2008).

Singh, Nikhil. *Black Is a Country: Race and the Unfinished Struggle for Democracy.* Cambridge, MA: Harvard University Press, 2004.

Turner, Frederick Jackson. "The Significance of the Frontier in American History." In *The American Studies Anthology*, ed. Richard P. Horwitz, 83–96. Wilmington, DE: Scholarly Resources, 2001.

Williams, Raymond. *Keywords: A Vocabulary of Culture and Society.* New York: Oxford University Press, 1985.

Wortham, Jenna. "'Obey' Street Artist Churns Out 'Hope' for Obama." *Wired*, September 21, 2008.

Yue, Lorene. "Chicago Designers Create Obama's Logo." *Crain's Chicago Business*, February 7, 2007. http://www.chicagobusiness.com/cgi-bin/news.pl?id=23974 (accessed March 5, 2009).

## SECTION TWO

# FILM AND TELEVISION: CHANGE TELEVISED

# Character-in-Chief
## Barack Obama and His Pop Culture Predecessors
### JUSTIN S. VAUGHN

*Introduction: Idealized Fictional Black Presidents and the Public Response*

At some point during the 2008 presidential election between Barack Obama and John McCain, it became fashionable for various journalists and essayists to craft articles on the notion that the genesis of now–President Obama's success was owed not to the Illinois Democrat's impressive 2004 DNC convention speech but rather to a handful of African American actors that had come before him. In particular, writers credited figures like Bill Cosby, Morgan Freeman, and Sidney Poitier with preparing broad swathes of the white electorate to imagine black executive leadership as not only possible but also positive. Actor Dennis Haysbert further gave voice to this position, arguing that his own work portraying a black president in the hit television program *24* was instrumental in Obama's election.

In mid-summer 2008, during a promotional conference call with entertainment reporters across the nation, Haysbert, who spent three years as *24*'s President David Palmer, said, "If anything, my portrayal of David Palmer, I think, may have helped open the eyes of the American people. And I mean the American people across the board — from the poorest to the richest, every color and creed, every religious base — to prove the possibility there could be an African-American president, a female president, any type of president that puts the people first" (Sonner, 2008).

Haysbert's contention was seconded by D.B. Woodside, who played David Palmer's brother Wayne, who later became *24*'s second black president: "David Palmer had a huge impact on the country being open to an African-American president" (Callahan 2008). Although Haysbert might be the first actor to link directly his portrayal of a fictional black leader to the subsequent political success of an actual African American politician, he is far from alone in making the claim that filmic and televisual portrayals of black presidents increased acceptance for the real thing among white members of the electorate.

Three years before Haysbert presided over the first of Kiefer Sutherland's long days on *24*, Morgan Freeman played a supporting role in the science-fiction disaster film *Deep Impact*. As President Tom Beck, Freeman led the nation in its space-based defensive action against an asteroid hurtling toward Earth and, after the failure of the effort, in its pre-apocalyptic preparation, with gravitas and command. Although the race of President Beck was never mentioned in the film, it was a subject of considerable attention after it screened, much of it largely positive. Freeman himself noted that white viewers often commented to him that they wish he was the president in real life, and he was quoted in a 2008 *Los Angeles Times* article saying, "If you think of these roles and how the country reacted, you kind of get the notion that perhaps they could handle it" (Stein, 2008).

Journalists and culture critics pick up where actors like Freeman and Haysbert leave off, and in the very same article that quoted Freeman, columnist Joel Stein boldly pushes this argument: "American is ready for a black president because we've seen them before. Black presidents, in fact, have been our awesomest presidents ever: Morgan Freeman in *Deep Impact* and Dennis Haysbert in *24*." Hyperbole aside, Stein's contention is not unique. A year later, Manohla Dargis and A.O. Scott (2009) wrote in the *New York Times*, "The presidencies of James Earl Jones in *The Man*, Morgan Freeman in *Deep Impact*, Chris Rock in *Head of State*, and Dennis Haysbert in *24* helped us imagine Mr. Obama's transformative breakthrough before it occurred. In a modest way, they also hastened its arrival." Writing for the *Jerusalem Post* in the summer of 2008, Solomon Israel remains agnostic about the impact of individual roles, but he does attribute an aggregate effect to the collective effort, noting, "If life truly does imitate art, Barack Obama can rest assured that the long-standing American tradition of black presidents on both the big and little screens has accustomed Americans to the idea of an African-American leader" (Israel, 2008). Months later, writing on the day of Obama's historic victory, Miro Cernetig (2008) gives credit to Hollywood in the *Vancouver Sun*, noting, "In fact, you could say it was America's dream factory ... that first prepared Americans, and the rest of us, for the possibility." Greg Braxton (2008), treating the commentary as the actual cultural artifact, observed as much when he wrote in the *Los Angeles Times* about "a somewhat surprising consensus that admirable black fictional figures subtly might have conditioned the electorate to be receptive to a candidate like Obama."

The central problem with these assessments is that they are basing their conclusions on cherry-picked data. Although Haysbert's President Palmer and Freeman's President Beck were generally positive (though hardly perfect) depictions of African American political leadership, they are far from the only portrayals that the American viewing public has seen. If we are to believe that the character of black presidential characters in films affects individual voter decision making, we must also be ready to acknowledge that such portrayals can be both positive and negative and that the impact of both kinds of portrayals matters to the electoral calculus.

Unfortunately for those who attempt to advance the thesis that fictional presidential portrayals paved the way for the election of Barack Obama, there are many more cultural artifacts to draw upon than simply those featuring Dennis Haysbert and Morgan Freeman. In addition to them, there are also fictional presidents ranging from unimpressive to incompetent to infuriating. If we are to believe that the good fictional presidents made the idea of a real black president palatable to voters, we also must accept the fact that the negative portrayals reinforced bias-driven concerns and ambivalence about electing a minority president. In other words, imagination is not value neutral, and if fictional portrayals are able to make voters imagine new possibilities, the tone of those fictional portrayals also influences the extent to which those imagined possibilities are positive or negative, desirable or something to be avoided.

The central argument of this essay is twofold: that the tone of these cultural portrayals is important and that, while there has been some improvement in recent years, the preponderance of the portrayals presents the possibility of black presidents in an unflattering light. As a result, when looking at all fictional black presidents rather than a selected sample of only the positive depictions, and taking the messages sent by these portrayals into account, the argument that such portrayals paved the way for the election of Barack Obama fails. In the pages that follow, I examine these portrayals, gauging the message and tracking the evolution of it, before placing President Obama's ascension in its context.

## *Black Presidents in American Popular Culture*

The mass-market portrayals of black presidents on film and television are actually relatively few in number. The earliest such portrayal referenced is a 1933 short musical film titled *Rufus Jones for President* that starred jazz singer Ethel Waters as the mother of a seven-year-old Sammy Davis Jr. In the film, young Rufus Jones, the character played by Davis, becomes the president of the United States, albeit literally in his mother's dreams. During the dream, images of the black child president are interspersed with a seemingly endless parade of racist visual clichés. As cultural critic Louis Bayard (2008) wrote in salon.com, "A modern viewer barely has time to register the aspiration before recoiling at the racial slurs that were common to that day: black voters lured to the polls with free pork chops; Rufus celebrating his victory with a half-eaten piece of chicken; a presidential platform that calls for unlatching chicken coops and planting watermelon vines close to the fence." If the dream sequence nature of the film's narrative failed to make the point that the idea of a black president was mere fantasy in the early years of the Depression, three decades before the passage of landmark civil rights and voting rights legislation and a lifetime before the inauguration of Barack Obama, the sheer ridiculousness of the way black politics and politicians were portrayed in the film completed the task. Between the child president's mother declaring herself "presidentress" and vowing to make poultry stealing easier and a call from the floor of the Senate to fill the roll of "dice" president with a senatorial gambling aficionado, the story's key thrust is clear: a black president will not soon come to the United States and thankfully so, given the havoc it would wreak on the political order and society. Eight years later, Judy Garland performed in black male drag as "Franklin Delano Jones" in the musical film *Babes on Broadway*, cementing the notion that black presidents are a fantastical phenomenon.

## *Conspiracy and Farce in the 1970s*

In the seventy years since, portrayals have continued to adapt this fantastical dimension into plot after plot, with the only variation coming in exactly how the fantasy affected the story, whether through how the individual at hand became president, how he behaved as president, or with respect to the scenarios he had to face as president. In 1972, James Earl Jones starred in the film version of Irving Wallace's lengthy pulp tome *The Man*, portraying President Pro Tempore Douglass Dillon. After poor health and disaster wipe out the president, vice president, and speaker of the House, Dillon ascends to the office by virtue of the succession mechanism in the Twenty-Fifth Amendment to the U.S. Constitution. Political scientist Lilly Goren (2006) has argued that the way in which minority candidates, both in terms of race and gender, achieve high office in fictional portrayals matters, as it represents social comfortability with minority leadership. In her paper, she notes that *The Man*'s protagonist came to the Oval Office not through legitimate democratic processes, but rather through technical and constitutionally prescribed procedural accident, thus casting the shadow of electoral illegitimacy onto President Dillon's character. Add to this the concern the film's narrative has with Dillon's potentially radical politics, which are considerably muted in comparison with the original novel version of the story but still present, and *The Man* operates not as an engine of progress but rather as a cultural artifact of fear, with a powerful black man usurping control and engaging in policy behavior at the expense of the white majority who were unable to vote against his selection. At that point in American history, the likelihood of such a presidency in reality is still low, at least outside of supermarket-aisle fiction, but the viewing public is still conditioned to be both skeptical and fearful of any potential manifestation.

By the end of the 1970s, this duality of fictional black presidents as something both unlikely and unwelcomed had descended into farce and had become largely entrenched in the arena of edgy and profane urban comedy. In 1977, in the first episode of the *Richard Pryor Show*, seminal black comedian Pryor staged a mock press conference with himself playing the role of the first black president. The bit, which lasts less than seven minutes, introduces Pryor as the fortieth president of the United States (a spot occupied in history by Ronald Reagan) and proceeds at first in a serious manner with President Pryor receiving largely deferential treatment from a mostly white press corps and espousing well-reasoned and middle-ground policy positions on issues like the Middle East peace process and the development of the neutron bomb. Race does not enter the skit until the third question is asked, concerning the nation's unemployment rate, where Pryor differentiates between levels for white Americans and unemployed black Americans. Even then, however, his rhetoric and demeanor is calm and thoughtful, though with the laughter of the in-studio audience, it becomes clear that such poise from a black president is itself a humorous proposition.

A fourth question allows Pryor to settle a little deeper into his famed racialized humor, answering a black reporter from Chicago's question about increased funding for NASA with the statement about it being time for black people to go to space, noting that "white people have been going to space for years ... and spacing out on us as you might say," and goes on to say that he plans to add selections from Miles Davis and Charlie Parker to existing cultural caches making their way to distant galaxies. Midway through the press conference, Pryor takes a question from a female reporter representing *Jet* magazine, the politically influential black weekly. Pryor salutes the reporter as he listens to her question about whether President Pryor intended to include Huey Newton on his list of potential FBI directors. As most viewers of the day would know, Newton was co-founder of the controversial Black Panther Party and had spent much of the previous decade involved in legal wrangling over allegations of manslaughter and murder concerning the death of an Oakland police officer. Pryor played off this situation, noting that Newton would indeed be on his short list, saying, "Yes, I figure Huey Newton is the best qualified. He knows the ins and outs of the FBI, if anybody knows the ins and outs, and he would be an excellent director." This question is followed by one from a reporter from *Ebony* magazine wearing a beret and who greets the president with a black power salute and the salutation "Yo, Blood" and "As-Salamu Alaykum," to which the president responds with both a surprised facial expression and the traditional Islamic response, "Alaykum as-Salaam." The reporter then challenges a nearby white reporter, asking, "What you looking at, Snow White?" before asking about the president's position on blacks in the labor force, with specific interest in having black quarterbacks in the "National Football Honky League."

It is at this point that President Pryor finally becomes animated, straying from the dull policy rhetoric and making increasingly energized proclamations. As Teresa Wiltz (2009) writes in *The Root*, "Once the black reporters start asking questions, the rage beneath the sober façade starts to peep through, and the president's agenda becomes evident." Pryor says,

> I plan not only to have lots of black quarterbacks, but we are going to have black coaches and black owners of teams. As long as there is going to be football, there is going to be some black in it somewhere. Because I'm tired of this mess that's been going down. Ever since the Rams got rid of James Harris, my jaw's been uptight.

By the time he finishes his answer, Pryor is so riled up that when the next reporter, a white journalist representing the *Mississippi Herald*, introduces himself, the president orders him to sit down. The journalist next to him, a white woman representing a Christian women's publication, then asks the president about being photographed with and generally courting white women. As the audience oohs and ahhs, Pryor appears both nervous and amused and informs the journalist that he does intend to continue his associations with white women "as long as he can keep it up," following that statement up with a rhetorical question: "Why do you think they call it the White House?"

Finally, the stage is set for the skit's ultimate question, asked by a white male reporter with a slight southern drawl. The question is initially prefaced with a reference to President Carter's mother's occupation as a nurse, at which point Pryor interrupts to ask what his question is about before being informed that it is indeed about the president's mother. Chaos briefly reigns and violence in the press room seems to loom as a scuffle starts between the questioner and the black journalist next to him, and President Pryor himself moves to leave the podium and heads in the journalist's direction. The room soon calms and Pryor indicates that the question should go on, though not without giving the journalist a lengthy hard look. Once the question is finally posed, the hard look proves warranted, as the journalist points out that the president's mother used to be a maid in Atlanta and wants to know if, after the president's tenure in office ends, she will go back to work and, if so, if she will clean his house. The scene immediately devolves into a race riot, with security carrying a violent Pryor away from the room as the violence continues behind him and the skit comes to an end. In only a handful of minutes, Pryor has taken the notion of a serious black presidency and whittled it down to the point of nonsense, using the press room as a forum to exhibit continuing racial tension when it comes to issues of sexuality, wealth, and inequality.

## Black Presidents as a Stand-Up Comedy Staple

Six years later, in Eddie Murphy's 1983 classic comedy concert documentary *Delirious*, the stand-up artist continues commentary on this tension as he riffs on the likelihood of Jesse Jackson winning a presidential election (a possibility attributed to the chance that white voters might vote for the "wrong" candidate on purpose as a joke) and then on his need to be in shape in order to elude assassins in the audience during subsequent presidential speeches. Once again, the notion of an actual black president is presented as unlikely, even humorous in its ludicrousness, and now an additional layer of negativity surrounding the phenomenon is added: the fear that a black president somehow elected, whether through a misguided joke or some other inexplicable development, will be killed by whites who cannot tolerate such a progressive development in the narrative of American history.

Two decades later, stand-up comedian Dave Chappelle picks up the assassination thread from Murphy, beginning a brief bit about the possibility of the first black president, wondering about the safety of such a person. Chappelle goes on to note that he would serve as the first black president though, saying, "I don't think nobody would really, really hurt me. I'm sure somebody would want to hurt me, but I don't think they'd touch me because, uh, because my vice president would be Mexican, for a little insurance. You can shoot me if you want, but you're just going to open up the border, so you might as well leave me and Vice President Santiago to our own devices." As Chappelle's commentary suggests, in the intervening twenty-plus years since Murphy suggested the likelihood of a fatal attack against a sitting black president, the risk involved with being the first black president is still present, even if the notion of a first Latino president remains even less palatable for white voters.

## Recent Takes on the Notion of a Black Presidency

The apparent rise of American ambivalence toward Latino executive leadership was not the only difference in the years between Murphy's Reagan-era pondering of the assassination question and Chappelle's George W. Bush–era response. In the interim, there was a relative explosion in Hollywood portrayals of fictional black presidents, with as many coming in the 1990s and 2000s as in the sixty years between *Rufus Jones for President* and *Delirious*. However, even as the frequency of such portrayals increased, the fantastical dimension of such portrayals stayed the same. Moreover, they did so in three discrete ways. First, films dealt with the unreality of black presidents being elected by the American public. Second, films featuring fictional black presidents were frequently set well into the future in decayed and degraded settings when black leadership co-existed with a declining civilization. Third, films set in real time or the imaginable near future pitted black presidents against threats of such epic proportions that the very fate of the nation, if not the world, was in the president's frequently under-matched hands.

## Farfetchedness and Undesirability in Chris Rock's Head of State

The prime example in the first category of films, 2003's *Head of State*, is in many ways a continuation of the stand-up genre merely transferred to the silver screen. Written by, produced by, and starring stand-up comedian Chris Rock (with a co-starring role by fellow stand-up artist Bernie Mac), the film's entire narrative revolves around the low likelihood that a black politician would ever be nominated by a major party as its presidential candidate, much less elected to the office by the American people. Indeed, *Head of State* has more in common with *Rufus Jones for President* than any other fictional portrayal of black presidents, particularly in the way it portrays both black politicians and black citizens. The film begins with a BET-style video introduction as an R & B singer narrates the theme of the film alongside bikini-clad dancers in front of images of Mount Rushmore and various monuments on the National Mall in Washington, D.C. Later, when we first meet Rock's character, Alderman Mays Gilliam, we find him in a montage of constituent service that relies upon a series of derogatory black behavioral stereotypes as he fields calls about a "Million Baby Mama's March" and using food stamps to buy tires. Later, as we see Gilliam out and interacting with his public, we see him point out a street corner where generations of bicycles have been stolen before he interacts at a gas station with a stolen meat fence and car thieves.

Throughout the film, the idea of a black presidential candidacy is presented in a cynical manner. After the party's chosen candidate perishes in a plane crash and it becomes clear that their opponent is destined to win the election, a closed-door session of strategic functionaries decides to improve the party's relationship with minorities by fielding a black candidate to run the destined-to-lose race. The electoral logic is so transparently crass in this conversation that a rather addled member of the group speaks up to suggest a "cripple" as a candidate. Later, when the first campaign ad for the candidate is screened, there are only white actors in it. At another point in the film, viewers learn that the polls suggest Gilliam's opponent has a 91 to 9 percent advantage; later the figures change to 84 to 10 percent, with 6 percent undecided except for being certain they won't vote for the black candidate.

Much of the film is clearly influenced by the comedic takes on black presidents that preceded Rock's writing. Once Gilliam is informed that he will be the party's nominee, his first thought is an echo of the stand-up of Murphy (and presages Chappelle's) as he imagines getting shot at a podium while "Hail to the Chief" plays in the background. Later, viewers are confronted by a montage of magazine covers that ask in different ways whether America is ready for a black president, except, in homage perhaps to the aforementioned Richard Pryor sketch, *Ebony*, which runs the headline, "About Time."

Throughout the film, even as Gilliam's run becomes increasingly plausible and, eventually, successful, the screenplay trots out trope after trope representing sensationalized white fears of black leadership. Dismissive hip-hop references abound, from Gilliam telling his bodyguard that Tupac could have used someone like him, to being passed a demo tape by a caterer at a fundraising event, to playing Nelly and manning turntables as white donors do the electric slide before coaching guests through Prince's "Do Me Baby" and then starting a mass exodus from the party by ad libbing to Rock Master Scott's "The Roof Is on Fire."

In later scenes, Gilliam's bail bondsman brother and future vice presidential running mate thanks God for crime, Gilliam starts commissioning rap video–style campaign ads, security is taken over by Nation of Islam types, Gilliam receives endorsements from Raekwon and Ghostface Killah and asks his manager about M.C. Hammer being his running mate, he wears a FUBU suit to a presidential debate, he says his opponent who refuses to debate him is avoiding him like he owes child support, he tells a white woman she has to ride in the back of the bus, and after a strong response during the debate on a gun control question, he receives dap from his brother who has run out on stage. The journalistic response to Gilliam's candidacy is equally racialized, with conservative radio talking heads admonishing that Gilliam is running for president and "not talking about running a rib shack," while a black magazine claims Gilliam is half white — an issue that appeared during Obama's campaign — at a low point in the campaign. Even in the ultimate scene where Gilliam is celebrating his improbable victory and declaring that "for the first time in history a black man will be president of the United States of America," his body double is shot, and his brother/vice president elect says that Gilliam's enemies won't dare assassinate him because they don't want him to be president.

While *Head of State* is obviously and transparently silly, light humor, it serves to reinforce the notion that black presidential leadership is unlikely, and should the unlikely event come to fruition it is not something to be taken seriously, as evidenced by the closing image of Gilliam's face added to Mount Rushmore, with sizable bling in his diamond earring stud, and potentially something to be feared, as evidenced by the experience of the elderly white woman who found herself relegated to the back of the bus, where African Americans were forced to sit forty years before. The film, which is the only one in recent years to directly consider the merits of a black presidential campaign, does nothing to advance positive ideas about the phenomenon and instead says quite a lot to set them back. As a result, even five years before the eventual electoral victory of Barack Obama, the notion of a viable mainstream presidential candidacy by a black politician is seen as anything but a serious enterprise.

## *A Black President? Only in Outer Space*

A second category of fantastical portrayals of fictional black presidents concerns portrayals of declining civilizations degraded to the point where anything, including black presidential leadership, is possible. Two Hollywood films fit this category: 1997's *The Fifth Element* and 2006's *Idiocracy*. In both cases, viewers are treated to narratives that occur in the distant future; in *The Fifth Element*, it is 2214, while *Idiocracy* takes place in 2505. In both cases, the world is dirty, dingy, and dangerous, and the individuals who portray the black presidential characters are both imposing and ineloquent, if not outright incompetent.

The president in *The Fifth Element* is portrayed by Tommy "Tiny" Lister, a former professional wrestler best known for his acting work in the urban comedy *Friday*, where he played a menacing thug named Deebo. Lister's President Lindberg is still physically imposing in the film, though the indomitable air of Deebo is missing, as his presidential character is frequently anxious, flummoxed, and powerless throughout the film. The plot of *The Fifth Element* largely revolves around the search for an alien artifact that has taken the form of a young woman and that must be found before an attack by an opposing evil alien force takes place. Lindberg's attempts to deal with the situation are consistently unsuccessful, and throughout the film his emotional and physical reaction is always as inappropriate as it is unpresidential, whether in his over eagerness to celebrate a false success or his cowering at the end of the film from an attack that never comes. Lindberg's society is one that is highly technologically advanced yet corrupt, filthy, deteriorated, and filled with equal parts rubble and militaristic police forces. The lack of success as a leader of government and the military is evident throughout, most notably when he is referred to on the phone as an idiot by the mother of the film's central protagonist.

The president in *Idiocracy* is played by Terry Crews, a former professional football player turned actor. His character in the film, President Camacho, is a former professional wrestler and porn star that has become president of an America five hundred years in the future, where reverse natural selection has led to the complete bottoming out of human intellect. The film's introduction notes that during the intervening half millennium, "mankind became stupider at a frightening rate." It is in this state of intellectual demise that they selected a black president, though the race of the president is never directly addressed in the film. The first scene featuring the president takes place in a decrepit White House where we learn that the president was a five-time champion of an event called Ultimate Smackdown, an accomplishment that matches the other behaviors he exhibits throughout the film, including cursing, brandishing weapons, singing, dancing, crotch grabbing, stupid promise making, drinking and driving, and wearing outsized "bling" with a presidential seal. The president's interactions with the public are predictably inane, as he makes statements ranging from "This guy just got his ass a pardon" to a drunken declaration that "I got some presidential decrees to make."

As is the case in *The Fifth Element*, humanity is eventually saved, thanks to a white central protagonist, and while Bruce Willis heroically saved the planet in a blazing gun battle while President Lindberg cowered in a command center, this time a sardonic Luke Wilson adopts a Kennedyesque countenance and issues rhetorical promises of rebirth as President Camacho retires to a life of frolicking and partying. In both films, the black president is portrayed as an undesirable function of a devolved world teetering on the precipice of oblivion, until white characters usurp their control, whether officially or physically. Once again, the message of the portrayal posits black presidential leadership as equal parts fantasy and comic horror. As Bayard writes, "Rufus' minstrel trappings have long since faded away, but the freak principle has proven more tenacious.... In both movies [*The Fifth Element* and *Idiocracy*], the joke is essentially unchanged from the days of Rufus Jones: These are the last guys in the world — or any world — you'd want to vote for" (Bayard, 2008).

## *The Black Presidential Apocalypse*

The final category of films trade comic themes in for science fiction drama, casting black actors in roles featuring presidents dealing with crises that threaten to eradicate if not the human species then at least large swathes of the American populace. The two key films in this category include 1998's *Deep Impact* and 2009's *2012*, while the now landmark television portrayal of a black president by Dennis Haysbert in *24* also fits the bill. In both *Deep Impact* and *2012*, Earth is threatened by natural forces well beyond the control of mankind, and the presidents in office, played by Morgan Freeman and Danny Glover, respectively, are forced into somber ceremonial roles remembered more for their solemn poise in delivering mankind's eulogy than for policy leadership in combating the problem at hand. In *24*, Dennis Haysbert's David Palmer navigates a series of difficult scenarios all taking place in separate twenty-four-hour increments over the course of several years, including an assassination attempt as a presidential candidate, biological warfare with a drug cartel, and nuclear threats from both Central European and Middle Eastern terrorists too numerous to count.

The recent preponderance of these films prompted comedian Jon Stewart to crack at the 2008 Academy Awards, "Normally when you see a black man or a woman president, an asteroid is about to hit the Statue of Liberty" (Braxton, 2008). Similarly, *The Onion* posted in February of 2008 a fake op-ed warning voters against voting for a black candidate since fictional black presidential portrayals correlate with the destruction of America. As the "author" of that post argued, "We can't deny the facts, people. All we will get by electing an African-American is Texas-size space particles crashing into the Earth's surface, mega-tsunamis that barrel into the Appalachian Mountains, and 6.6 billion dead people." He then went on to draw an art-precedes-reality conclusion, stating, "If history is any indicator, a vote for Barack Obama in 2008 is essentially a vote for the complete and total obliteration of the human race" (Henry, 2008). These two comedic references only underscore the serious point that the ubiquitousness of this portrayal only further serves to cement the notion of black presidents as unreal fantasy.

The first of this trio, *Deep Impact*, features Morgan Freeman's President Tom Beck, whom Bayard refers to as "a commander in chief of such unquestioned authority that he can impose martial law the way other presidents declare commemorative holidays and, without triggering a single riot, can inform the American people that all but a million of them will be demolished by an asteroid seven miles wide." This description, if slightly more flip, is representative of virtually all journalistic commentary on the portrayal, highlighting exclusively Freeman's solemn and empathic demeanor. Such writing forgets, of course, that Freeman's character is first introduced to the viewer under a cloud of possible scandal, which proves to be narrative discretion and definite corrupt horse-trading with the press for future access in exchange for immediate silence. Later, we see the president's every policy effort fail, despite significant black-op funding hidden from the general public and most legislative leaders, forcing him to preside over the national panic that ensues when he finally tells the public of their fate and the militarized separation of a chosen few survivors (determined by both elite standing and random lottery). We last see Freeman's Beck addressing a crowd in front of the ruined Capitol after the damage proved less than anticipated, thanks to the heroic and sacrificial efforts of a shuttle crew who earlier failed to stop the approaching asteroid. Thus, rather than laudable leadership described by Bayard and his colleagues, American viewers saw a failed administration that, visually, was contrasted against a destroyed national capital and, narratively, had to be salvaged by a team of technocrats led by a heroic white male (Robert Duvall's out-of-retirement astronaut Spurgeon Tanner).

A clear parallel to *Deep Impact*, Danny Glover's portrayal of President Thomas Wilson in *2012* also must cope with an apparently unconquerable natural threat to humankind. Although Wilson's threat comes from inside the planet, thanks to an overheating core and the subsequent destabilization of Earth's crust, rather than from outer space as his fictional predecessor Beck's did, the character-based continuities, both commonly acknowledged and otherwise, are striking. Both Presidents Wilson and Beck are made well aware of the planetary threat, both lead major secret policy responses designed to cope with the devastation that privilege elites over the masses, and both see those policy initiatives initially flounder, though they ultimately succeed thanks to the heroic efforts of a non-political white male (in the case of *2012*, it is John Cusack portraying a failed writer, father, and husband). Like *Deep Impact*, the president's most presidential moments are when he announces the certain doom that awaits the American people. Members of the audience know nothing of how Glover's character became president or even of his politics, meeting the character two years into his administration and only observing him through the prism of his response to the central crisis.

Glover's Wilson is somewhat more self-aware and contemplative, however, as he verbally acknowledges to himself that he'll be the last American president and later prefaces his message to the public at large with the statement, "This will be the last time I address you." Indeed, populist fatalism is a central component of Wilson's portrayal. He elects to meet the disaster and die with the citizenry rather than evacuate with his daughter to the planned survival operation in China, and in his message to them, he notes that "today they are one family stepping forward into the darkness together," a point underscored moments later when the feed is interrupted as he begins reciting the Lord's Prayer. His final minutes are spent caring for the suffering refugees huddled on the White House lawn, coated with a layer of volcanic ash that had blown in from a massive rupture at Yellowstone hours before. Wilson survives the dramatic collapse of the Washington Monument onto the shelterless crowd below, but he ultimately succumbs to the crisis as the White House is crushed by the aircraft carrier *John F. Kennedy*, which rides the crest of a tsunami well past the shoreline. Thus, the way in which the ultimate demise of the first black president comes about doubly reinforces some types of fears. The first black president becomes the last American president, and symbolic representations of his more legendary institutional predecessors become the missiles aiming to send him to his maker. While film critics may see a Freemanesque performance of nobility and grace, viewers must balance those dimensions against the linkage of black presidential leadership and national ruin.

The final entry in this category of fictional black presidents is the one that originally motivated this project: FOX's *24*, which features not only the aforementioned work of Dennis Haysbert as President David Palmer in seasons 1 through 5, but also D.B. Woodside's portrayal of Wayne Palmer, whom viewers first meet as his brother David's chief of staff before he becomes president himself in season 6. Initially, Wayne is yet another addition to the flock of untrustworthy and immoral intimate advisors that David Palmer tends to surround himself with, a crew that includes his dastardly wife, later estranged, and his craven chief of staff. Wayne is corrupt personally as well as politically; initially embroiled in the lingering consequences of an illicit romp with a previous mentor's young wife, one that places his brother's administration in a vulnerable position. As his character expands over the four dozen episodes he appears in, his righteousness starts to rebound, but his weakness as a leader and a man become more central to his narrative. Prior to his own time as president in season 6, we see Palmer repeatedly in a junior partner position, often injured and in danger, taking orders from more decisive characters. This timidity continues into his presidency, as he continually turns to advisers within his administration and agents like Jack Bauer outside to solve problems.

Such executive indecision is a hallmark of *24*'s presidents, but particularly so during Wayne Palmer's term, when he consistently vacillates between policy options. His lack of determination is rewarded with a season's worth of existential threats, and Wayne's tendency toward physical distress continues when an assassination attempt nearly kills him. A more decisive vice president initially replaces him after the attack and, when Wayne returns to command, nearly unseats him with a Twenty-Fifth Amendment challenge (similar to one his own brother faced in a previous season) that convinces a full half of Wayne's own administration and goes to the Supreme Court before ultimately failing, not because of Palmer's successfulness but rather because the insurgent vice president falls victim to another man's blackmail. The peace is short-lived, however, as Wayne's health continues to fade, and he eventually falls into a coma that lasts through the rest of the season. In a subsequent between-series television movie (*Redemption*), we see the reins handed from his usurping vice president to the new president, indicating that Palmer was not able to finish his term and, in fact, may never have been able to return to office.

Interesting, in the commentary about Wayne Palmer's role in *24*, he is hardly ever characterized as a role model for black political leaders. His year as President Palmer preceded the 2008 election by only a year, whereas David Palmer's administration on television had ended while Barack Obama was still an Illinois state senator. While writers focused heavily on Wayne's flaws and moral foibles, it was David Palmer who not only made American voters comfortable with the notion of a black president, but actually led them to yearn for one. A perfect example of the typical journalistic description of Haysbert's Palmer can be found in a column written by Tony Norman (2003) in the *Pittsburgh Post-Gazette* in the run-up to the 2004 presidential election. In that essay, Norman was thinking more about Al Sharpton than he was Barack Obama when he wrote that "presidential candidates of all persuasions should take note of Palmer's decency and savvy and how it co-exists with his steely resolve to do the right thing," but even as the real black candidate changed in the intervening years, the description of Palmer as resolved and righteous permeates all discourse surrounding the character. A close observation of the character, however, uncovers recurring themes that, rather than reassuring voters that black presidents are a desirable thing, instead reinforce age-old concerns and threats. Every season has Haysbert's character involved in some moral scandal, and though he is never the one with the dirtiest hands or the worst intentions, his consistent half embraces of the flawed choice undermine the accuracy of journalistic claims that his brand of leadership is all roses and honor. Instead, Haysbert's Palmer is frequently blindsided and confused, hallmarks not of a president in command, but rather one out of his element. Further, although some writers describe Palmer's character as post-racial, implying that the character's race rarely, if ever, affects the story line, we see it in episode after episode throughout the five seasons in which Palmer appears. The first time we are introduced to Palmer, as he campaigns as a sitting U.S. senator for the office of the presidency, it is under the auspices of a death threat that is initially perceived to be motivated by domestic racist groups. Years later, in the first episode of the fifth season, Palmer is indeed assassinated, building on the comedic legacy of Murphy, Chappelle, and Rock by putting a tragic face on it.

This is not to say that President Palmer, were he a real president, would not be a good one. Clearly his efforts as portrayed in *24* were imperfect and occasionally corrupt, but probably no more so than the kind of action and decision making that has come out of every other real presidential administration and far more benign and righteous than most. It is this better-than-average presidential leadership, combined with Haysbert's stately demeanor and graceful dignity, that leads so many writers to the kinds of shortcuts that celebrate the portrayal of David Palmer (and Morgan Freeman's Tom Beck) as one-dimensional hero presidents. Even if those portrayals were correct, however, and they are clearly not, the end result would still be negative in terms of perpetuating the white hegemonic status quo. As Stephanie Greco Larson (2005, 31) argues in *Media & Minorities*, a key way that black film and television themes reinforce the status quo is to "deny racial inequalities by focusing on individuals and ignoring social structures. In this way, films can tell viewers that race does not matter. Some of these films present a rosy picture of racial relations where blacks and whites live equally and cooperatively together."

When films like *Deep Impact* and *2012* portray tragic hero presidents without consideration of the political system they came up within, it serves to pretend the social forces arrayed against minority citizens and candidates either do not exist or have been vanquished. Thus, such "positive" portrayals can have negative consequences as they send effectively post-racial messages that, rather than supporting future black politicians, allow white voters to feel off the hook. To the extent that race and especially racial violence have composed sub-themes in the plot development of various seasons, the writers of *24* are less guilty of this sin of omission; however, by portraying David Palmer as a savior type and not a compromised and morally complex individual, the writers who cast for cultural linkages between the fictional predecessor and the actual sitting chief executive do a similar disservice to the viewing and voting public who view such political perfection to be as likely as the meteor strikes, time travelers, and stand-up comedians that have so far dominated pop-culture approximations of black presidential scenarios.

Instead, a comprehensive theoretical argument concerning the notion that popular culture can causally precede political reality must grapple with the fact that audiences consume these portrayals of fictional black presidents through multiple senses. Simply seeing black presidents on-screen is only part of the viewing experience; audiences also receive the messages in the narratives that those television programs and films advance. As a result, the image of a fictional black president alone is not value neutral, but rather, the degree to which consumers (and voters) will find the prospect of black presidential leadership appealing depends on the context of the portrayal. The fact that the current assortment of fictional black presidential portrayals ranges from morally ambivalent to offensively absurd does little to support the argument that these portrayals, whether by Haysbert or Rock or Pryor, paved the way for our current actual president.

## *Conclusion*

Upon consideration of the actual substance of the few portrayals of black presidents in American film and television history, it becomes quite evident that the journalistic trope about how the David Palmers and Tom Becks of Hollywood paved the way for America's first African American president are not only poorly supported; they are flawed and false. When the narratives of these films do not directly underscore an alleged ridiculousness to the idea of black presidential leadership (*Rufus Jones for President, Idiocracy, The Fifth Element, Head of State*), they put the protagonists in positions where they are either battling the impossible (*Deep Impact, 2012, 24*) or are under threat of assassination and removal from office (*The Man, 24*). Rather than preparing the viewing public for a future real black president, the catalogue of fictional black presidents instead prepared generations of viewers to consider it farcical, impossible, and undesirable. Indeed, a far more plausible statement to make is that Barack Obama became the nation's forty-fourth president not because of Dennis Haysbert's portrayal of his fictional predecessor, not to mention those by Chris Rock and Deebo, but rather in spite of it. Stated otherwise, the 2008 election was less an example of life imitating art than of it defying the expectations of popular entertainment.

## REFERENCES

Bayard, Louis. "Black Presidents We Have Known." *Salon.com*, November 3, 2008.
Braxton, Greg. "A Black President? Art Precedes Life." *Los Angeles Times*, June 30, 2008.
Callahan, Maureen. "A President in Real-Time: Did '24' Help Obama's Candidacy?" *New York Post*, February 24, 2008.
Cernetig, Milo. "A Black President: From Fantasy to Fact." *Vancouver Sun*, November 4, 2008.
Dargis, Manohla, and A.O. Scott. "How the Movies Made a President." *New York Times*, January 16, 2009.
Goren, Lilly J. "The American Presidency and Cultural Curveballs: Women and Minorities in

Hollywood's Oval Office." Paper presented at the annual meeting of the American Political Science Association, Philadelphia, PA, August 31, 2006.

Henry, Kevin. "Do We Really Want Another Black President after the Events of *Deep Impact*?" *The Onion*, February 13, 2008.

Israel, Solomon. "Precedent for Black President in US Film and TV." *Jerusalem Post*, June 4, 2008.

Larson, Stephanie Greco. *Media & Minorities: The Politics of Race in News and Entertainment*. Lanham, MD: Rowman & Littlefield, 2005.

Norman, Tony. "A Black President? Only on Television." *Pittsburgh Post-Gazette*, February 11, 2003.

Sonner, Scott. "Haysbert on '24' Presidency: You're Welcome, Obama." *Chicago Sun-Times*, July 2, 2008.

Stein, Joel. "A Black President? Seen a Few." *Los Angeles Times*, January 11, 2008.

Wiltz, Teresa. "Hollywood's Leading Man." theroot.com, January 17, 2009.

# Barack Obama or *B. Hussein*?
## The Post-Racial Debate in *Boston Legal*

JENNY BANH

> DENNY CRANE: *The basket has made its way all around the table. Denny takes a roll.* So Turnip, tell me, what do black kids like to eat?
> *There is a murmur of protest.*
> SHIRLEY SCHMIDT: For God's sake! Denny!
> ALLEN SHORE: What do black kids like to eat?
> DENNY CRANE: Well, I wanna know! Koreans like Korean. Greeks like Greek.
> *Shirley lifts her eyes to heaven as the protesting gets louder.*
> SHIRLEY SCHMIDT: I've had it with you two!
> MELVIN PALMER: Feisty bunch.
> ALLEN SHORE: RACIST!
> DENNY CRANE: Racist?
> ALLEN SHORE: Yes. Racist.
>
> —Boston Legal, Episode "Thanksgiving,"
> Scene "Systemic Racism"

## Barack Obama and Post-Racial Debate on *Boston Legal* Episode "Systemic Racism"

President Barack Obama's election spurred popular cultural artifacts from Ben and Jerry's new commemorative ice cream flavor "Yes Pecan" and Jay-Z's rap video "History," to the ubiquitous appropriation of Shepard Farley's "Change" poster, which some argue has contributed to the *post-racial* debate. The Emmy-winning television show *Boston Legal*'s "Thanksgiving" episode, scene "Systematic Racism," which aired in its final season, presents a unique popular-culture debate taking place across the United States, namely, does the election of Barack Obama as president signal a move of the United States into a new "color-blind" (post-racial) society? This essay is grounded and framed by one singular Thanksgiving dinner-party argument that takes place in the fictitious television world of writer David E. Kelley's *Boston Legal*, which ran from 2004 to 2008 on ABC. In this episode a ferocious argument occurs between the five principal lawyer characters on the show at a Thanksgiving dinner party set in Boston, Massachusetts, over whether America is post-racial. The essay argues that we are not a post-racial society yet, but that Barack Obama's election has completely changed all of the racial parameters and may hearken a new age.

The heated argument opens with Denny Crane—a character played by William Shatner—asking a young African American nine-year-old, "What do black people eat?" This elicits a response that he is "racist" by Allen Shore. The fractious conversation swings toward whether the election of Barack Obama signals a new dawn for race relationships in the United States. In a nutshell, the idea of the *post-racial society*—with race no longer a factor—is being bandied about by the characters. On one side of the debate is the ethics challenged Allen Shore—a character played by James Spader—who scoffs at the idea that America is now color-blind. Shore's statement is vehemently opposed by all the other Anglo American characters, who argue that African Americans have turned a significant corner. This essay goes over this singular real-time ten-minute argument line by line and unpacks the veracity of the contentious statements by the characters about whether indeed the election of Barack Obama has brought about a new age where race is no longer salient (post-racism). While other popular-cultural artifacts reference the current debate, few do so in as nuanced a manner as *Boston Legal*, including the use of contemporary statistical data on the socio-economic realities of Anglo Americans and African Americans. This essay ultimately takes the side of Allen Shore in that we are not (yet) in a post-racial state, but with the caveat that President Obama's election does change and complicate the parameters of all racial discussions hereafter.

Using the *Boston Legal* television episode as a unique framework, this essay highlights both sides of the debate and charges that many popular-cultural pieces are debating this topic since the election of Barack Obama. The argument in this episode of *Boston Legal*, "Thanksgiving," pushes a long-standing academic argument into a new mainstream public consciousness. For example, this dovetails with Theodor Adorno and Max Horkheimer's Culture Industry theory (1944), which argued that all humans are duped into constant consuming that feeds the capitalistic system. Their ubiquitously quoted culture industry thesis — that the mass media is a form of capitalistic "mass deception"—is a piece that uniquely brings an academic argument out into mainstream popular culture for people to debate. Analogously, Walter Benjamin's *The Work of Art in the Age of Mechanical Reproduction* (1935) argues that mass media and production releases the "aura" of fine art to be more democratic, which I charge is what this *Boston Legal* scene is doing for this debate. Benjamin is trying to say that before mass media, "fine art" was only for the elite to peruse, but after it became mass produced, more people could participate in its dialogue. The post-racial debate has been bandied about in academia like this; however, now the popular culture post-racial debate is evoked further by President Obama's election, pushing it to the forefront where more people can democratically debate. Now the academic and popular-culture dialogues finally overlap, undermine, and collide with each other in this debate.

In academia, the post-racial contrarians use evidence that we are not color-blind because of the unequal systems of prison, health and education. The other side argues that we are color-blind because there are no longer any racist de jure laws. One side of the popular-culture front argues that we are *not* in a post-racial state because of the election of Barack Obama using varied evidence: such as a cartoon of Obama depicted as a runaway gorilla; Rush Limbaugh's song, "Barack the Magic Negro"; Anne Coulter ad nauseam calling Obama "B. Hussein"; and Congressman Joe Wilson screaming, "You lie! You lie!" Some might argue that these examples are merely rude and petty events, but in fact these examples neatly fit into age-old racist stereotypes of African Americans that were used to justify slavery. These heinous stereotypes are that African Americans are non–intelligent, apes, mystical, disloyal, and dishonest. The other side of the post-racial popular-culture debate argues that the fact that a "black man" has been elected by the United States indicates that race is no longer a defining characteristic of a country that used to enslave its African American citizens. We have moved beyond seeing race, using evidence such as: (1) rising multi-racial marriages of which Obama is one of its progeny, (2) non-biological discreteness and (3) changing non–Anglo American demographics.

## Boston Legal *Layout of Characters: Allen Shore, Denny Crane, and Shirley Schmidt*

In the *Boston Legal* "Thanksgiving" (2009) episode, scene "Systemic Racism," one of the show's principal characters, Allen Shore, attends a Thanksgiving dinner party hosted by his law firm boss Shirley Schmidt, played by Candice Bergen. While they are giving grace, Shirley mentions that she cried when Barack Obama was elected. Adorned with self-congratulatory smiles, the other liberal white lawyers, Denny Crane, played by William Shatner; Carl Sack, played by John Larroquette; and Jerry Espenson, played by Christian Clemenson, heartily agree. Edwin Poole, played by Larry Miller; Katie Lloyd, played by Tara Summers; and Melvin Palmer, played by Christopher Rich, also attend the dinner party and agree that America has turned a significant corner. All the Anglo American lawyers at the table reflect upon how far *we* have come as a nation in terms of race relations. The only minority at the table is a nine-year-old African American boy named Justin "Turnip" Graves, played by Kwesi Boakye, who earlier in the episode attempted to rob Shirley in the grocery store parking lot. Turnip now is under the guardianship of Edwin Poole. Hilarity and discomfort ensue when Allen, who is also Anglo American, launches into a diatribe about how little has changed for African Americans in the forty years since the apex of the civil rights movement, citing the continued lack of quality health care and education and the persistent poverty that continues to plague African American citizens. He further references the perception some Americans hold that Barack Obama is an Arab, not born in America ("birthers"), or is secretly a "Muslim terrorist." Allen also cites the various examples of coded racial language used during the presidential campaign, including Joe Biden's reference to Obama as "clean and articulate" and the Fox News Channel's reference to Michelle Obama as "Obama's baby's mama." Through the different parts of this chapter, a snippet of the dinner party will be quoted and analyzed in the order of the real-time argument.

African Americans, in contrast to Anglo Americans, do have alarmingly unequal wealth, health care, and education patterns, as Allen Shore argues. On the other side of this debate, some groups, such as West Indian and African immigrants, have made significant strides, and no one can deny the historic feat of a partially African-descended man now sitting as the president of the United States of America. However, both sides of the color-blind debate are not typically found in one popular-culture piece so comprehensively. This essay will charge that although there has been little change in the parameters of wealth, education, and health care since the 1960s for most African Americans, Barack Obama's election invites popular-culture pieces that give the opposite impression. Popular-culture entities are taking dramatically different sides in this debate, namely in recent television shows, newspapers, magazines, the Internet, songs, and YouTube videos.

## *Systemic Racism: Different Academic Views of Inequality*

> ALLEN SHORE: Yes, racist. This is a holiday. Please let's not extend the systemic racism of the firm to the dining room table.
> — Awkward Pause for three seconds
> *Carl is taken aback, as are others.*
> SHIRLEY SCHMIDT: What systemic racism of the firm?
> ALLEN SHORE: Oh! Come on, Shirley!
> —Boston Legal, *Episode "Thanksgiving," Scene "Systemic Racism"*

Here the *Boston Legal* character Shirley Schmidt seems dumbfounded when the character Allen Shore announces at the Thanksgiving dinner party that there is systemic racism at the law firm that she, Edwin Poole, and Denny Crane founded. Shirley absolutely does not believe that her law firm is biased in any way against African Americans, which plays into a larger debate over whether or not America is racist toward minorities. The producer, creator, and writer of this episode, David E. Kelley, wrote this "Systemic Racism" scene which uses Shirley's offended question to argue that racial inequality in the United States is over. But before we go into Shirley's view, let us digress to what theories of inequality preceded her. There are varying academic theories of why there is a large poor underclass group and a small powerful elite group. Theorists state that the reason for inequities is because of class, power, and status differences which affect life chances.

The academic sociological basis of the "inequality" debate is well trod. The founders of sociology, Karl Marx, Max Weber, and Emile Durkheim, did not see racial differences as playing a large role in the understanding of inequality between different groups. Marx argued that the *base* or economic forces, and how one is positioned in the *means of production*, explained how and why one is exploited. To Marx, "race" was relegated to the *superstructure*, which consisted of culture and ideas and was tangential to the all-important base. Weber emphasized *status* and *power* as the main predictors of inequity; while Durkheim studied how the psychologies of suicide, religion, and social organizations could indicate unfair outcomes. W.E.B. DuBois, Harvard-trained African American sociologist very famously objected to these three theorists by stating, "The most significant problem of the twentieth century is the color line" (DuBois, 1896). While DuBois very much agreed with the importance of the economic factors, he also indicated the importance of how race has had a detrimental effect on individuals such as African Americans. He argued that there are real historical and structural barriers (read: systematic racism) that prevented African Americans from moving up in economic class.

## *Post-Racial America: "It Doesn't Mean We Are Racist!" Says Shirley Schmidt*

    SHIRLEY SCHMIDT: No, I'd like to hear this.
    ALLEN SHORE: Well, look around the table. Or the office! You see any black attorneys?
    SHIRLEY SCHMIDT: It doesn't mean we are racist!
    ALLEN SHORE: Right!
    DENNY CRANE: Do you ever think for one second that maybe black attor-

neys do not want to work with us? Maybe they wanna be with their own?
ALLEN SHORE: Oh God.
SHIRLEY SCHMIDT: Denny! Don't help me, please.
—Boston Legal, *Episode "Thanksgiving," Scene "Systemic Racism"*

The proponents of the pop-culture post-racial thesis such as *Boston Legal* characters Shirley Schmidt and Denny Crane argue that America is now *equal*. Here in this dialogue they defend their firm against charges of racism much in the same way that others defend contemporary American society and culture from similar charges. Here one can make the inference that Shirley views racism as the David Duke, KKK (Ku Klux Klan) style in which hooded white men lynch innocent African Americans. Neither she nor her colleagues would ever think to engage in these abhorrent acts; thus they consider themselves a non-racist law firm. Can there be racism without racists?

Eduardo Bonilla-Silva's *Racism without Racists: Color-Blind Racism* (2006) discusses this phenomenon of not having explicit racists or racist act as an indicator there is no racism. Dr. Bonilla-Silva argues that there is still a lot of inequality based on the color of your skin. He charges that the structures that permeate American society are unequal and biased against minorities. Bonilla-Silva calls it "color-blind racism," which is when Anglo Americans internalize their sense of privilege or racist beliefs about minorities.

Analogously, Ian Haney López argues in his book chapter "Colorblind White Dominance" (2009) that color blindness masks white dominance and makes racial inequality permanent. He argues that color blindness is a "sham" to mask continuing racial subordination. In tandem with Bonilla-Silva, López asserts,

> Our faces and our racial ideology maybe changing but the fundamental racial dynamic of White dominance in this country will not end anytime soon. Instead, it will continue even as the definition of who counts as White expands, in large part because the material interests of so many demand it, but also the ideology of contemporary colorblindness protects and perpetuates White dominance [chapter 8, p, 212].

López's quote argues that the core values of white dominance will continue because too many people benefit from it. She says that there may be an expansion of who counts as "white," but the racist ideology of white dominance is the same. Disagreeing with Shirley, López and Bonilla-Silva would assert that there are still systematic inequalities affecting all minorities psychologically and structurally, which prevents them from full participation in many fields, including law firms.

## *"We Just Had a Black Man Elected President!"* and Other Popular Culture Arguments That We Are Now Post-Racial

> TURNIP GRAVES: Could you please pass the...?
> SHIRLEY SCHMIDT: No! We just had a black man elected President and you still think?
> ALLEN SHORE: *Oh please?*
> SHIRLEY SCHMIDT: What? Oh, please."?
> ALLEN SHORE: Never mind...
> —Boston Legal, *Episode "Thanksgiving," Scene "Systemic Racism"*

Shirley argues that America has turned a corner by citing the election of "a black man" as president. What she neglects here to augment her argument is the use of Barack Obama and other African Americans in the popular-culture realm. Since the election of Barack Obama, there have been a plethora of references to the idea of a post-racial state. One could argue along with Shirley that this post-racial discussion is more apparent since Obama's election than ten years ago. One thing that Shirley can cite is when, just a few years before, Kanye West had famously ranted that "George Bush doesn't care about black people!" after Hurricane Katrina; this comment resonated more than today. West was complaining that the ill treatment African Americans were getting from the government was because of the color of their skin. So when Tracy Morgan made his joke at the 2009 Golden Globes, it was ever so much more poignant.

When *30 Rock* star Tracy Morgan accepted the 2009 Golden Globe for best comedy series, he killed the crowd with this uproarious joke. "Tina Fey and I had an agreement," he said. "If Barack Obama won, I would speak for the show from now on. Welcome to post-racial America! I am the face of post-racial America! Deal with it, Cate Blanchett!" (2009 Best Television Series—Musical or Comedy Award for *30 Rock*). Only Tracy Morgan with his random stream of consciousness could pull off a joke that would delight the Hollywood foreign press and insider audience. He directly stated that America is now post-racial, but was the crowd's laughter an indication of incredulousness or agreement, or just confusion over another Tracy Morgan random joke?

Shirley could have argued that other popular cultural renditions of Barack Obama in an arguably post-racial setting include: the Marvel Comics "Spidey Meets the President!" (#583), Ben and Jerry's ice cream flavor "Yes Pecan," and Shepard Fairey's "Change" poster. Even before the popular-culture post-racial debate, Shirley Schmidt might argue that there has been a long global appreciation of African Americans arts, namely hip hop and African

American artists such as Jay-Z (Sean Carter), P. Diddy (Sean Combs), and Michael Jackson.

Indeed many Americans have grown up watching shows with African American casts such as *Good Times*, *The Jeffersons*, *Sandford and Son*, *The Cosby Show*, *A Different World*, and *The Fresh Prince of Bel-Air*. Watching these African American shows every day on television can arguably have a great positive psychological effect on how individuals view minorities if they do not have any interactions. Direct descendants of these shows are *My Wife and Kids*, *The Bernie Mac Show*, and *Everybody Hates Chris*. While there may have been some race-themed episodes, not all the shows were about racism directly, which might be used as an argument that we are now moving to a post-racial state.

## *Academic Post-Racial Arguments Shirley Neglects to Use: Sociology and Anthropology*

> SHIRLEY SCHMIDT: No, I'd like to hear this, Allen.
> CARL SACK: I don't.
> EDWIN POOLE: Neither do I.
> SHIRLEY SCHMIDT: I do. Say it, Alan. I wanna hear what you have to say.
> —Boston Legal, *Episode "Thanksgiving," Scene "Systemic Racism"*

In the dialogue here, Shirley wants to hear evidence on why America is still a racially unequal society. She does not give any further academic points to her argument. The point of this section is to use academic arguments that Shirley did not use in her argument that we are now post-racial. This part of the chapter will look at post-race theories that Shirley did *not* use in her argument that we are now a post-racial America — namely the biological anthropological and sociological arguments.

One vocal sociologist, William Julius Wilson, argues in his book, *The Declining Significance of Race: Black and Changing American Institutions* (1980), that "class" plays a larger role in African American lives than race. When other factors are controlled, it is *class* that determines how far you will go in life; thus middle-class Anglo and African American people have the same life chances if all variables are the same (1980). Another sociologist, Herbert Blumer, agrees that it is not always racism that drives inequality. Blumer argues that it is not necessarily racism but the "logic" of maintaining group privilege that maintains inequality.

The Association of American Anthropologists (AAA) officially stated that "race is not a biologically real entity but is a social reality for people"

("Statement on Race," May 17, 1998). The AAA argues that race is a "social construction" with three key pieces of evidence: (1) genes co-vary, (2) there are more differences within groups than between groups, and (3) all humans evolved from Africa. The AAA further clarifies that although race is constructed, racism based on perceived differences is quite real, along with genuine structural racism which exists on many levels.

Other books such as the *Mismeasure of Man* (1981) by Steven Jay Gould also document how *biological race* is not real. The multiple lines of evidence he uses are the mitochondrial DNA and the overlapping genes loci. Gould's world-renowned book proved that European scientists made a priori assumptions and made their data fit these assumptions, which were chiefly that Europeans were superior. All of these theorists would agree that there is no such thing as a biological essentialist notion of race. These sociological and anthropological academic arguments are something that Shirley could have used in her contention that we are now "color-blind."

## *"[Y]ou Think We Have Really Turned a Corner?" Post-Racial Debate in Terms of Barack Obama*

> ALLEN SHORE: What, you think we've really turned a corner? Of a hundred senators, one is black. One! And that is Barack Obama; come January there will be none! Of fifty governors, two are black and one of those is in New York by default because Eric Spitzer got caught with his hooker. This country hardly seems willing to elect black leaders on a regular basis.
> —Boston Legal, *Episode "Thanksgiving," Scene "Systemic Racism"*

The 2008 U.S. presidential election results showed that African American Illinois senator, Barack Obama, did win the state of North Carolina, a decidedly red state, which some argue indicates that race is no longer salient. Allen Shore disagrees and says that "the country hardly seems willing to elect black leaders on a regular basis." Allen's statement holds if one were to look at the election of Obama in comparison to other black candidates. Shore's point is that there is a difference in electing Obama and regularly voting for black candidates for other offices.

According to the CNN exit poll on November 5, 2008, all the different races voted for Barack Obama. He won overwhelmingly with all demographics, especially with the youth and minority vote. The only demographic that he did not win was the sixty-five and older demographic. "Race played less of a role in the election than age, exit polls showed" (CNN exit poll, November 5, 2008). Bill Schneider, senior CNN political analyst, comments on this story, saying, "Race was not a decisive factor in this election," but instead the economy, the Iraq War, health care and terrorism were.

Although all the different races voted for Obama in the presidential election, Allen Shore is correct that historically African Americans have not had a large political presence in the United States. To this day there have only been six African American senators in American history: in 1870, Hiram Revels; 1875, Blanche K. Bruce; 1967, Edward Brooke; 1993, Carol Moseley Braun; 2005, Barack Obama; and 2007, Roland Burris (United States Senate, 2010). Similarly, we have only had three African American governors: L. Douglas Wilder, Virginia, 1990–1994; Deval Patrick, Massachusetts, 2007–present; and David Paterson, New York, 2008–2010.

## *Post-Racial Debate in Politics: Bradley Theory, Huxtable Theory, Palmer Theory*

> CARL SACK: But the people of the firm are. They overwhelmingly voted for Obama.
> ALLEN SHORE: How the hell do you know what happened in the privacy of those polling booths?
> —Boston Legal, *Episode "Thanksgiving," Scene "Systemic Racism"*

Some argue Obama's election completely defeats the often-touted *Bradley theory*. The Bradley theory is a political-science theory that argues that whites will often express support for minority candidates and racially progressive issues, or say that they are "undecided" in polls, but end up voting against minority candidates and racially progressive issues in actual elections. This is particularly apparent when the minority candidate is running against an Anglo American candidate. This theory is named after popular African American Los Angeles mayor Tom Bradley, who ran for the California governorship in the 1980s. In the weeks leading up to the election, he was shown to be ahead in the polls but ended up losing the election, much to the surprise of pollsters. Bradley theorists argue that Anglo Americans lied in the polls when they were asked if they would vote for him. Many have taken this example and applied it to other voting situations when an Anglo politician runs against an African American politician, such as Barack Obama against John McCain. This is significant because a candidate's race could conceivably cost him votes.

Other political scientists argue that the Bradley effect means that white voters will always vote predominantly for white politicians. But does the Bradley effect focus too much on race, and why did it not work in the election of President Barack Obama? Some journalists and popular-cultural theorists answer that it is because of the *Huxtable effect* and the *Palmer effect*.

Many Americans grew up watching the top-rated African American television program *The Cosby Show* on NBC (National Broadcasting Corporation) in the 1980s to the early 1990s. The show was about an upper-middle-class African American family named the Huxtables. The patriarch of the show was Heathcliff "Cliff" Huxtable, an obstetrician who lives with his wife, Clair Huxtable, an attorney, and their five children. The award-winning actors who played those roles were Dr. Bill Cosby and Phylicia Rashad. Although the show was not about African American race issues directly, it was Afrocentric in showing its pride in great African American artists. Alisa Valdes-Rodriguez, a *Chicago Sun-Times* journalist, wrote about this show and how it directly affected the election of Obama in an article titled "The Huxtable Effect: How Cosby Paved the Way for Obama's Candidacy" (*Chicago Sun-Times*, 2008, November 3). Valdes-Rodriguez coined the phrase "The Huxtable effect," which refers to the fact that many young Americans grew up with a positive African American father image on television every day in the form of Cliff Huxtable, which in turn made them comfortable voting for an African American candidate. There also has been a fictionalized popular African American president on the television show *24*, which some argue contributed to Obama's election in what is called the Palmer effect.

On the popular show *24*, Dennis Haysbert portrays America's first African American president, David Palmer. This fictionalized African American president was decisive, ethical, and competent; each week he dealt with Jack Bauer's dramatic antics with aplomb and calm grace. Simon Reynolds' article titled "Haysbert: '24' president helped Obama" (July 2008) quotes the fictional *24* actor as saying that he had a positive effect on the election of Obama. The actor said that he would be eating in all–Anglo settings and people would come up to him and thank him for his positive portrayal of an African American president. Nick Bryant coined the term "Palmer effect," which argues that many Americans were willing to vote for an African American candidate because they were used to seeing an African American chief executive on the hugely successful *24*. The larger point here is that the political-science theory of the Bradley effect may not have been as effective as the popular-culture theories of the Huxtable effect and the Palmer effect in the election of Barack Obama.

## *(Post) Racial Disparities? Life Expectancies and Cancer*

> SHIRLEY SCHMIDT: Get out of this house! You will not say things...
> ALLEN SHORE: But I haven't eaten yet!

> SHIRLEY SCHMIDT: I don't care!
> CARL SACK: Ho, ho, ho. Let's just slow down.
> SHIRLEY SCHMIDT: You will not say things like that...
> ALAN SHORE: What did I say?
> *Shirley doesn't answer.*
> JERRY ESPENSON: Maybe since Barack Obama was just elected we can celebrate the progress that blacks have made in this country, instead of...
> —Boston Legal, *Episode "Thanksgiving,"*
> *Scene "Systemic Racism"*

At this point Allen Shore is being kicked out of the Thanksgiving dinner party by Shirley. Shore states that he has not eaten yet and does not want to go. Allen just wants to make the point that race permeates everything in the United States and has detrimental effects on people of color. Carl then states that maybe we can celebrate how far African Americans have come. If Carl and Shirley are correct, then there should be few or no differences between the races in all different social, economic, and political categories. Outside of the *Boston Legal* law firm, there are many who agree with Allen Shore's position that race is still important, and it shows up in, among other areas, health disparities.

Michael Omi and Howard Winant's racialization theory challenges the post-racial thesis and argues that Obama's election masks the fact that "race" still permeates nearly all aspects of American society and has real (negative) costs for the nation's non-white population. This is seen in disparities in health care, schooling, and imprisonment rates. Winant's *Racial Formation in the United States: From the 1960s to the 1990s* (1994) argues that indeed race has historically and still is the main structuring medium in how the United States has treated its non-white inhabitants. The point of this part of the chapter is to reveal that Shore is correct by citing health-care disparities between white and black Americans.

In *Race, Socioeconomic Status, and Health: The Added Effects of Racism and Discrimination*, David R. Williams charges that racism is the chief reason for higher disease rates of African Americans over Anglo Americans. Williams argues that this is because of African American (1) residence in poor neighborhoods, (2) medical care that is racially biased, and (3) stress over daily discrimination (Williams, 1999).

Another example of health disparities is mortality rates as reported in the study titled, "Eight Americas: Investigating Mortality Disparities across Races, Counties, and Race-Counties in the United States" (Murray, et al., 2006). This study divided America into eight separate pieces based on race, location of the county of residence, population, race-specific level of per capita income, and cumulative homicide rate. The census and national health statistics found that "the life expectancy gap between the 3.4 million high-risk urban black males and the 5.6 million Asian females was 20.7 years in 2001." Furthermore, *A Cancer Journal for Clinicians: Statistics for 2006* provides evidence for disparate cancer survival rates between Anglo and African Americans. The larger point of this section of the chapter is that if Carl and Shirley were correct that we are post-racial, then the cancer and life expectancy would be the same, but it is in fact the opposite. This fits into the larger argument that we are not post-racial, even if we did elect "a black man."

## *(Post) Racial Disparities? Prison Rates and Death Row*

> ALLEN SHORE: Celebrate? In this country black people are still incarcerated almost six times the rate of white people. Turnip here seems well on his way.
> TURNIP GRAVES: Hey!
> —Boston Legal, *Episode "Thanksgiving," Scene "Systemic Racism"*

Allen Shore argues that the country still jails more African Americans than Anglo Americans. To follow the last piece, if America was truly post-racial as Carl and Shirley contend, then the prison rates of different races should be equal. Allen Shore is correct when he states the prison rates for the different racial groups are uneven. Angela Davis, in an evocative article in *Colorlines* magazine titled "Masked Racism: Reflection on the Prison Industrial Complex" (Fall 1998), charges that prisons are big profit-making businesses for states and private industries. Prisons employ a large number of people and make minorities and undocumented people disappear like "magic." There is even a new crop of private-profit prisons that are interconnected with America's big industries. She calls this big profit-making prison business the "Prison Industrial Complex" (PIC) which she charges is a holding and *disappearing* tank for society's least privileged. "Homelessness, unemployment, drug addiction, mental illness, and illiteracy are only a few of the problems that disappear from the public view when the human beings contending with them are relegated to cages" (Davis, Fall 1998). Unfortunately, the least privileged are still people of color and the undocumented.

Following this is Alfred Blumstein's (1982) seminal article, "On the Racial Disproportionality of the United States Prison Population," which argues that there are gross inequalities in the incarceration rates between whites and blacks. "Although Blacks comprise roughly one-eighth of the population, they represent half of the prison population." Blumstein argues that this inconsistency suggests gross injustices in the American criminal system.

Another injustice that a 2007 sociological article gives credence to is that black and white prisoners are not only incarcerated at different rates but are sentenced to death differently. In the article "Who Survives on Death Row? An individual and Contextual Analysis" (Jacobs, et al., 2007), the authors provide some startling findings. They find that in the United States, blacks who kill whites are more likely to get executed. Whites who kill blacks have better life chances than blacks who kill whites. This gives credence to Allen's point that African Americans are treated differently in who survives the death penalty.

## *(Post) Racial Disparities? Allen Says, "Blacks Have Double the Unemployment Rates as Whites and Have for Forty Years"*

> ALLEN SHORE: Blacks have double the unemployment rates as whites and have for forty years now! Whether it's that or the government's underwhelming response to AIDS among blacks, or racial profiling, the black community continues to get screwed.
> DENNY CRANE: Allen!
> ALLEN SHORE: Let's not even discuss the public funding for black neighborhoods. Or how the Supreme Court is eviscerating *Brown versus Board of Education*.
> —Boston Legal, *Episode "Thanksgiving," Scene "Systemic Racism"*

Allen Shore here is arguing that black employment and education are not adequate in America. He is right about the inequality in schooling, but his number for the unemployment rates for African Americans is debatable. In the working paper titled "Public High School Graduation and College Readiness Rates in the United States," Jay Greene and Greg Forster (2003), funded by the Bill and Melinda Gates Foundation, make some startling statements on which American students are or are not "college ready." Students who are not college ready, which means they do not fulfill the minimum requirements to go to a four-year college, are then relegated to the lower social, political, and economic career choices. Unfortunately, the authors contend that non-college-ready students tend to be people of color, excluding Asian Americans. Their executive summary findings detail the following:

> Only 70% of all students in public high schools graduate, and only 32% of all students leave high school qualified to attend four-year colleges. Only 51% of all black students and 52% of all Hispanic students graduate, and only 20% of all black students and 16% of all Hispanic students leave high school college ready. The graduation rate for white students was 72%; for Asians, 79%; and for American

Indians, 54%. The college readiness rate for whites was 37%; for Asian students, 38%; for American Indians, 14% [Greene & Forster, 2003].

This is evidence for Allen Shore's statement that educational opportunities are not the same for all high school students. If one does not go to college, there is a higher chance of being unemployed. The 2000 Census indicates that black unemployment is still higher than whites. "In 1994, a higher proportion of whites (67 percent) than Blacks (63 percent) 16 years old and over were in the civilian labor force (U.S. Census Bureau, 2008; Angela Davis would dispute these numbers because she would argue that they do not include African Americans who are incarcerated and "disappeared").

Unemployment is also a big issue that Allen Shore touches upon in his tirade. "The civilian unemployment rate for Blacks was more than twice that of Whites in both 1994 and 1980 (11 versus 5 percent and 14 versus 6 percent, respectively) (U.S. Census Bureau, 2008). Allen Shore is correct according to the 2000 Census that black unemployment is double that of whites. These statistics go against Shirley's and Carl's argument that African Americans should be proud of how far they have come because of the election of Barack Obama. The virtual numbers of unemployment for African Americans are the same as before, with no measure of lessening since Obama was elected president. These are not statistics of a true post-racial America.

## *Post-Racial Politics? Political String of Apologies Over Coded Terms About "Race"*

> ALLEN SHORE: Let's not forget that we've got the Republican congressman Lynn Westmoreland from Georgia who referred to Obama as "uppity." Not once! Twice! Uppity!
> —Boston Legal, *Episode "Thanksgiving," Scene "Systemic Racism"*

This penultimate part of the essay will first go over a string of political apologies for racist comments about President Obama that Allen Shore mentions in his tirade. The first one is the only one that Allen mentions, which is when Lynn Westmoreland, a Republican representative from Georgia, calls Michelle and Barack Obama "uppity." The Associated Press cites *The Hill* newspaper, where Westmoreland is quoted: "Just from what little I have seen of her and Mister Obama, Senator Obama, they're a member of an elitist class, individuals that think they are uppity." When the reporter asked him to explain again the term "uppity," Westmoreland reiterates, "Yes, uppity" (*The Hill*, September 4, 2008). Many people were incensed by this comment, and Congressman Westmoreland defends it by saying that the dictionary definition of "uppity" is putting on airs or an elite attitude. Anyone, though, who grew up in the South knows what the term "uppity" means an African American individual who does not know his "place" and acts equal to a white person.

The second in a long line of apologies is by Senator Harry Reid, who was quoted in the book *Game Change* (2010), by *Time* magazine's Mark Halperin and *New York* magazine's John Heilemann, as saying that Obama was "light skinned" and "had no Negro accent, unless he wanted to have one." The Republicans were quick to call for his resignation as the Democrats did when then senator Trent Lott was accused of perceived racist comments. In 2002, Trent Lott attended the South Carolina senator Strom Thurmond's (R–SC) one hundredth birthday party bash and said, "I want to say this about my state: When Strom Thurmond ran for president, we voted for him. We're proud of it. And if the rest of the country had followed our lead, we wouldn't have had all these problems over all these years, either." Many people thought that Senator Lott was hearkening back wistfully to the times of segregation in America. Lott was eventually pushed to resign his leadership post over this issue.

Another Obama racial incident concerned South Carolina congressman Joe Wilson's inappropriate behavior of shouting "You lie! You lie!" during Obama's health-care address to a joint session of Congress when he said that undocumented immigrants would not have access to his health-care plan. Former president Jimmy Carter referred to the Wilson incident as being a racist affront because he said that if President Obama was not African American, he would not have gotten so much disrespect. These racially coded comments were directed at Obama, but there were also other "racial" comments that have left a popular-culture stain. Unlike these issues, there were other obvious racial incidents that had no distinct apologies attached to them, such as the conservative talk show host Rush Limbaugh's radio skits.

## *Rush Limbaugh's "Barack the Magic Negro" and "Light-Skinned" Verbal Incidents*

Circles on the left cite racially prejudiced incidents against the president such as Rush Limbaugh's radio skit "Barack, the Magic Negro," a parody written by Paul Shanklin playing off the Peter, Paul, and Mary hit song "Puff, the Magic Dragon"; Limbaugh argued that he aimed to satirize the fawning media and white liberal guilt. The song had a faux Al Sharpton voice-over contending that Obama is not successful because of any of his political accomplishments but instead because he represents the "spiritual" African American trope. Many people were outraged by the song and said it was very racially offensive in many ways, especially in using such antiquated terms as "Negro." Additionally people were offended by the *Esquire* (February 2010) magazine interview (in which former Illinois governor Rod Blagojevich claimed he was "blacker than Barack Obama" because he shined shoes as a child.

CNN reported that Republican Chip Saltsman distributed a CD which had "Barack, the Magic Negro" as a track to Republican supporters. There was a storm of criticism that came at him from both white and black Republicans who said it was out of place for the inclusive Republican Party. He made a speedy mea culpa but was later forced to withdraw from the Republican National Convention. Limbaugh never apologized and instead said that it was the "left-wing media's" and "drive-by" listeners' fault for not getting his humor of satirizing political events. Limbaugh followed this up months later by saying that Obama was trying to appear "compassionate" to both the "light-skinned and dark-skinned black community in this country," which was a play on Senator Reid's poor choice of words to authors of the book *Game Change*.

## *Conclusion: Pop-Cultural Dreams of Obama*

> ALLEN SHORE: Even Obama's own running mate during the primary, Biden, praised Obama for being clean and articulate. What was that? We can give thanks for a lot of things today, but the defeat of racism in America is not one of them. Especially at liberal white-collar law firms like Crane, Poole, and Schmidt. Look around the table.
> *There is a moment of silence. Shirley sighs.*
> CARL SACK: Bet you don't get invited to a lot of dinner parties.
> —Boston Legal, *Episode "Thanksgiving," Scene "Systemic Racism"*

The character of Allen Shore quoted the 2007 incident when then senator Joe Biden of Delaware told the *New York Observer* that Obama was "the first mainstream African-American who is articulate and bright and clean and a nice-looking guy." Does Obama's presidency transport us away from these negative images into new neutral color-blind ones? Allen Shore eye-rollingly says, "Oh, please." Shirley Schmidt disagrees and emphatically states, "We just had a black man elected president!" implying that racism is now over. Here the post-racial thesis comes in. The post-racial thesis is simple: America is now color-blind, and the election of Barack Obama is proof.

Allen Shore is correct that we are still not a post-racial United States even with the election of President Barack Obama. The evidence that we are not color-blind is seen in the persistent black-white inequalities of prison, health care, cancer, education, and unemployment rates. It is also seen in racially coded terms such as "uppity" and "Negro" directed at President Obama. The inequality statistics are very simple and straightforward to see.

On the other hand President Barack Obama's story is everything but simple. His life story is complex and cannot be stuffed into the compact sound bites that many try to place him into. Is he black, white, biracial, or other? Is he the son of a Kenyan Harvard graduate or the son of a white Kansas single mom who raised him partially in Asia? The popular-culture renditions of Obama are even more myriad; is he a crime-fighting comic book character alongside Spider-Man, or is he the Rush Limbaugh–spoofed "Obama, the Magic Negro"? His election on November 4, 2008, ignited global excitement and expectation when suddenly he became the physical embodiment of the motto *E pluribus unum*—"Out of Many, One," which has led to his international and pop-cultural fame. This also has led many people, like the fictional Shirley Schmidt, to say that we are now a post-racial America. Although this essay showed that we are not, Barack Obama's election has completely changed, compounded, and complicated all of the racial conversations hereafter. Looking to the future of Barack Obama's legacy one can argue that his election has pointed America and the world, still presently riddled with the wounds of discrimination, in the right direction of a true color-blind society.

## Note

"Whites" and "Anglo Americans" are used interchangeably throughout this essay.

## References

Adorno, Theodor, and Max Horkheimer. *The Culture Industry: Mass Culture as Mass Deception.* Dialectic of Enlightenment. Palo Alto: 1944; Stanford University Press, 2002.

Association of American Anthropologists. "Statement on Race." *Anthropology Newsletter*, Arlington, VA, May 17, 1998. http://www.aaanet.org/stmts/racepp.htm.

Blumer, Herbert. "Race Prejudice as a Sense of Group Position." *Official Journal of the Pacific Sociological Society* 1, no. 1 (1958): 3–7.

Blumstein, Alfred. "On the Racial Disproportionality of the United States Prison Population." *Journal of Criminal Law and Criminology* 73, no. 3 (1982): 1259–1281.

Bonacich, Edna. (1973). A Theory of Middleman Minorities. *American Sociological Review.*

Bonilla-Silva, Eduardo. *Racism without Racists: Color-Blind Racism.* Lanham, MD: Rowman & Littlefield, 2006.

Bryant, Nick. "Ten Quick Lessons from the US Elections." BBC, November 8, 2008. http://www.digitalspy.co.uk/showbiz/a106486/haysbert-24-president-helped-obama.html (accessed November 9, 2008).

Cohen, Ben, and Jerry Greenfield. Ben and Jerry's Ice Cream Flavor, "Yes Pecan." 2008.

Davis, Angela. "Masked Racism: Reflections on the Prison Industrial Complex." *Colorlines Mag-*

*azine*, September 1998. http://www.colorlines.com/archives/1998/09/masked_racism_reflections_on_the_prison_industrial_complex.html.
\_\_\_\_\_. *Women, Race, and Class.* New York: Vintage, 1981.
DuBois, W.E.B. *The Souls of Black Folk.* Oxford: Oxford World's Classics, 2009.
Durkheim, Emile. *On Suicide.* New York: Penguin Classics, 2007.
"Exit Polls: Obama Wins Big among Young, Minority Voters, November 4, 2008." CNN.com, November 5, 2008. http://www.cnn.com/2008/POLITICS/11/04/exit.polls.
Golden Globes Acceptance Speech, 2009 Best Television Series — Musical or Comedy Award, for *30 Rock*, January 11, 2009.
Gould, Steven Jay. *The Mismeasure of Man.* 1981; New York: Norton, 1996.
Jacobs, David, Zhenchao Qian, Jason T. Carmichael, and Stephanie L. Kent. "Who Survives on Death Row? An Individual and Contextual Analysis." *American Sociological Review* 72, no. 4 (August 2007), 610–632.
Jemal, Ahmedin, et al. "2006 Cancer Statistics." *Cancer Journal for Clinicians*, 56 (2006): 106–130.
Kelly, David E. "Thanksgiving." Season 5, disc 3. *Boston Legal.* Aired November 24, 2008.
Lopez, Ian Haney, ed. *Colorblind White Dominance: White by Law.* New York: New York Press, 2006.
Lyman, S. M. "The Race Relations Cycle of Robert E. Park." *Pacific Sociological Review* 11, no. 1 (2006), 16–22.
Marx, Karl. *Capital.* Vol. 1, *A Critique of Political Economy.* Ed. Ben Fowkes. New York: Penguin Classics, 1992.
Mukhopadhyay, Carol Chapnick, Yolanda Moses, and Rosemary Henze. *How Real Is Race? A Race Sourcebook.* Lanham: Rowman & Littlefield, 2007.
Murray, C.J.L., et al. "Eight Americas: Investigating Mortality Disparities across Races, Counties, and Race-Counties in the United States." *PLoS Med* 3, no. 9 (2006).
Omi, Michael, and Howard Winant. *Racial Formation in the United States: From the 1960's to the 1990's.* 2nd ed. New York: Routledge, 1994.
Reynolds, Simon. "Haysbert: '24' President Helped Obama." *Digital Spy*, July 2, 2008. http://www.digitalspy.com/showbiz/news/a106486/haysbert-24-president-helped-obama.html.
"United States Census Bureau: Population Profile of the United States." Census Bureau Home Page. http://www.census.gov (accessed July 8, 2008).
United States Senate. "Breaking New Ground: African American Senators." http://www.senate.gov/pagelayout/history/h_multi_sections_and_teasers/Photo_Exhibit_African_American_Senators.htm (accessed February 25, 2010).
Valdes-Rodriguez, Alisa. "The Huxtable Effect." *Chicago Sun-Times*, November 3, 2008.
Weber, Max. *The Protestant Ethnic and the Spirit of Capitalism.* New York: BN Publishing, 2008.
Wells, Zeb, Todd Nauck, Frank D'Armata, et al. "Spidey Meets the President: Marvel Bonus Back Up Feature." *Amazing Spider-Man 583.* New York: Marvel, March 2009.
Williams, David R. "Race, Socioeconomic Status, and Health: The Added Effects of Racism and Discrimination." *Annals of New York Academy of Sciences* 896 (1999): 173–188.
Wilson, William Julius. *The Declining Significance of Race: Blacks and Changing American Institutions.* 2nd ed. Chicago: University Of Chicago Press, 1980.

## SECTION THREE

# HIP-HOP CULTURE: REMIXED RESPONSE TO OBAMA'S POPULARITY

# "The Audacity of Dope"
## Rap Music, Race, and the Obama Presidency
### Travis L. Gosa

*Introduction*

The election of Barack Hussein Obama as the forty-fourth president of the United States provides valuable insight into the construction of contemporary racial discourse. Since 2008, popular race-talk has been saturated with "post-racial" logic, as many predicted that a black president would signal a new era free of anti-black prejudice and discrimination (Crowley). The audacious hopefulness of "Obama-mania" imagined a post-racial America in which access to employment, education, and the American Dream would be available to all. So far, statistics on the demography of poverty, wealth, education, and incarceration do not support the claim of a post-racial or post-black America (Roediger; Wingfield & Feagin). Ironically, the election of the first black president is making it difficult for many Americans to talk about race (Wise).

This essay explores how the post-racial myth is being constructed and challenged. Building on previous studies of contemporary race-talk (Bonilla-Silva; Pollock), I examine the discursive strategies, symbolisms, and linguistic manners surrounding the myth of a post-racial America. How the post-racial meme is forwarded by Obama and the mainstream press has received some attention (Marable). Here, I am interested in how hip-hop, a pop-culture movement obsessed with race and black authenticity (Boyd), is responding to Obama's image. Are rappers embracing the idea of post-racial America, or are they rejecting it?

My study uses the cultural field of rap music to explore the discursive battle over the racial implications of the Obama election. Rap music, a diverse eco-culture of musical styles and subgenres, is a useful proxy for public discussions of race in this era of alleged color-blindness (Jackson; Rose). Elsewhere, I have documented the impact of Obama-mania on hip-hop culture, as evident in the hundreds of Obama-inspired rap songs, mixtape compilations, and music videos released since the election (Gosa). In this essay, I argue that the "Obamification" of rap has resulted in conflicting depictions of race relations in America. Mainstream, more popular artists like Jay-Z or will-i-am (of the Black Eyed Peas) label Obama the beginning of post-racial America. Conversely, members of hip-hop's "conscious" left (think Immortal Technique or dead prez) have challenged this optimistic interpretation of Obama since the election. I also present evidence of a broader anti–Obama backlash in hip hop.

## Race-Talk and Obama's Post-Racial America

Racial inequality is (re)produced at the intersection of large-scale, historical structures and micro-symbolic interactions. That is to say, race works in "big ways" and "little ways." Social structures such as economy and violence create racial hierarchy, but race is also maintained by symbolic meaning systems embedded in language (Bonilla-Silva). Each day, we tell stories about race, and this "discursive racial framing" can disguise our racist assumptions. Race-talk involves reducing the complexities of race into easy-to-grasp definitions, social actors, and story lines. Patricia Hill Collins observes that these stories construct a powerful "common sense" about race:

> To maintain their power, dominant groups create and maintain a popular system of "commonsense" ideas that support their right to rule. In the United States, hegemonic ideologies concerning race, class, gender, sexuality, and nation are often so pervasive that it is difficult to conceptualize alternatives to them, let alone ways of resisting the social practices that they justify [Collins, 284].

Social scientists refer to this commonsense knowledge as an "ideology" or "paradigm." Ideology means that it is difficult to talk or think without relying on deeply entrenched story lines. In terms of racial ideology in the U.S. before the 1960s, it was difficult to talk about race without repeating the myth of biological differentiation by race and black inferiority. Before the candidacy of Barack Obama, race-talk tended to invoke a "color-blind" or "color-mute" ideology (Bonilla-Silva; Pollock). Much like Stephen Colbert's fictional character on Comedy Central's *The Colbert Report*, we pretended not to see or care about race. Instead, we mask our racial anxieties in coded and race-neutral language about "hard work" or "educational values." This, of course, can be a clever way to talk bad about non-white people without sounding racist.

Our attempts to stay silent on the issue of race were shattered by the candidacy and election of Obama. More precisely, it was the discourse surrounding Obama — the music, Internet clips, and the twenty-four-hour news banter — that exposed our preoccupation with race and the unhealed wounds of the past. Race-talk's transition from color blindness to post-racialism is the story of "Obama Girl booty shorts," "the long-legged mack daddy," and rap music — the latter is the main focus of this essay.

White America's fear of black men as sexual predators and the defilers of white women's "purity" has maintained from slavery, to emancipation, and past Jim Crow segregation. Explicitly voicing these beliefs in color-blind America would be seen as supporting the old-style racism of the Ku Klux Klansmen in D. W. Griffith's *Birth of a Nation* (1914/1915). Enter Obama supporter and actress Amber Lee Ettinger, and her tight red "Obama booty shorts." The "Obama Girl" provided a sexy ode to Obama called "I Got a Crush on Obama." Stricken with a bad case of Obama jungle fever, the songstress promised to "Ba-rock" the black presidential hopeful all night long. With more than 75 million views on the Internet, the Obama Girl positioned Obama as the "new" and "young" candidate. She also caused America to begin talking about inter-racial sex. In response to Obama Girl, Pastor James David Manning flooded the Internet with videos calling Obama a "Kenyan mack daddy" and "long-legged pimp of white women." According to the viral videos of the ATLAH World Missionary Church pastor, no black man could resist a white woman with a "54 double D" cup size. Mixed-race heritage made Obama especially susceptible to the lure of white women, Pastor Manning proclaimed, because his Kansas-born mother was also "white trash." On the eve of the election, some Americans began asking out loud, is Obama really a Muslim-terrorist, Kenyan-born, socialist hell-bent on pimping white women? Is America really ready for a black president? In the logic of post-racialism, an Obama victory would be evidence that the country had moved away from these fears and racial innuendos once and for all.

The "post-racial," "trans-racial," or "post-black" America paradigm is elusive, but it typically involves three interrelated ideas. First, Obama represents a new era in which a person's race no longer matters. As Crowley (2008) observes of post-racial America, white behavior is based on rational assessments — not on prejudice, fear, or hate — because they no longer "see" race. Therefore, as Crowley declares, it is possible for neo–Nazis to appreciate Obama's intellect and moral fiber. While Obama has never used the phrase "post-racial," his campaign embraced the label of "Democratic presidential candidate who *happens to be black*" (Marable, 2–6, emphasis added).

Second, post-racial logic also constructs a historical narrative for situating the 2008 election as the end of the black liberation struggle. The "two warring ideals in one dark body," as W.E.B. DuBois characterized the African American double consciousness over a century ago, are now reconciled; no longer are blacks hyphenated Americans. It establishes a binary timeline of two broad epochs of "blackness" and "post-blackness." In the former, African Americans struggled with the hybridity of competing identities as hyphenated Americans. In the latter stage of post-blackness, blacks have achieved full inclusion into the American polity and now possess a generic American identity. Now that blacks are truly American, racial redress, agitation, black nationalism, or radical defense against racism are anachronisms of the past.

Third, post-racial thought embraces the ideology of meritocracy, the belief that the "winners" and "losers" of society are determined by individual effort, morality, and hard work. The subtext of Obama's (2006) *Audacity of Hope* narrative adds the immigrant optimism of "hope" and "believing" to this story, but the point is the same. Post-racial America means that any black child, regardless of socio-economic background, can now grow up to become president of the United States.

In the rest of this essay, I explore how hip hop, specifically rap music, has dealt with this narrative about race in the Obama era. My observations about rap music's take on Obama are derived from cataloging and analyzing hundreds of rap songs, digital mixtapes, and music videos since the spring of 2007. This includes spending too much time and bandwidth downloading MP3s from file-sharing sites and clicking on YouTube videos. In addition, I've been reading the hip hop blogs, online message boards, and, increasingly, the Twitter stream ("tweets") of artists. I have attempted to maintain an ear for talk related to Obama, politics, and race. Rappers have contributed to the Obama craze by saying so much, and they don't appear to be stopping anytime soon. The following sections provide an overview but are not meant to be exhaustive of everything in the wide world of rap music.

## *We Are Now Livin' the American Dream*

If rap has anything to say about racial politics, it is that Obama is "black," with a capital *B* and exclamation point. Obama's blackness has been the organizing discursive frame in rap music. Much of hip hop since Obama has celebrated a collective identity of blackness based in progress, prosperity, and optimism for the future. The deeply entrenched story line found in most "Black President" and "My President Is Black" tracks since the election is that the election represents an important step forward for blacks.

According to the tribute songs, it is exciting to have a president who simply "looks like me" or "looks like us," as Obama's phenotypical dark skin is the source of empathy and similarity between the hip hop generation and Obama. In a country defined by anti-black racism, the election of a black man is deemed a moment to pop champagne bottles, and throw money in the air. Rappers have spared no allusion to conspicuous consumption when expressing the significance of the Obama election. While yelling "my president is black," they contrast Obama's black skin with the color of "green presidents" (money), black Mercedes Benz Maybachs, and American Express black cards. Picture in your mind the following scene: a video of young black men flashing white diamonds, riding on yellow-tinted car-rims, in a nation controlled by a black man. The not-so-subtle message is that it's an exciting time to be young, black, and rich in America.

The discourse surrounding Obama has involved an interesting tension between celebrating Obama as authentically black and yet transcendent of the old boundaries of black identity. Rappers want the world to "see" and acknowledge Obama's blackness. Expressions of racial pride in Obama have arrived with some colorful depictions of what it means to have a black family in the White House. For example, the significance of having a black First Lady, according to Lil' Flip, is that the White House kitchen will have Kool-Aid and fried pork chops ("A Letter to Obama," 2008)—authentic soul food fare, to be sure. This embrace of Obama as an icon for black progress has corresponded with the claim that Obama represents "everyman." During the election year, rappers used the meme "I am Obama" to declare that all Americans have a bit of Obama in them. The use of this refrain can be found in Double DZ's track entitled "I Am Obama" (2008). The song features different ethnic-sounding voices repeating, "I am Obama," reminiscent of the "I am Tiger Woods" Nike commercials or the Michael Jordan "Be Like Mike" Gatorade commercials. Like Jordan or Woods (before the sex scandal), Obama has come to represent a new, transcendental black identity.

The influence of post-racial ideas on rap music has resulted in a nuanced political theme about race, American identity, and even patriotism. Being authentically black, or even a "gangsta," no longer excludes civil participation and responsibilities. That is, the black president has resulted in many rappers embracing a more mainstream, less alienated black identity. Since Obama, popular rappers seem a lot less angry at the world. Indeed, during 2007 and 2008, rappers like Jay-Z and Young Jeezy became de facto sloganeers for the Obama campaign. They could be found smiling at political rallies chanting "One America" and "Change we can believe in." Our favorite ghetto celebrities still continue to rhyme about guns and women, but they also seem to drop a few Obama-inspired verses about fixing the "environment," "health care," or the economy. Given the political nihilism that has plagued hip hop since the mid–1990s, this is a major shift in the framing of race and politics.

The post-racial influence on hip hop discourse can also been seen in the explication that the Obama presidency represents the conclusion of the black liberation struggle. Hip-hoppers review the long scope of black history and posit that Obama represents getting "there" or to "the promised land." The rapper Freeway provides a useful example of how the Obama election is imagined as the conclusion of black struggle in his 2008 song "Change." Freeway details the legacy of black oppression from slavery, to "the back of the bus," to Obama. Obama is not only linked to the freedom fighters of the 1960s but is predicted to complete the three hundred year struggle for liberation. This historical narrative is a particularly pluralistic one, as "all races" are part of the struggle, and the goal is the unification of all Americans.

In the post-racial frame, race no longer circumscribes the life chances of black Americans. The election of the first black president reconciles the promise of equal opportunity for black Americans in the public sphere. Obama, in this respect, represents the inclusion of blacks in the "American Dream." No longer is one's Africanity a barrier to mainstream America. Obama's life story is said to demonstrate that any black person, regardless of circumstance, can make it. Hip-hop-pioneer-turned-Hollywood-sensation Will Smith has been a vocal proponent of this post-racial viewpoint:

> You know, I don't think America is a racist nation. I think there are racist people that live here, but I think as a whole America is not a racist nation. You were Uncle Tom if you ever said that before.... I think [Obama's election] completed a cycle of African-American citizenship. It was like the last stamp on African-American citizenship, and no longer are we African-Americans. We are Americans of African descent [Caro].

The Fresh Prince of Bel-Air has been a moderate voice in hip hop for almost twenty-five years. But the self-proclaimed American gangster Jay-Z has made similar comments about the implications of the election. "You can be anything you want to be in the world. Black people are no longer left out of the American Dream," he told reporters after the Democratic National Convention (Jay-Z, "The American Dream," 2008). On the *Blueprint 3* (2009) album, Jay-Z brags about his involvement in the Obama victory, and his ability to hit up Obama on text message. On the intro track, "What We Talking About," Jay-Z describes the election as the completion of Martin Luther King Jr.'s dream of racial equality.

These high-profile representatives of hip hop say that we are living in a new era of American life. The black president provides an opportunity for blacks to take responsibility for reforming inner-city neighborhoods. For example, the Chicago emcee Twista rhymes that it's time to restore family values in the black community, to encourage black women to attend college (instead of stripping), and to attack consumerism ("Waiting to Change the World," 2008). Rappers have called for a renewal of individual responsibility by demanding better parenting among blacks, especially black fathers.

"Positive" messages have been floating around since the election, causing some to predict an "Obama effect" in the world of hip hop. One of the first advocates of the Obama effect thesis is rapper/actor Common Sense. In CNN interviews, Common provides a three-part working definition of the Obama effect. First, the optimism of the Obama campaign will rub off on rappers, leading to more positive lyrics: "Hip-hop artists will have no choice but to talk about different things and more positive things, and try to bring a brighter side to that because, even before Barack, I think people had been tired of hearing the same thing (quoted in McLaughlin). Second, Common predicts that Obama will lead to a decline in gangsterism as the dominant expression of blackness in hip hop. "Gangsta talk," as Common put it, is "super played out." Third, the Obama effect will decrease the influence that record companies and corporations have on the production process of rap music.

Many in the hip hop community have embraced this optimism that rap might return to its radical, nationalist politics of Public Enemy's "Fight the Power" in 1989, or even the "Peace, Unity, Love, and Having Fun" electro-funk of Afrika Bambaataa in 1979. But are there any signs that the spirit of Obama has altered the direction of popular rap music? In the three years since the election, there has not been a resurgence of racialized poetics in the music, and judging from the success of artists like Wacka Flocka Flame, Rick Ross, Gucci Mane, and Nicki Minaj, "gangsta talk" about sex and expensive liquor are still viable. There are some indications that Obama-era hip hop has adopted an explicitly multi-cultural, or non-racial pop sound far removed from ghetto-scape narratives about black strife. Mainstream radio and music charts in 2009 and 2010 were dominated by acts like Drake, Kid Cudi, B.o.B., and the Black Eyed Peas, which have focused on dancing, and having a good time.

## *Ambivalence and the Anti-Obama Backlash*

Most attempts by rappers to construct alternative narratives on the meaning of a black president have been overshadowed by the celebrations of a new era. However, a few artists are attempting to raise critical questions about Obama's politics and whether a black president will signal a new stage of race relations. In this section, I highlight some of the strategies rappers have used to counter the racial optimism of the Obama moment.

These artists acknowledge that a black president is symbolically important, but they are ambivalent that Obama represents a major shift in the life chances of black and poor people. To reject this premise of post-racialism, rappers recount how the lived experiences of poverty, racial inequality, and government inaction make it difficult to believe in a new America. Joel Ortiz and Dante Hawkins' track "Letter to Obama," for example, uses the letter format to question the president's policy intentions. The song describes life on drug-infested corners, racial discrimination from employers, and young black girls forced to become strippers. The duo, like other artists, acknowledge the symbolic significance of a black president, but are they ambivalent that the politics of hope — in which positive thinking and community service will help all Americans "reclaim the American Dream" — will apply to the urban poor.

While the post-racial frame obscures the interaction of racism and socioeconomic disadvantage, political rappers are asking hip hop to refocus attention on the margins of society. In his "Open Letter on Media, Messages & Pimps," released on the Internet at the beginning of 2011, Public Enemy frontman Chuck D chided American rappers as rich businessmen disconnected from the plight of everyday people:

> It does the people of the planet little good to hear that an artist is famous and rich, will wear expensive jewelry straight from the mines, show it off, stay at the hotel, ride in limos, do the VIP with chilled champagne in the clubs, ape and monkey the chicks (meaning not even talking) and keep the dudes away with slave paid bodyguards when real people come close. The mimic of the VIACOM-sanctioned video has run tired, because it shows off, does NOT inspire and it says NOTHING [Chuck D].

In the Obama era of rap, Chuck D says that rappers are being "pimped" by corporations and are too busy wanting to be the power instead of fighting the power on behalf of black communities. Brooklyn emcee Talib Kweli has suggested that hip hop was exploited by the Obama campaign (Langhorne). The disingenuous use of rapper endorsements, he says, has distracted attention away from politicians that have a sincere policy agenda aimed at addressing the problems of the hip hop generation. Lupe Fiasco's 2011 single "Words I Never Said" is highly critical of Obama. On the track, he accuses Obama of bombing people of color in the Middle East, and he declares that he will not vote for Obama in the 2012 election.

I suspect that these grumblings at the start of 2011 represent a growing backlash against Obama. Caught up in post-racial Obama-mania, it was "obvious" to most rappers that a black president would result in improving the conditions of black people. As the novelty wears off, it is likely for more artists to start asking tough questions. In February of 2011, Sean "P. Diddy" Combs, once a staunch supporter of Obama, began putting pressure on the president via Twitter and interviews with hip hop blogs (Rutter). The black president, Diddy exclaims, owes black America and the hip hop community for getting him elected. In return, he must abandon the color-blind policies and direct attention to the problems facing his black and poor constituents.

It should be recalled that before the election, rap's political left attempted to raise these types of critical questions about Obama's post-racial image. Recall the notably anti–Obama song entitled "Politrikkks" (2008) by Dead Prez. The track describes how poor blacks were tricked into believing that they will enjoy the benefits of full citizenship under an Obama administration. Party politics and elections are a ruse, according to the lyrics, because all candidates represent the will of white supremacy. The misspelling of politics with the triple *K* is a not-so-subtle suggestion that politicians are the enemy of black people, much like the Ku Klux Klan. Dead Prez's race- and class-based critique suggests that Obama will only benefit the white elite and a complicit black middle class. On behalf of the black proletariat, Dead Prez argues for a new black nationalism to benefit the black masses.

Lyrically, rappers have been keen on opposing the image of a post-racial America by rhyming "Obama" with "Osama." The allusion to Osama bin Laden, the Saudi national responsible for attacks on domestic and overseas U.S. interests, is used to express disdain for the U.S. government's treatment of blacks. The message is that blacks continue to be treated like enemy combatants at home and have no choice but to seek revenge against America. Underground rapper Morg Parks, for example, declares war on America in his 2008 song "Obama Intro." Parks acknowledges the courage of a black man becoming president in America, but he argues that Obama's immigrant optimism does not apply to native, inner-city blacks who are treated like criminals in their own country. Given a racist opportunity structure, Park laments that violent crime and sex trafficking are the only options for the black underclass.

In the light of cultural inversion, the symbolism of Osama bin Laden takes on a powerful meaning. During the election, white racist organizations and the political right leveraged Islamophobia to portray Obama as a potential Muslim terrorist. The injection of bin Laden into the discourse plays on these popular fears by usurping what was once a racial affront and using it to attack the symbolisms of white power structure. The artists are not advocating literal violence or the embrace of radical Islam; rather they are exploiting post–9/11 fear of Arab "Others" to challenge popular interpretations of the Obama election.

Another strategy used to critique Obama is to claim that the president has little power to change racial inequality in America. Post-election tracks decode the language of "Hope" and "Change" as the hidden agenda of individuals much more powerful than the president. According to political rappers such as Immortal Technique, Chuck D (of Public Enemy), and KRS-One, Obama is the puppet of a secret organization that will enact a "New World Order" (global governance). This is the theme of Trends' mixtape *The*

*Inauguration* (2009). The tracks warn that blacks have to see beyond the "rock-star" image of Obama ("Cold Winter") and realize that Obama works for a New World Government that plans sterilization and enslavement for the poor ("What's Really Real?"). The album doesn't reveal much about the composition of this shadowy organization, only that the same group was behind both the 9/11 attacks and the installation of Obama.

If hip hop's borrowing of New World Order conspiracy theories is not meant to be taken literally, it may be a way to exploit anxiety about Obama's citizenship and race by portraying him as the ultimate outsider. The metaphor dramatizes black distrust of politicians and uneasiness about Obama's dedication to black America. The narrative expresses the fear that blacks have been tricked into believing in a system that is inherently corrupt. Instead of a new post-racial world, the warning is that the New World Order may reflect the same old status hierarchy in which people of color are subordinate.

## *Discussion and Conclusion*

This essay examined contemporary racial discourse surrounding Barack Obama and post-racialism. Through a discussion of rap music since the 2008 presidential election, I explored the rhetorical and symbolic strategies used to support and challenge the post-racial narrative. While most mainstream rappers tend to repeat the meme that Obama represents black progress and the weakening of racial stratification, a few artists are using this moment to re-race public discourse. In this essay, I highlighted three strategies used to reframe the significance of the black president. Rap narratives of the black underclass try to show how race and socio-economic inequality continue to matter. The terrorist motif is used to reconstruct an oppositional black identity that resists assimilation into mainstream, post-black politics. And, contrary to the belief that Obama represents a new era of black progress, conspiratorial language is used to challenge the pretext that racial inequality is negated by a black president.

The findings contribute to a growing literature which seeks to examine how racial stratification is preserved and challenged through discourse. This exploration of race-talk shows that it is possible to find rappers challenging the myth of a post-racial America. Given the popularity of color blind ideology and post-black politics, rap music's ability to maintain an ongoing conversation about the importance of race and social class is promising. However, this affirmative interpretation of rap music is tempered by the illusiveness of the deconstructionist counternarrative. The tracks that problematize Obama appear to be a minority in the larger rap discourse.

The rappers described in this essay have a difficult time discussing the Obama election outside of the post-racial frame. But it is important to remember that very few academics and public intellectuals of color offered serious assessments of Obama during the election year. Criticizing other blacks in public while in the gaze of white America has always been a faux pas; thus, many rappers were likely cautious to avoid sabotaging Obama. Also, we should keep in mind that contemporary rap is popular culture and mass media and therefore tends to replicate the likes, wants, and desires of the masses. Post-race offers a convenient storyline for dealing with the complexities of race, but it can also offer a (false) sense of pride and accomplishment for all Americans. The performance side of hip hop, despite its racial diversity, is still the realm of young black men. It is likely that these rappers, like most Americans, were also swept up in Obama-mania and the emotional symbolism of a black president. Perhaps as the initial euphoria continues to fade, celebration will give way to critical conversations in the 2012 (re)election. This appears to be happening already with the public comments of Talib Kweli and P. Diddy. Is a backlash against Obama and post-racialism on the horizon? Future research will be needed to determine if and how rap's race-talk shifts in a second Obama term, or in a post–Obama America.

## References

Bonilla-Silva, Eduardo. *Racism without Racists: Color-Blind Racism and the Persistence of Racial Inequality in the United States*. 3rd ed. Lanham: Rowman & Littlefield, 2009.

Boyd, Todd. *Am I Black Enough for You? Popular Culture from the 'Hood and Beyond*. Bloomington: Indiana University Press, 1997.

Caro, Mark. "How Will President Obama Affect Entertainment and the Arts?" *Chicago Tribune*, January 7, 2009, PopMatters. http://www.popmatters.com/pm/article/68764-how-will-president-obama-affect-entertainment-and-the-arts (accessed February 2, 2011).

Collins, Patricia Hill. *Black Feminist Thought: Knowledge, Consciousness, and the Politics of Empowerment*. Rev. 10th anniversary ed. New York: Routledge, 2000.

Crowley, Michael. "Post-Racial: Even White Supremacists Don't Hate Obama." *New Republic: A Journal of Politics and the Arts*, March 12, 2008. http://www.tnr.com/article/post-racial (accessed October 5, 2009).

D, Chuck. "Chuck D's Open Letter on Media, Messages & Pimps." AllHipHop, January 3, 2011. http://allhiphop.com/stories/editorial/archive/2011/01/03/22542191.aspx (accessed February 2, 2011).

Gosa, Travis L. "Not Another Remix: How Obama Became the First Hip Hop President." *Journal of Popular Music Studies* 22, no. 4 (2010): 389–415.

Jackson, John L., Jr. *Racial Paranoia: The Unintended Consequences of Political Correctness; The New Reality of Race in America*. New York: Basic Civitas, 2008.

Langhorne, Cyrus. "The Obama Campaign Used Hip-Hop Very Effectively." SOHH, January 31, 2011. http://www.sohh.com/2011/01/the_obama_campaign_used_hip_hop_very_eff.html (accessed February 3, 2011).

Marable, Manning. "Racializing Obama: The Enigma of Post-Black Politics and Leadership." *Souls: A Critical Journal of Black Politics, Culture, and Society* 11, no. 1 (2009): 1–15.

McLaughlin, Eliott C. "Common: 'Obama Effect' Steering Rap away from Rims, Bling." CNN.com, 2009. http://www.cnn.com/2009/SHOWBIZ/Music/09/23/common.obama.hip.hop/index.html (accessed November 10, 2009).
Pollock, Mica. *Colormute: Race Talk Dilemmas in an American School.* Princeton, NJ: Princeton University Press, 2004.
Roediger, David. "Race Will Survive the Obama Phenomenon." *Chronicle of Education Review* 55, no. 7 (2008). http://chronicle.com/free/v55/i07/07b00601.htm (accessed May 20, 2008).
Rose, Tricia. *The Hip Hop Wars: What We Talk About When We Talk About Hip Hop — and Why It Matters.* New York: Basic Civitas, 2008.
Rutter, C.J. "P Diddy: 'Obama Owes Us!' Hip Hop Mogul Wants the President to Stand Up..." Taletela, February 1, 2011. http://www.taletela.com/news/4770/p-diddy-obama-owes-us (accessed February 3, 2011).
Wingfield, Adia Harvey, and Joe R. Feagin. *Yes, We Can? White Racial Framing and the 2008 Presidential Campaign.* London: Routledge, 2009.
Wise, Tim J. *Between Barack and a Hard Place: Racism and White Denial in the Age of Obama.* Open Media Series. San Francisco: City Lights Books, 2009

# DISCOGRAPHY

dead prez. "Politrikkks" [Song]. *National Uprising*, vol. 1. 2009.
Double DZ. "I Am Obama!" [Song]. *Gorilla Music*, vol. 1. 2008.
Freeway. "Change" [Song]. *Change Is Now.* 2008.
Jay-Z. "The American Dream" [Song]. *Barack Obama: Yes We Can.* 2008.
_____. *Blueprint 3* [Album]. Roc Nation, Atlantic Records. 2009.
Joel Ortiz and Dante Hawkings. "Letter to Obama" [Song]. *Audacity of Hope Mixtape.* 2008.
Lil' Flip. "A Letter to Obama" [Song]. *Obama '08*, vol. 1. 2008.
Lupe Fiasco. "Words I Never Said" [Song]. *Lasers.* 1st & 15th, Atlantic Records. 2011.
Morg Parks. "Obama Intro" [Song]. *War Room*, vol. 1. 2008.
Trends. "Dear Obama," "Cold Winter," "What's Really Real?" [Songs]. *The Inauguration.* 2009.
Twista, Joe Budden, and John Mayer. "Waiting to Change the World" [Song]. *Obama 08*, vol. 1. 2008.

# The Politics of Tagging
## Shepard Fairey's Obama
### Erika Schneider

In 2008, the "Barack Obama for President" campaign tapped graffiti artist Shepard Fairey to design the official campaign poster. Fairey, an enthusiastic supporter of the candidate, designed a series in print and collage of the most resonant and evocative images in recent campaign history. Borrowing ideas from a number of movements ranging from constructivism to pop art, Fairey's representations of Obama plastered billboards and bumper stickers across the nation. This essay seeks to show that Fairey, while working within the post-modern art historical context of appropriation, endeavors to expand the appeal of fine and graphic arts by engaging popular-culture consumer's knowledge of graffiti. Unlike contemporary campaign posters which tend to use only the candidate's name in various shades of red, white and blue, Fairey's image and text reference earlier styles and evoke the visual popularity of the first African American primary victor. In the Obama campaign, Fairey found an engine to promulgate his political art just as he was about to have his first museum retrospective and just as Obama was poised to surge ahead in the 2008 presidential race, pivotal moments for both artist and politician.

The Obama campaign poster effectively "tagged" the future president's territory with its distinctive signature, serving at least several purposes. First, it identifies the maker, spreading renown. Second, it potentially defaces another's work. Lessening another's renown also can increase one's own. In this case, it's not necessarily the artist's expertise that captivates, but the artist's proliferation, at the expense of the previous resident. Additionally, it claims the territory marked out by the original artist. Therefore, within the dialogue of graffiti art, appropriation is part of the cycle. But unlike most graffiti artists, Fairey exploits canonical sources from the annals of twentieth-century art. By including Obama's image in this milieu, both with street and fine art, Fairey broadens the candidate's appeal by giving him credibility outside of the campaign setting.

Inspired by Barack Obama's Democratic primary campaign as well as his keynote address at the Democratic National Convention in 2004, Fairey created his first image of the junior senator from Illinois in 2007. According to Fairey, he had wanted to work with the Obama campaign but didn't want to taint the candidate with an unwanted association. He explained, "I actually knew that Obama's support was probably going to be people who are fairly progressive and an endorsement from someone like me might not actually be a welcome endorsement if it made Obama seem like the fringe, street-artist, radical types were his supporters" (Arnon). Having been arrested numerous times for illegal postings, Fairey wasn't sure he would be an asset. He overcame his reservations after connecting with the campaign publicist Yosi Sergant, who recognized a kindred spirit.

Fairey's identification as a "radical type" demonstrates precisely what the Obama campaign appreciated about the artist. By using the street artist's work, the campaign excited members of the youth culture, a demographic courted by the senator. Street art offered hipness because of its outsider status. In the 2008 presidential campaign, with the troops in Iraq and an economy in crisis, no one wanted to be associated with the status quo. In addition, Sergant commented that "Fairey's free distributive model fit well with Obama's bottom-up, technologically-oriented, self-starting organization and base" (Arnon). The artist regularly promotes his work through his website, where people from art collectors to college students can access his designs and either purchase or download his images for free.

Fairey himself borrowed a photograph from a website to ignite the poster campaign, a consistent application of his views on the distribution of digital images (not necessarily shared by the taker of the photograph in question). From this photograph, he created a stenciled image design for the Obama poster. For the screen print and offset prints, he used a four-layer Rubylith, a screen printing film, of red, white, and two shades of blue composed digitally (Reaves). In the lower right appeared Fairey's characteristic Obey star which dates back to his notorious 1989 street art campaign using Andre the Giant's image. By including his own tag, rather than the Obama campaign's sunrise logo, he laid claim to the image, effectively marking his creation. As the artist explained,

> I included my Obey star embedded in the Obama logo, not to try to highjack Obama's credibility as some people have said. But rather, because I know that my hard-core collectors would feel that they had to buy the poster just because it had an Obey logo. Therefore, I was more or less forcing my audience to fund further perpetuation of the image [Arnon].

Rather than "hijack Obama's credibility," Fairey commandeered the image as his own, thus effectively linking his identity with the candidate's. In Fairey's interpretation, he did this to maximize sales. With the Obey tag, he claimed the message and candidate as his own, thus linking his popularity to Obama's. The title "Progress" which he emblazoned in capital letters at the bottom of the image refers to the artist's belief that Obama stood for improvement, but at the same time could also refer to his own evolution from renegade street artist to official campaign artist. The Obama campaign's acceptance of the poster legitimized Fairey's work, while Fairey asked his own supporters to accept and support Obama's bid for the Democratic nomination and ultimately presidency. Paradoxically, by gaining legitimacy, Fairey risked losing his appeal as an outsider, an illegitimate artist.

The Obama campaign reclaimed the image a few months later, having noticed its resonance. While half of the original seven-hundred-print run were put up on the street, the other half were immediately sold. Due to the enthusiastic response from the public, the Obama campaign requested another edition of the print for fundraising, this time stipulating that the campaign logo replace the Obey star and that the "Progress" title change to "Hope." Thus the campaign reclaimed its identity by supplanting the Obey logo and by tagging the image as the official campaign poster. The image became a potent cost-effective marketing tool. With the proceeds from the original 350-print sale, Fairey printed three thousand more posters for distribution at campaign rallies where participants proudly displayed and waved them in front of national camera crews (*Obey: Supply and Demand*, 272). By the time of the arrival of Super Tuesday in February 2008, the extent of public knowledge of the Obama poster had elevated its stature to the level of the "iconic."

The relationship between the artist and the campaign is a story of mutual benefit and exploitation. Despite the popularity of the "Progress" and "Hope" posters, neither became the official authorized campaign image. Fairey explained, "[T]hey couldn't use what I'd done because they didn't have the rights to the photo and because it was something that had been disseminated illegally at times" (*Obey*, 271). The campaign's association with a street artist conferred the benefits of alternative distribution while at the same time affording the requisite distance. The campaign could not be held responsible for unauthorized images of Obama. For the official poster, Fairey employed a sanctioned image of Obama with the word "Change." However, this is not the image that most people know. The work that made it into public consciousness is an appropriated image which gained popularity through a grassroots movement, fully supported but not in the truest sense authorized by the campaign.

As a street artist, Fairey promoted the work in nontraditional ways and thus reached a larger population than previous campaigns. By posting the image on his website, he automatically reached his own fan base as well as people who might, for example, search the internet for "Obama." During the primary, he even included a personal message with the images:

> I believe with great conviction that Barack Obama should be the next President. I have been paying close attention to him since the Democratic convention in 2004. I feel that he is more a statesman than a politician. He was against the war when it was an unpopular position (and Hillary was for the war at that time), Obama is for energy and environmental conservation. He is for healthcare reform. Check him out for yourself www.barackobama.com. Proceeds from this print go to produce prints for a large statewide poster campaign.

Unlike traditional graffiti artists who typically let their work stand alone as a political message, Fairey used his website as another means of communicating his endorsement. *LA Weekly* editor and writer Joshuah Bearman observed that with people moved by the image, "Fairey's Web traffic spiked as thousands of people downloaded the image, applying it to their own sites and printed materials" ("Street Cred," 70). Although previous presidential candidates had used the internet, the transfer of information had never been faster or easier as people appropriated the "original" image for their own. This ease of ownership allowed individuals to feel invested in the campaign, to fancy themselves as campaign operatives instead of merely as donors or supporters. Not only did people post the image on their websites and blogs, but they also embraced the guerrilla dissemination of street artists by posting the work in public locations. Fairey explained:

> We sent posters to Philadelphia and they got put up all over — on abandoned buildings and on street corners. That's something you don't normally see — that level of motivation in people to spread an image. There are a lot of graffiti artists who are motivated enough to spread their own work and their own name — I'm one of them — but this is that unique case where all we had to do was make the materials and disseminate them to some sort of hubs around the country and the rest of it pretty much took care of itself [Arnon].

By posting someone else's image, these individuals went outside the conventional confines of street art, which is usually limited to self-promotion. Fairey himself takes pride in the fact that he puts up his own work. His arrest in Denver during the Democratic National Convention while posting an Obama poster illustrates the artist's personal investment in the image even when it did not have his signature Obey tag. Thus Fairey and the public tagged the country for Obama.

In addition to the flat campaign poster, Fairey also created large-scale collages, one of which the National Portrait Gallery acquired for its collection. Due to their large scale, Fairey's Obama collages have a major presence within a gallery or exhibit, just as the legendary wrestler, Andre the Giant, towered above his puny foes. For example, the collage in the National Portrait Gallery is sixty by forty-four inches. During the Democratic National Convention, he made a ten-by-fourteen-foot backdrop of hand-painted copies with modular screen prints. Like advertising billboards, the works dominate the space and herald a message. With his flair for the commercial, his images advertise the artist's own personal messages, this time his support for Barack Obama.

The collages reveal a complex layering more typical of the artist's gallery production. Although outside the domain of his street art, the collages demonstrate the artist's creative process as legible text appears behind the stenciled image. Mostly drawn from vintage sources, the background creates an intricate tapestry of articles, advertisements, and wallpaper. In this interwoven cacophony, the Andre the Giant star logo mushrooms all over in various sizes and locations. By reintroducing his tag, Fairey reasserted his street identity in the collage works. The main stenciled work still has the campaign's rainbow logo, but the Andre the Giant logo is embedded in the whole work. While each collage has variations, Fairey's tag remains consistent.

The fragmentary layering behind the image also references billboard posting, where multiple posters overlap one another. Fairey's collages mirror this experience as viewers can read partial headlines and article scraps. In the National Portrait Gallery's collage, one can read "Player" over Obama's left shoulder, "Stay Up" to the left of his head, and "Kills Dandruff" along with a cartoon of two morphed women's heads below his right eye. As a result of this layering, the collages underneath look timeworn and trafficked while the bold Obama image clearly trumps the underlying older messages.

The artist says he likes the organic quality of the ripped papers and chipped paint as well as the multiple meanings suggested in the collage (Reaves). Paying homage to the neo–Dada style of Robert Rauschenberg, Fairey uses the found objects to create a layered subtext open to free association to read or obfuscate meaning. Borrowing from newspapers from the Victorian to World War II eras, he orchestrates a concert of texts. He confesses, "I use some text that's relevant to the image and some that has nothing to do with the image" (Reaves). Like all of his work, he says "everything has multiple agendas"—obvious and subversive. The Obama collages are no different.

Puzzling through the semiotics of the ephemera and image placement in Fairey's Obama collages yields a number of recurring trademarks and revealing text. For one, Fairey always includes a large Obey logo in blue over Obama's shoulder. In graffiti, this tag is a creator's signature. Fairey reinforces this by signing his name below the recognizable tag in the fine-art tradition. Thus he unites the two traditions of street and fine art.

Fairey's most legible sources derive from advertisements. The words "Stay Up" appear in at least two of the Obama collages, perhaps as encouragement to the candidate or as a repetition of the ceaseless call to "stay up" in the polls during a campaign. One can read the word "Sale" in a number of the collages. Here again, Fairey gets to have it both ways. He both broadcasts his suspicion of the commercial world even while he reveals his business acumen time and again through his clothing line and web sales. By including "Big Special" on the "O" of "hope" and repeating prices with dollar signs, Fairey comments on the selling out of American politicians to lobbyists and special interest groups (or perhaps ironically the selling out of artists to lobbyists for campaigns). Although he unequivocally supported Obama's street campaign, he infused the gallery campaign with his self-awareness as an artist tempted by the big money of politics.

The National Portrait Gallery's acquisition of one of the collages, the third one created by Fairey, allowed public access to a version usually more restricted to private collection. By the time the museum purchased the work, the poster image had become part of popular culture. In terms of accessibility, the federally funded Smithsonian Institution site offered the most public venue due to the popular tourist destination of Washington, D.C. Usually, the museum acquires a portrait of the president after he takes office. However, in this case, the curators sought and installed the work in time for the inauguration. Deputy director and chief curator Carolyn Carr explained the choice: "It is clearly the iconic image of the campaign. It is an image that is ubiquitous" (Perry). The public's recognition of the work significantly contributed to the acquisition; the museum sought to benefit from both the candidate's and the artist's popularity.

Presidential portraits have always been part of the museum's permanent collection, which includes a dedicated hallway for their display. However, this is the first presidential collage portrait. Many of the museum's collection, from Gilbert Stuart's 1796 unfinished painting of George Washington (*The Athenaeum Portrait*), owned jointly with the Museum of Fine Arts, Boston, to Mathew Brady's photographs of Abraham Lincoln, are well-known images. Carr even likened the Fairey image to Brady's February 27, 1860, photograph of Lincoln taken the day he spoke at the Cooper Union in New York. The widely disseminated image allowed the public to see the yet-to-be-nominated presidential candidate in the same way that Fairey's work gave Obama higher visibility. Of course, the rapid dissemination of images in the twenty-first century dwarfs that of previous attempts, but the use of technology to broaden a candidate's popularity links the two. The curators believe that the public will first recognize the image and be drawn in and then "be impressed by the artistry" (Perry). Graffiti is a gateway for fine-art appreciation.

The sheer prevalence of graffiti serves Fairey's multitude of aims. The familiarity of graffiti shortens the distance between viewer and artist, boosting the artist's appeal. The hipness of street art grants the artist credibility as an "outsider." The illegality of street art grants the artist even more credibility as an "outsider." The Obama campaign liked Fairey's design for the trendiness of hip-hop culture. Spray-painted images and stencil designs associated with graffiti appear regularly in its couture as well as the media. However, the destructiveness of street art probably did not attract the Obama campaign. Many people see graffiti as nothing more than vandalism, evidence of urban decay, and the work of juvenile delinquents and of gangs marking territory. By regularly posting his own work without permission in urban settings, Fairey only reinforces these negative associations.

Usually one tag will lead to another mark until a building becomes plastered with different messages, but graffiti is about more than defacement. The history of graffiti demonstrates its associations with the Obama image. In graffiti's previous incarnations, it existed primarily as a medium for the written word rather than images (Walde, 24). Dating back millennia, scratched words and phrases appear as early as Roman times and throughout history, with soldiers in Napoleon's armies scrawling their names and dates on the Egyptian tomb of Perneb or American soldiers inscribing "Kilroy was here" throughout Europe during World War II. These pre-contemporary graffiti writers left their marks to broadcast their existence or nationality in places far from home.

In the late 1960s, the ubiquitous "Taki 183" left his signature all over New York City, prompting a writer in the *New York Times* to publish an article about him in 1971, which heightened the profile of the tag and of graffiti artists. Although the teenager varied his ink and lettering almost constantly, the tag, based on a Greek diminutive for his name, Demetrius, and the street where he lived in New York, remained the same. "Taki 183" revealed that the campaign postings of 1968 and 1970 supplied the impetus for his widespread marking, a method appropriated by a number of his imitators. When questioned about the destructive nature of his writing, the seventeen-year-old asked, "Why do they go after the little guy? Why not the campaign organizations that put stickers all over the subways at election time?" ("'Taki 183' Spawns Pen Pals"). In his own estimation, Taki 183's writing was no different than election campaign postings. Like the candidates, he wanted to publicize his name. Without official campaign approval, Taki 183 did not have the same authority as Fairey, whose presidential tags escaped the scrutiny of his Obey tags. Thus, the Obama campaign's use of Fairey's graffiti-like image returns to the origin of a pivotal example of contemporary graffiti.

"Taki 183" and many later graffiti tags had more obstacles to overcome in the artists' quest for fame than Fairey's presidential tag. Artistically, one is handwritten at the site and the other is a screen print prepared in a studio, so one artist had the support of a studio, and the other was on his own on the street. Taki 183 was just a teenager when he gained notoriety, whereas

Fairey has been creating art for more than twenty years, so one artist was untrained while the other had the benefit of a career in art. "Taki 183" acted on his own when he placed his tag on various public locations; Fairey had the support of a presidential campaign to create the image. So one artist worked independently while the other enjoyed the support of a presidential campaign. Yet the nature of illegal posting links the two and begs the teenager's question about the nature of illegality.

Indeed Fairey's solo exhibition in 2008 at the Institute of Contemporary Art (ICA) caused some controversy among locals who decried the artist's illegal postings as equivalent to condoning graffiti. After the press the "Taki 183" tag garnered, the graffiti movement exploded in urban areas, most visibly on the New York City subways. The 1982 documentary *Wild Style* followed some of the graffiti artists in their pursuit to cover the subway cars with their names and images. *Wild Style* was the first film to trace the major original elements of the hip-hop movement, of which graffiti is one, along with deejaying, emceeing, and breakdancing. Not limiting himself to one mode of expression within hip-hop, Fairey also deejays and emcees. In fact, Fairey was on his way to deejay an event at the ICA in Boston when he was arrested for an outstanding warrant (Valencia and Shanahan). The artist's arrest confirmed to the already skeptical public that Fairey's work was not fine art but merely graffiti, as seen in subsequent columns and letters to the editor (Cullen).

Fairey has tried to combat the negative image of graffiti. "Street art is made in anger," Fairey says. "You're supposed to be against everything. Even in 2004, the statement was anti–Bush, not pro–Kerry. The Obama image is the opposite, and it's refreshing to create something out of inspiration" (Arnon). For example, one of his 2004 images of George Bush, "One Hell of a Leader," depicts a grinning, blood-dripping vampiric likeness of the president. Another work, "War, Everyone Wants It, Except Smart People and the UN," shows Bush with a Hitler moustache leading gas-masked troops. In 2008, he avoided negative depictions of the Republican candidate, John McCain, and instead focused on positive images of Obama.

There was yet more controversy for the artist after Obama's election when the Associated Press accused Fairey of unlawfully using one of its photographs for the artwork. Freelance photographer Mannie Garcia took the photograph of Obama in April 2006 (Gralish). Fairey originally argued that he altered the original photograph enough to avoid charges of copyright infraction, further claiming that he had not even used Garcia's work but a January 2007 Reuters photograph by Jim Young. In August 2009, Fairey admitted that he lied and had used Garcia's image (Smee). The system of stealing another's work is not only part of graffiti practice, but also fits within the post-modern art historical context of appropriation, which reached its height in the 1980s.

Fairey's image borrowing resembles two of the most well-known appropriation artists, Richard Prince and Jeff Koons. In the late 1970s, Prince attained fame for reproducing the iconic cowboys in Marlboro cigarette advertisements by cropping and aggrandizing them to dramatic sizes. Without their contextual references, the images lose their original meanings as both advertisements and celebrations of the free spirit of the American West which Philip Morris undoubtedly wanted to evoke. As French philosopher Jean Baudrillard declared, the original does not exist because in the post-modern era the copy becomes the only known reality or simulacrum (6–7). Appropriation artists thus highlight the disparity between the original and the copy as well as declare the primacy of the artist who manipulates the image. Despite lawsuits from the original photographers and an out-of-court settlement, Prince commented, "I never associated advertisements with having an author" (Kennedy). To Prince, it was not stealing because he did not acknowledge commercial designers as autonomous artists. When Fairey borrowed the Associated Press image, he negated the journalist's work as art, much like graffiti artists do when they plaster over someone else's designs.

The other well-known case of copyright infringement came with the 1989 case of *Rogers v. Koons*. Art Rogers sued Koons for using his 1985 black-and-white photograph *Puppies*. Koons asserted that he significantly changed the meaning behind Rogers' work when he translated the photograph into a polychrome sculpture, *String of Puppies*, 1988. At the end of the trial, the court ordered Koons to relinquish all material related to the work, including an artist's proof copy. Although Koons lost the case, his lawyers pursued an appeal, subsequently lost, citing the tenets of postmodernism as extenuating circumstances. They wrote,

> For the first time, this Court must attempt to reconcile the fair use doctrine with various widely recognized elements of what is called the post-modern art movement. More so than their traditional forebears, post-modern artists incorporate in their works existing art and commercial images, thereby putting these artists on an apparent collision course with the Copyright statute [Traub].

They went on to argue for the flexibility of fair use laws in this new era. It is an argument that Fairey continues to pursue. Within the context of hip-hop culture and graffiti, using the Obama image makes perfect sense. Today, hip-hop artists in the music industry regularly use riffs from other music, reorganizing and reworking it into their own recordings (Thompson, 481). As Prince commented, what was once "pirating" is now "sampling" (Rosenberg).

Although Prince and Koons, as well as many of the other appropriation artists of the 1980s, continue to produce work in a similar style, in the last two decades, appropriation art has faded in popularity. Fairey's Obama campaign image demonstrates a sense of irony as well as a reflection on the 1980s, the Reagan years, and the paranoia of the Cold War era. This engagement with the 1980s recurs throughout Fairey's work, and the Obama image references them as well. The feeling of surveillance conjured by the Orwellian Big Brother and Soviet Union propaganda posters looms large in many of Fairey's works.

In addition to appropriating current imagery from the media for the Obama campaign poster, Fairey borrowed from Russian constructivism and pop art. His tribute to Russian constructivist Alexander Rodchenko appears in many of his works. The sans serif lettering, reduced color palette, bold graphic quality, and dramatic diagonal compositions are all hallmarks of Rodchenko's style. Constructivism originated during the Russian Revolution as a means of broadly communicating the Bolshevik agenda to a mostly illiterate population. To limit costs in a time of severe economic hardships, colors were used sparingly, the party red being the most dominant. Text was kept to a minimum, letting powerful imagery and graphic shapes broadcast the message, as seen in Rodchenko's *Books in All Knowledge* poster. At first, revolutionary leaders in the new Soviet Union embraced the new constructivist style as an abrupt break with past styles associated with the now toppled elitist aristocratic powers. Under the Department of Agitation and Propaganda, hence the term agitprop, the Communist government eagerly employed artists in the championing of the proletariat. However by the end of the 1920s with the rise of Joseph Stalin, constructivism was denounced as formalism (Clark, 73–74).

Fairey shares the Soviet artists' conviction that art can foment social change. As in both constructivism and socialist realism, where artists focus on party leaders as icons, Fairey used Obama's face and simple text as the main means of expression. In many socialist realist works, the solitary representation of Lenin or Stalin aggrandizes the leaders. However, these propaganda posters usually include the happy crowd of workers to demonstrate solidarity to the leader. Fairey has directly borrowed from the sources a number of times, as in *Giant Lenin*, 1997, and *Giant Stalin*, 1998, where each of the leader's faces is superimposed over a halftone image of the Andre the Giant tag; *World Influence* from 1998 which features both Lenin and Stalin standing against the outline of factory silhouettes; and *Obey Lenin Money* from 2003 and *Obey Lenin Album* from 2005. In each example, he removes the extraneous material of the original image.

As for the communist or socialist message, the artist is quick to assert that his work transcends such labels. In an interview with the ICA curator, Emily Moore Brouillet, Fairey claimed, "A lot of people are beyond that association with my aesthetic because it's just good design, and the Works Progress Administration used it under FDR, they just didn't use red. I used the flag colors. It's red, white, and blue.... But I don't think the poster looks communist anyway, so it's sort of a moot point" (*Obey*, xi). Even though he espouses some of Marx's philosophy, he avows that he is a capitalist; he's in it for the design more than the ideology. Fairey's focus on just Obama's face streamlines the image, ultimately aligning the message with the tenets of pop art more so than Russian constructivism.

Andy Warhol's celebrity portraits share a similar style to Fairey's work in their brightly colored silk-screen format. Like the Soviet propaganda posters, the Warhol images iconize the sitter by spotlighting the face. Raised a Roman Catholic, Warhol took this similarity further when he gilded a publicity image of Marilyn Monroe, like Byzantine icons. The Marilyn series begun in 1962 was followed by similar portraits of Elizabeth Taylor and Jacqueline Kennedy. These early portraits both celebrate and depersonalize the star in their mass production. They are gaudy in their neon colors, flashy in their large scale, and attractive because of the subjects. All these women were known for their beauty, but with Warhol's repeating images, they became a commodity. Through emphasizing certain recognizable characteristics such as Monroe's blond hair and toothy smile and Taylor's dark eyebrows, he reduced them to their trademarks. He also highlighted the messiness of a rapidly produced silk screen, as colors are irregular and sometimes bleed outside the edges. Although they are recognizable, he cheapened the idea of fame through mass production. Like his myriad of Campbell's soup cans or Coca-Cola bottles, the women are yet another object for public consumption and its insatiable appetite. Despite this interpretation or perhaps even because of it, many celebrities clamored for Warhol to immortalize them in a similar style. Because of the popularity of these portraits, Warhol has become synonymous with blurring the boundaries between fine art and popular culture, much as Fairey has done with his crossover from street art to the gallery (Dyer, 33).

One might argue that Fairey's slickness is also akin to Warhol's opportunism. Because of his highly successful marketing campaigns, Fairey has been criticized for selling out and losing touch with the revolutionary spirit associated with street art (Vallen). The artist acknowledges his initial formalism. "To be honest," he says, "I started with a surface appreciation of hip graphic nature and rebel posturing. But it sparked curiosity and exposed me to substance later" (Bearman, *Huffington Post*). The posters, with which people are most familiar, do seem relatively simplistic. They read like familiar advertisements in their bold graphics and reduced colors. In Fairey's recognizable style, Obama becomes an icon and a superstar. Regardless of how the street- or fine-art world perceives him, Fairey's commitment to politics has remained strong throughout his twenty-year career.

Like Fairey, Warhol also lent his support to the political arena. In 1972, he created a single image of Richard Nixon for a benefit auction, with the words "Vote McGovern" (National Gallery of Australia) (Heller). The work features an unflattering image of Nixon with a green face, blue five o'clock shadow, and yellow eyes and teeth. The sickly shades made the grinning incumbent look sinister, while the blue shadow alludes to the historic 1960 Nixon-Kennedy television debates in which Nixon appeared haggard and unkempt compared to the young senator. In addition, the bright colors and handwritten script give the image the appearance of a vandalized campaign poster, similar to the Obama image over the ripped-up advertisement and wallpaper collages. As Warhol had done with the Monroe, Taylor and Kennedy portraits, he used a magazine illustration for the silk screen. However, he started taking his own pictures when Patricia Caulfield and others sued him for using their photographs (Search, 193). Fairey readily acknowledges his indebtedness to earlier sources, including Warhol. In fact, "Supply and Demand," the exhibit which included one of the Obama collages and an image of Warhol and premiered at the ICA in Boston in 2008, then traveled to the Andy Warhol Museum in Pittsburgh in 2009. And this time Fairey got to deejay at the opening reception without the police arresting him.

In the creation of the silk-screen poster and subsequent fine-art collages, Fairey made Obama look famous. Although the Illinois senator was already a rising star in politics, the general public needed a celebrity to win their votes. Through the distribution method, Obama gained not only superstar status but also street presence. By tagging the nation with the image, Fairey claimed a greater territory and reached a new constituency. Obama is now president, and Fairey is an internationally known artist. It was a mutually beneficial relationship.

# REFERENCES

Arnon, Ben. "How the Obama 'Hope' Poster Reached a Tipping Point and Became a Cultural Phenomenon: An Interview with the Artist Shepard Fairey." *Huffington Post*, October 13, 2008.
Baudrillard, Jean. "The Precession of Simulacra." In *Simulacra and Simulation*, trans. Sheila Faria Glaser. Ann Arbor: University of Michigan Press.
Bearman, Joshuah. "Behind Obama's Iconic HOPE Poster." *Huffington Post*, November 11, 2008.
\_\_\_\_\_. "Street Cred." *Modern Painters* 20, no. 9 (October 2008): 69–73.
Clark, Toby. *Art and Propaganda in the Twentieth Century*. New York: Harry N. Abrams, 1997.
Cullen, Kevin. "Fairey's Art of Hypocrisy." *Boston Globe*, February 12, 2009, B1.
Dyer, Jennifer. "The Metaphysics of the Mundane: Understanding Andy Warhol's Serial Imagery." *Artibus et Historiae* 25, no. 49 (2004): 33–47.
Gralish, Tom. "Found —AGAIN— the Poster Source Photo." *Scene on the Road*, January 21, 2009.
Heller, Steven. "Beyond Red, White and Blue." *New York Times*, February 15, 2008.
Kennedy, Randy. "If the Copy Is an Artwork, Then What's the Original?" *New York Times*, December 6, 2007.

*Obey: Supply and Demand, the Art of Shepard Fairey*. Boston: The Institute of Contemporary Art, 2008.
Perry, Warren. "Interview with Carolyn Carr." *National Portrait Gallery*, January 14, 2009.
Reaves, Wendy Wick. "Interview with Shepard Fairey." *National Portrait Gallery*, January 17, 2009.
Rosenberg, Karen "Artist: Richard Prince." *New York Magazine*, May 21, 2005.
Search, Patricia. "Electronic Art and the Law: Intellectual Copyright Laws and Cyberspace." *Leonardo* 32, no. 3 (1999): 191–195.
Smee, Sebastian. "A Threatened Closing; an Arrest, a Striking Year." *Boston Globe*, December 27, 2009, N6.
"'Taki 183' Spawns Pen Pals," *New York Times*, July 21, 1971.
Thompson, Krista. "The Sound of Light: Reflections on Art History in the Visual Culture of Hip-Hop." *Art Bulletin* 91, no. 4 (2009): 481–505.
Traub, James. "Art Rogers vs. Jeff Koons." In *Subjective Reasoning: A Series of Ten Publications*, ed. William Drentell and Paula Scher. Stamford, CT: Champion International, 1992.
Valencia, Milton J., and Mark Shanahan. "Street Artist Arrested on Way to Event at ICA." *Boston Globe*, February 9, 2009, B1.
Vallen, Mark. "Obey Plagiarist Shepard Fairey." *Cultural Shifts*, January 23, 2008.
Walde, Claudia. *Paper Graffiti Art*. New York: Thames & Hudson, 2007.

SECTION FOUR

# COMIC BOOKS: OBAMA'S POPULARITY AND THE ORIGINAL SUPERHERO MEDIUM

# Obama and Spider-Man
## A Meta-Data Media Analysis of an Unlikely Pairing
### ROBERT G. WEINER AND SHELLEY E. BARBA

*Introduction*

In early January of 2009, Marvel Comics revealed that President-elect Barack Obama would be starring in a story with their flagship character Spider-Man. This announcement ran worldwide in print, on television, and throughout the Internet. *Amazing Spider-Man 583* is not only the first time a president-elect made the cover of a Marvel comic book magazine, but it is also the first time a political figure has been teamed up with a Marvel character as an equal. The story, written by Zeb Wells, Todd Nauck, and Frank D'Armata, features Obama's inauguration and Spider-Man thwarting an attempt by the Chameleon to impersonate the incoming president. In actuality the story is not that exceptional, but the magazine has become one of the best-selling comic books of all time. This issue of Spider-Man is now in its fifth printing, and the first print now commands hundreds of dollars for sale.

Although the history of comic books is rich with the blending of politics and superheroes, at first glance, this pairing seems unlikely. By using meta-data—the way the media describes the comic book—this essay will show how this pairing of a popular-culture icon coincided with a political icon and the country's expectations of him. We will look at the various media outlets and how the media portrayed this teaming of a politician and a major superhero. Because of the popularity of the two icons, the press was completely taken with this little story. We will examine just what it was the press found so fascinating.

*Presidents in Comics, a Brief Summary*

During the last half century, presidents have appeared in numerous, varying styles of comics. While some of the magazines have been little more than illustrated histories or propaganda pieces, others have the presidents as supporting or background characters, enriching the plot of the superhero. Comic book writers have been using those in the White House as far back as the 1940s when President Franklin D. Roosevelt appeared in multiple World War II–era comics like *Captain America*. Published in 1963, *Action Comics 309* features President John F. Kennedy's presidency — a This Is Your Life parody issue in which Kennedy, dressed as Clark Kent, helps Superman by standing in for him on the game show. Later that year, in another story, "Superman's Mission for President Kennedy," Superman helps Kennedy by supporting his physical fitness programs (*Superman 170*, July 1964). However, real-life events altered the publisher's plans, and the story, originally scheduled to appear in an earlier issue, was held for over half a year because of Kennedy's unexpected death.

Later presidents have had varying degrees of panel time in comic books and graphic novels. Alan Moore's 1986 *Watchmen* series prominently features President Richard Nixon as America's commander-in-chief, but President Jimmy Carter only has a face cameo as a part of the crowd on the cover of the oversized comic book *Superman vs. Muhammad Ali*. Subsequent leaders are found throughout popular pieces of the past twenty years. President Ronald Reagan appears in Frank Miller's *The Dark Knight Returns*; President Bill Clinton in *Superman Man of Steel 20*; and President George W. Bush in Marvel's *Civil War* series.

Other comic books feature the presidents as the main focus; some are like the illustrated history pieces alluded to above, and others are a bit more fantastical. There are numerous biographical graphic novels on American presidents, including Presidents John F. Kennedy, Ronald Reagan, and Barack Obama. Even outside of the comic book medium, presidents have been linked to superheroes. One well-known example is *The X-Presidents*, a parody of other superhero teams such as the X-Men, which originally appeared as an animated skit series on television's *Saturday Night Live* in 1997. Featuring former presidents Gerald Ford, Jimmy Carter, Ronald Reagan, and George H.W. Bush defeating super villains, Random House Books published this series as a graphic novel a short time after its television appearance.

## *President-Elect Obama in Comics, a Brief Summary*

In the first week of January 2009, a Marvel Comics press release revealed that President-elect Barack Obama would star in a story with their flagship character Spider-Man. The president-elect would even appear on one version of the cover of the comic. The original cover would feature Spider-Man in a style typical of the series, but the variant cover would feature President-elect Obama. The press release and reporters' commentaries about this issue instantly ran worldwide in print media, on television, and throughout the Internet.

*Amazing Spider-Man 583* was going to be the first time a president-elect was on the cover of a major comic book magazine in such a prominent way. The teaser panels released by Marvel also revealed that the comic book would be the first time a president (or president-elect) teamed up with a comic character instead of just appearing as a cameo or to establish the superhero in a real-world setting. The Obama-centered story is actually just a backup strip, written by Zeb Wells, Todd Nauck, and Frank D' Armata, and only five pages long. However, because of all the media attention the comic received, or perhaps something else, the magazine became one of the best-selling comic books of all time and the biggest-selling comic for 2009 (Melrose, 2009). The issue *Amazing Spider-Man 583* has had at least five printings, and the first printing commanded hundreds of dollars from collectors within the first week. The story has since been republished in a graphic novel *Amazing Spider-Man Election Day* in both paperback and hardback. This graphic novel also had a variant cover, but this time the variant cover was of the typical Spider-Man villain variety featuring a Green Goblinesque villain known as Menace strangling Spider-Man (Guggenheim, 2009). The phenomenal popularity of President-elect Obama at the time Marvel published the comic carried over to anything with his image on it, and this particular piece of memorabilia was boosted by Obama stating publicly and repeatedly that Spider-Man was his favorite superhero.

Obama has appeared in a number of sequential art books — another term for comic book — before and after his meeting Spider-Man. Published before Election Day in 2008, Obama appears in IDW Publishing's biography, *Presidential Material* (2008). *Savage Dragon 137*, printed in the summer of 2008, features and endorses Obama for president on the cover. Taking a cue from Marvel, *Youngblood 8*— released after the *Amazing Spider-Man* issue — also features Obama on its cover, and writer and artist Kyle Baker is currently at work on a new graphic novel biography of President Obama ("'ASM #583' Gets 5th Printing, Other Obama Comics Also Reprinted," 2009). Aspects of Obama's personal life are even being drawn as his family members get their own comics. In April 2009, Blue Water Comics gave Michelle Obama the sequential art treatment in their ongoing biographical series *Female Force*. Later that year, the First Family's dog made it to print in *Bo Bama*.

Publishers have also printed some parody comics within the past two years, including *Barack the Barbarian* (a Conan knockoff, done because

Obama confessed to collecting *Conan the Barbarian* comic books); *Drafted One Hundred Days* (in which aliens foil Obama); and *Army of Darkness: Ash Saves Obama* (an *Evil Dead* and Obama mash-up). One can also find a vast collection of online Obama cartoons ("The Barack Obama Cartoons" and "Comics from the Cartoonist Group," 2009). Despite the abundance of Obama comic material available, and despite the weakness of the actual story line, it is the *Amazing Spider-Man* issue that has become a mass-cultural touch point for America and a comic book industry milestone.

## *Amazing Spider-Man 583:* "*Spidey Meets the President*"

Two versions of *Amazing Spider-Man 583* were originally published; one has a regular Spider-Man-type cover, and the other has a variant cover by artist Phil Jimenez.[1] The Jimenez cover features a huge drawing of Obama giving a thumbs-up in the foreground, with Spider-Man hanging upside down in the background. Spider-Man says, tongue in cheek, "Hey if you get to be on my cover, can I be on the dollar bill?" This quip sets the tone for the Obama short story inside.

The story, "Spidey Meets the President," begins with President Obama's inauguration ceremony in Washington, D.C. Peter Parker is there taking photos, and suddenly two men looking like Obama show up to the appointed spot. Parker, as Spider-Man, quickly springs into action, and although the Secret Service is skeptical at first that this costumed figure can help, one Obama says, "Let's hear him out." Spider-Man suggests that a question be asked that only the "real" Obama will know the answer to. The question asked is about Obama's nickname on his high school varsity basketball team. The imposter does not know the answer, and in a wave of emotion he wails in lament about being so close to the presidency. The Chameleon, a frequent villain in the Spider-Man series, was trying to take Obama's place as the leader of the free world. Spider-Man, in his usual wisecracking manner, says, "The President-elect here just appointed me Secretary of shuttin' you up" as he punches the Chameleon in the jaw. Spider-Man is about to leave as the Secret Service takes the villain away, but Obama stops Spider-Man, saying, "I've been a fan of yours for a long time," then "Thanks ... partner" as he bumps fists with Spider-Man (Wells et al., 2009).

The story is reminiscent of older comic book plotlines from the 1960s and 1970s with its simplistic resolution and cheesy dialogue. There is even a retro ambiance with shades of the Cold War because Spider-Man devotees know that the Chameleon trying to take over America is really Dmitri Smerdyakov, a born citizen of Russia.

Obama appearing in *The Amazing Spider-Man #583* was so popular, Marvel Comics printed multiple variations and editions of the issue (courtesy Marvel Entertainment, LLC).

Throughout its history (from the 1940s onward), Marvel has put real-life public figures in their comics alongside their fictional characters, creating a sense that the events in the books are more real. The comics have settings in actual locations; for example, Peter Parker lives in a real place, New York City. Therefore, it is logical he will meet real people. So, it does not seem unnatural that Obama would show up in a Marvel story as opposed to previous presidents' appearances with DC Comics characters such as Superman.

While the story itself is not special, it is unique in that the president-elect calls Spider-Man a partner, as though they are equals. In the comic books, Spider-Man has often had an unsteady relationship with law and governmental officials; so having the leader of the free world calling him a partner is certainly a first for the series. Usually, superheroes are not portrayed as equals with their presidents or leaders, whether they are real public figures or fictional characters. In most comics previous to this one, the presidents are limited to a cameo role, requesting help from the superhero or congratulating his or her job well done. Typically, the superhero is a person of action who saves the day without too much trouble, and the president oversees the results as the commander-in-chief. However, the Spider-Man series has never really followed the traditional formula. Obama himself had this to say about Spider-Man and superheroes:

Obama and Spider-Man fist bumping is not only a fun image, it is one of many examples of President Obama's popularity turning him into an icon equivalent to Spider-Man and other touchstones of American popular culture (courtesy Marvel Entertainment, LLC).

> I was always into the Spider-Man and Batman model. The guys who have too many powers — like Superman — that always made me think they weren't really earning their superhero status. It's a little too easy. Whereas Spider-Man and Batman, they have some inner turmoil. They get knocked around a little bit [Sarasohn, 2009].

President-elect Obama's discussion of Spider-Man, with his appearance in the comic, fueled many discussions between comic fans and political followers alike on the similarities between the two figures.

## Obama and Spider-Man: Comparisons

With the rise and success of superhero movies in the past ten years, especially the *Spider-Man* movies, it makes sense to have an extremely popular President-elect Obama with Marvel's flagship character. This short story being included in the regular issue is a step toward introducing sequential art to those who may never have thought about buying a comic book or graphic novel. Despite the prevailing maxim that comics are something only for children or geeks, there is a new perception of the format as being hip and cool taking shape across the country. David Sarasohn (2009) goes on to state,

> For Obama, comic-book stardom is an extension of his legendary appeal to youth, and he's the first president in memory who could flourish in the comic book medium. Nobody could imagine George Bush having extraordinary abilities, and nobody would want to see Bill Clinton in tights.

For many, the election of Obama is nothing short of fantastical. Many pour their hopes and dreams into what he stands for like one would for a superhero.

However, not every superhero story comes out with a happy ending, and real-world problems impact today's sequential art storytelling. Our modern world is one where even superheroes cannot lead us to a life where everyone lives happily ever after. Our world feels bigger and more complicated than in the past, and our superheroes seem to echo the complicated new reality in which contemporary America finds itself living. The readers place a lot of expectations on our superheroes to give us a little hope between the horrific events perpetrated by villains in real life and in the stories.

To many, Obama seems like a superhero that can do this. When running for office, he acted and looked like a superhero, just without the cape and tights. While he does not give off so much an aura of invincibility like Superman, to his supporters he appears to be a hero that will be there when the chips are down, someone who will never give up. During his campaign for the presidency, his supporters touted his super powers, pointing to his seemingly perpetual energy, his intelligence, and his ability to solve a problem long before the problem has been fully acknowledged by others. Because as president, Obama will deal with world and domestic issues such as the war in Iraq, the war in Afghanistan, the economy, and unemployment — in addition to facing members of the government who do not agree with his policies — the Obama and Spider-Man story becomes even more poignant.

Spider-Man, a young man with limited capabilities, often fails in his attempts to save the day. We have yet to see how successful Obama will be. Through his close to fifty-year history, various authors have made Spider-

Man one of the most human of the superhero canon. His experiences are not farfetched but grounded in real-life occurrences. For example, he must deal with people he cares about dying, including his onetime girlfriend Gwen Stacy and, of course, right at the beginning of his mythology, his Uncle Ben. He must face his own fears and limitations as he deals with insane villains such as Kraven, the Green Goblin, and Venom. He even struggles with his inability to fully control situations, as when his beloved Aunt May was going to marry Doctor Octopus. Because his crime-fighting duties often come before his personal life and desires, Peter Parker must be late for appointments or even stand up dates. In his relationships, he must be guarded to protect those he loves, making his romantic life less than satisfying. Throughout all his struggles for happiness, control, and balance, Spider-Man repeatedly fails. He makes the wrong choices, says or does the wrong thing, and ultimately must learn from his mistakes.

Just as Peter Parker has to deal with J. Jonah Jameson, his boss, who constantly barrages Spider-Man with insults in his newspaper, the *Daily Bugle*, Obama has to deal with political pundits such as Debbie Schlussel and Rush Limbaugh who criticize him mercilessly. While Peter Parker's personal life is often a mess with worries about money, school, and the perception of others, he still tries to do the right things. Obama's supporters believe that he will act in a similar fashion when faced with the pressures of leading the country; he may fail and make mistakes, but the point is that he is trying to mold the country and the world into what he believes will be a better place. Both Obama and Spider-Man have enemies on every side, and their good intentions may bring results that are less than satisfying.

## Amazing Spider-Man 583: *These Phenomena*

When *Amazing Spider-Man 583* went on sale on January 14, 2009, large crowds of people all over the country, many of whom were not traditional or usual comic book buyers, waited in line for hours. In Manhattan, it was reported that "hundreds" stood in line waiting for a comic shop to open (Chan, 2009). Those in line confessed to a variety of reasons they desired a copy of the comic: some bought the issue as a keepsake of Obama's election they could pass on to their children, some felt it would be an investment piece they could sell to future collectors, and others simply wanted the comic to read and add to their established *Amazing Spider-Man* collections.

The issue set sales records as the best-selling comic since 2001; it grossed $1,408,282.47 at $3.99 per copy (Simmons, 2009). For a title that usually sells 70,000 copies of a title, this issue sold an astounding 352,953 copies and is still going ("Amazing Spider-Man #583 Sets Sales Record," 2009). One comic store owner predicted that even on the first day of sales the issue would begin selling at $20.00 per copy (Colton, 2009). The price, however, rose much higher, and by the afternoon it was selling on eBay for $299.00 (Tucker, 2009). One store owner even called the Obama issue a "stimulus package" of its own (Janega, 2009).

One of the most interesting aspects of the public debate in the media concerns whether or not the Obama and Spider-Man comic will be a good investment. With five printings, and depending on Obama's popularity, it is possible that the issue could be worth little more than $3.00 despite those who paid hundreds of dollars for it. If Obama can retain his popularity, the comic could indeed be a collector's item, but if he loses his popularity, it is possible that the issue may lose its value (Peters, 2009). One investment broker, who was not a supporter of Obama (and said that he did not vote for him), commented, "The significance of the comic outweighs whoever I voted for." He further stated, "To have Spider-Man have such a pinnacle moment as meeting the president.... It's [a piece of] history" (Montemurri, 2009).

Taken as a group, graphic novel sales have skyrocketed over the past ten years, but individual comic book sales are not nearly as high and tend to primarily cater to a small niche market. This book seems to go against that trend. Despite great sales in January and February, Marvel decided to make the Obama story available for free online at their website, *Marvel.com*, less than two months after the print books were released. The free digital story also included a brand new comic called "Gettysburg Distress" featuring Captain America and Spider-Man going back in time to see Abraham Lincoln recite the Gettysburg Address. Even with the story available to the digital public, copies of the print edition continued to sell.

## *Obama and Spider-Man: The Coverage*

Of the over one hundred newspaper, newswire, blog, and magazine stories surveyed for this article, few of them made a judgment call on the literary merits of the Obama and Spider-Man story itself; most only rehashed the same Marvel press release. However, in the desire to stand out, assorted news media tried to cover different aspects of the comic book's release, and they tended to fall into five categories.

The first wave of news stories covered the actual mass purchasing of the comic book. The only real variation in these kinds of news stories is based on the use of different quotes from people waiting in line to buy the comic. Many of the folks who were interviewed by reporters were not traditional comic buyers and said they had no plans to sell the issues they purchased. Instead, they intended to keep it in their scrapbooks for posterity. As one buyer, Phaniel Rigaud, commented, "I'm not a big collector, but I want these. They're something you can take out 50 years from now and remember that you were part of something historic. They're also something I can pass down to my kids" (Sholley, 2009). There were stories even covering who was buying it. Even a purchase by the actress who portrays Aunt May in the Warner Bros.' *Spider-Man* films, Rosemary Harris, was seen as newsworthy (Clodfelter 2009). On the news site *The Huffington Post*, comments on the story were overwhelmingly positive, with multiple posts about how this would be the first comic book the commenter had purchased in ten, fifteen, or twenty years. A larger percentage claimed this would be the first comic book he or she had ever bought (Tolin, 2009). This kind of news story, that people were buying a comic book, was the most frequent news coverage and spanned worldwide. It made the news in the UK, France, Mexico, Australia, Egypt, and Canada.

The second group of stories are actual book reviews. While few mainstream media outlets commented on the actual story itself, some did mention plot points. In the rush to cover this comic book frenzy, some sloppy reporting did occur, and one news story stated that it was the Vulture not the Chameleon whom Obama and Spider-Man team up to fight (Frenette, 2009). On the news magazine program *Red Eye with Greg Gutfield*'s January 9, 2009, episode, panelists discuss the comic book's plot, claiming the comic's use of basketball to identify Obama as racist, focusing on Obama and Spider-Man's parting fist bump, and joking, "Later the real Obama picks up Wonder Woman and does a rail of blow off her belt" ("Friendly," 2009).

The real analysis of the actual comic itself comes from niche media outlets that specifically cater to graphic novel fans. Both *Ain't It Cool*'s and *IGN Comic Blog*'s reviewers found the plot to be paper thin and the illustrations poorly drawn. "[The Obama story] that has garnered national attention was about as entertaining as one of those old Hostess super hero ads of old. In fact, those old ads at least were fun to read" (Bug, 2009). The highest praise the critics had for the actual plot was, "It's hard for me to really begrudge something so innocuous" (Joel, 2009).

The third category of the news articles are meta-commentary: discussing others' reactions to the comic rather than the comic book itself. Salon.com commentator Alex Koppelman was one of the few on a general-interest news site who wrote as if he actually looked at the piece, saying the comic looks "corny and all around awful"; however, his review heavily goes on about reactions to the book. He points out the irony in right-wing commentator Debbie Schlussel's vehement attack on the comic, which was posted on the website *Big Hollywood*, because she had failed to mention the fact that Marvel hired

Karl Zinsmeister to write stories about the war in Iraq, after which he went on to be President Bush's chief domestic policy adviser (2009). News pieces such as these are frequently found on the Internet where such a style of reporting flourishes.

The fourth category of stories consists of many mainstream news sources and political-issue-focused blogs discussing the mixing of politics and comic books in general. Columnist Peter Bart argued in one of his columns that Obama had his work cut out for him, and he could learn from other superheroes. Bart opines that,

> If Barack Obama is going to bring this off, perhaps he should take note of a few of the traits of the superhero fraternity. "Iron Man's" gift is that he has a strong moral compass. And he knows how to handle the military-industrial complex (it's part of his family). "Spider-Man's" relevant gift is that he can swing from situation to situation with amazing dexterity, never quite leaving a mark [Bart, 2009].

All the while, the late-night comedian Jay Leno takes a more lighthearted approach to the Obama and Spider-Man teaming by commenting in his monologue: "The story is about how Spider-Man stops bad guys from ruining Barack's inauguration. And psychologists believe this comic book was actually very handy in helping President Bush understand the transition" (Leno, 2009). Reporters and editors were in agreement that superheroes are to be helpful and politicians could learn something from their example.

The fifth kind of news story focuses on Marvel as a company and their incentives for publishing the comic. While some of the articles were combinations of the different categories, the most prevailing angle in all the news stories was this false debate about whether Marvel was truly innocent in their inclusion of the president-elect or if they had dark alternative motives.

Obama's appearance in Marvel Comics' flagship character's book did not escape the notice of those who saw this as a publicity stunt despite Marvel's denial. The *Oregonian* even went so far as to say the reprinting of the comics made it "the first element of the Obama economic stimulus program," and that "Marvel seized its opportunity like a radioactive spider," grabbing on to the Obama bandwagon. More than just that, Marvel seems to prove that the sequential art format is a "powerful presidential tool," and it is still a relevant part of modern popular culture despite being a niche market (Sarasohn 2009).

On the entertainment media sites geared toward comic books and fans, the early commentary (before the comic was released) was split almost down the middle on if this pairing was a good idea. Many felt the idea of Obama and Spider-Man together was interesting or "cool," while others felt the issue was a gimmick or just inappropriate for the medium. While it is no secret that Marvel, a publishing company, is in the business of making money off of its creations, many felt that this "stunt" was cheap and rooted only in Marvel's desire to cash in on Obama-mania. One commenter posted on Marvel's digital press release, "Spiderman [*sic*] meeting with him seems to connote implicit support[;] leave the politics to the politicians" (Laz3rwolf, 2009).

Marvel has repeatedly stated that having Obama on the cover of *Amazing Spider-Man* was not an attempt to sell more comics or gather more press for the company. The former president of Marvel, and now publisher and chief operating officer, Dan Buckley, said those at the company "were blown away by the overwhelming response" to the Obama and Spider-Man comic (Clark, 2009). Marvel editor-in-chief, Joe Quesada, told reporters that the idea to do the issue came from Obama's confession that he once collected *Spider-Man* and is a fan of the character. "How great is that? The commander in chief to be is actually a nerd in chief," and "It was really, really cool to see that we had a geek in the White House. We're all thrilled with that" (Tolin, 2009). In the face of those critics who decried the comic as Marvel being politically partisan, Quesada responded that if John McCain had won the election and was a Spider-Man fan, he would have featured him. As it is, McCain is on the record as a Batman fan (Dobuzinskis, 2008).

The 583rd issue of *The Amazing Spider-Man* should not be seen as a political statement in favor of Obama (Colton, 2009). Marvel's editor-in-chief Joe Quesada hypothesized that Spider-Man's appeal to Obama could be the creed by which nearly all Spider-Man incarnations have adhered, "With great power comes great responsibility." This philosophy is one the American people have expected of the office of the president since the founding of our country, and it is this repeatedly stated ideal that sets the character of Spider-Man apart from all the other superheroes available in literature. Naturally, Quesada goes on to quip that President Obama *should* live by that same principle ("Spider-Man Swoops to Save Obama," 2009).

## *Conclusion*

By the end of 2009, *Comic Book Resources* reported that *Amazing Spider-Man 583* was the most ordered comic, and the best selling comic of not only 2009, but of the last decade (Melrose, 2009). Comic book art is the quintessential American modern art form. "It's pop culture. Thus it is somehow fitting that Americas' first black president be on the cover of the *Amazing Spider-Man.* It's history in your hands" (Sholley, 2009). Thus Spider-Man is the perfect hero to tie with Obama precisely because, although he is admired as a superhero, he is imperfect and sometimes makes decisions that have negative side effects. Obama makes other appearances in mainstream comics, but these appearances did not make the national news with the fervor that the

*Amazing Spider-Man* appearance did. Earlier in 2008, DC Comics' seven-issue *Final Crisis* series saw Obama as not only president of the United States, but also as a version of Superman (Morrison et al., 2009). It is of note that turning Obama into a version of Superman did not generate the same kind of media interest that the Marvel comic did. As our article shows, the teaming of Obama with Spider-Man resonated more with the public at large and with the media on various levels. Despite Superman's popularity, Spider-Man has more of an appeal to the average citizen due to Peter Parker's personality and the Obama election being a milestone in the history of the presidency. No doubt the American presidency will continue to infiltrate the medium of sequential art, and it has a long history which warrants more study and scholarship.

Editors and bloggers alike debated what significance Obama's appearance in the comic had on the classic American institutions of the office of the president and Spider-Man. One faction holds that such an appearance diminishes the prestige of the White House, while the opposite side claims his inclusion tarnishes the appeal of Spider-Man to all Americans regardless of their political party line. However, as the awe-inspiring sales of *Amazing Spider-Man* 583 show, the real question is which figure helped the other in popularity the most. Could Obama's guest spot boost his popularity with the masses enough to make the changes he feels would be beneficial to the country? Did having President-elect Obama in his comic spur on Spider-Man's popularity to a new audience interested in seeing his new adventures, or even other comic books? A year after the title's issuing remains too soon to see what impact it will have had on Obama's and Spider-Man's popularity. In looking at the media coverage during this time, it is difficult to say which of the men is more beloved. In the final analysis, President-elect Obama's and Spider-Man's immense popularity is the same: they are two individuals working hard to do what they believe is the right thing even in the face of criticism.

## Note

1. For *Amazing Spider-Man 599*, Marvel put President Nixon on its variant cover giving the two-finger Nixon sign, saying, "Face it Tiger I am not a Crook," with Spider in the background taking a photograph. There is no actual Nixon content in the comic written by Joe Kelly, with art by Stephen Segovia and Marco Cehcchetto.

## References

"'Amazing Spider-Man' #583 Sets Sales Record." *ICV2*, February 17, 2009. http://www.icv2.com/articles/news/14314.htm.

"'ASM #583' Gets 5th Printing, Other Obama Comics Also Reprinted." *IVC2*, January 30, 2009. http://www.icv2.com/articles/news/14207.html.

*The Barack Obama Cartoons and Comics*. The Cartoonist Group, October 15, 2009. http://www.cartoonistgroup.com/bysubject/subject.php?sid=54.

Bart, Peter. "The Fast Action Hero: Obama's Heady Rise." *Variety* 413, no. 8 (January 12, 2009): 3.

Bug, Ambush. "AICN Comics Reviews *Final Crisis! Invincible! G.I. JOE!* And much more!" *Ain't It Cool News*, January 21, 2009. http://www.aintitcool.com/node/39833.

Chan, Sewell. "Lining Up for Obama and Spider-Man." January 14, 2009. http://cityroom.blogs.nytimes.com/2009/01/14/hundreds-brave-chill-for-obama-comic.

Clark, Cindy. "'Spider-Man' Comic Brought Forth Free." *USA Today*, February 16, 2009, Life section, 1D.

Clodfelter, Tim. "Bitten: Folks Drawn to Spidey-Obama Issue." *Winston-Salem Journal*, January 14, 2009, B1.

Colton, David. "Obama and Spider-Man on the Same Page; The President Elect Gets to Meet His Superhero in a Special Comic." *USA Today*, January 8, 2009, Life section, 9B.

Dobuzinskis, Alex. "Obama, McCain Both Endorse Batman, but Guess Which One Cried Over Bambi." *Toronto Star*, August 8, 2008, AA3.

Frenette, Brad. "Remember That if You Win an Election, Action Will Be Your Reward." *National Post*, January 9, 2009, PM8.

"Friendly Neighborhood President." *The Red Eye with Greg Gutfield*. Greg Gutfield, Fox News Network, January 9, 2009. http://www.foxnews.com/search-results/m/21744360/friendly-neighborhood-president.htm.

Guggenheim, Marc, John Romita, Zeb Wells, et al. *The Amazing Spider-Man: Election Day*. New York: Marvel, 2009.

Janega, James. "Comic Relief: Obama Issue of Spider-Man Boosted Failing Shop, Owner Says." *Chicago Tribune*, distributed by McClatchy-Tribune News Service, February 18, 2009. Lexis Nexus Academic.

Joel, Byran. "Amazing Spiderman #583 Review" *IGN Comics*, January 14, 2009. http://comics.ign.com/articles/945/945139p1.html.

Kelly Joe, Stephen Segovia, Marco Checchetto, et al. *Amazing Spider-Man 599*. New York: Marvel, September 2009.

Koppelman, Alex. "Quote of the Day: Right-Wing Commentator Debbie Schlussel Bemoans the Good Old Days of Comic Books, When the Heroes Weren't Obama Supporting Terrorist Lovers." Salon.com War Room, January 8, 2009. Lexis Nexis Academic.

Laz3rwolf. "Comment." *Marvel—Spidey Meets the President Comment Board.* http://marvel.com/boards/viewtopic.php?t=144308.

Leno, Jay, Conan O' Brien, and Jimmy Kimmel. "Late Night Political Humor: Last Laughs." *The Frontrunner*, January 21, 2009.

Melrose, Kevin. "Obama Issue of *Amazing Spider-Man* Was Most-Ordered Comic of Decade." *Comic Book Resources*, December 31, 2009. http://robot6.comicbookresources.com/2009/12/obama-issue-of-amazing-spider-manwas-most-ordered-comic-of-decade.

Montemurri, Patricia. "Pow! Zap! Spidey Saves Inauguration." *Detroit Free Press*, January 14, 2009. Newspaper source, EBSCOhost.

Morrison, Grant, J.G. Jones, Doug Mahnke, et al. *Final Crisis*. New York: DC Comics, 2009.

Peters, Mike. "Dynamic Duo: Obama/Spider-Man Comic a Big Hit." *Greeley Tribune*, January 19, 2009. Newspaper Source, EBSCOhost.

Sarasohn, David. "Spider-Man, Obama Build a World Wide Web." *The Oregonian*, January 16, 2009. http://www.oregonlive.com/news/oregonian/david_sarasohn/index.ssf/2009/01/spiderman_obama_build_a_world.html.

Schlussel, Debbie. "It's Official: Spidey in the Tank for Obama (& Ashford & Simpson, Too)." *Big Hollywood*, January 8, 2009. http://bighollywood.breitbart.com/dschlussel/2009/01/08/its-official-spidey-in-the-tank-for-obama-amp-ashford-amp-simpson-too.

Sholley, Diana. "Spidey-Fans Hailing Obama Too." *Inland Valley Daily Bulletin*, January 21, 2009. Newsbank: Access World News.
Simmons, Joshua L. "Catwoman or the Kingpin: Potential Reasons Comic Book Publishers Do Not Enforce Their Copyrights against Comic Book Infringers." *Columbia Journal of Law & the Arts*, August 18, 2009. Forthcoming. Available at SSRN: http://ssrn.com/abstract=1457388.
"Spider-Man Swoops to Save Obama." *Deutsche Presse-Agentur*, January 9, 2009. Lexis Nexis Academic.
Tolin, Lisa. "Obama, Spider-Man Appear in Inauguration Marvel Comic." *Huffington Post*, January 8, 2009. http://www.huffingtonpost.com/2009/01/08/obama-spiderman-to-team-u_n_156329.html.
_____. "Obama and Spider-Man Appear in Comic Together." Associated Press Online, January 10, 2009. Lexis Nexis Academic.
Tucker, Maria. "Fans Line Up for Obama Comic." *Knight Ridder Washington Bureau*, distributed by McClatchy-Tribune News Service, January 14, 2009. Lexis Nexis Academic.
Wells, Zeb, Todd Nauck, Frank D'Armata, et al. "Spidey Meets the President: Marvel Bonus Back Up Feature." *Amazing Spider-Man 583*. New York: Marvel, March 2009.

# Comics and Politics
## An Interview with Larry Hama, Creator of *Barack the Barbarian*

NICHOLAS A. YANES

Larry Hama is an American actor, musician, and comic book writer and artist. He has had minor roles on *M\*A\*S\*H* and *Saturday Night Live* and was in the Broadway musical *Pacific Overtures*. In regard to comic books, Hama entered the comics industry at the age of sixteen when he sold his first comic book work to the now defunct magazine *Castle of Frankenstein*. After serving in the United States Army Corps of Engineers during the Vietnam War between 1969 and 1971, Hama returned to publishing. Some of his venerable career highlights involve him working with legendary artist Wally Wood; drawing for *Esquire* and *Rolling Stone*; editing the Marvel Comics series *The Nam* from 1986 to 1993 and *G.I. Joe* from 1982 to 1994; and editing the DC Comics *Wonder Woman* series. During the 1990s he was the writer for Marvel Comics' *Avengers, Generation X*, the insanely popular *Wolverine*, and DC Comics' *Batman*. His most recent work is as the writer for *Barack the Barbarian*, a comic book mini-series that places President Barack Obama and other political figures in the world of *Conan the Barbarian*.

*Q: President Obama seems to have more comic books featuring him in some variation than any other president in U.S. history. The only president that I can think of who was frequently featured in different comic books was FDR during World War II. What do you think it is about Obama that has inspired so many comic book creators to write stories about him?*

A: It's probably about who the majority of current comics creators are. Rich old conservative white males don't generally want to make comic books. I'm not any of those things, except old — but I guess I still think of myself in my head as a kid. (I know I get very uncomfortable sitting in a room with guys in suits who want to talk about the stock market, sports and women as objects.) At the time of his election, Obama was generating the kind of excitement I had only ever witnessed before in regards to JFK. Let's face it, Nixon, Ford, Carter and Reagan did not make young people sit up and notice, or even keep them from falling asleep. Clinton managed to tarnish his own Camelot, Bush père was about as inspiring as an insurance salesman, and Bush fils had the hero quotient of a village idiot caught rifling the poor box. So, Obama was the one.

*Q: On this note, do you think Obama's extraordinary presence in comic books is rooted in his race or just in his personality?*

A: What personality? There hasn't been a more compelling cipher in office since Herbert Hoover. I think race has a lot to do with why the people who are opposed to Obama feel so threatened. Race is probably a lesser factor in his supporters — maybe because of the age, educational and economic gaps.

*Q: Most of Obama's depictions in comic books have shown him in a positive light. In contrast, Marvel's Ultimate titles featured President George W. Bush flustered around Captain America, then humiliated by Magneto by being stripped naked and forced to lick the villain's boots. Why do you think Bush and Obama have been presented so differently in comic books?*

A: It's back to the views of the people who make the comics. G. W. Bush inspires the same fear and loathing on the left as Obama inspires on the right. At the time I wrote *Barack the Barbarian*, I still held out a lot of hope — but lately, I have been disappointed by his handling of Guantanamo, BP, and Afghanistan. Where's the change? Not to say that my hope and trust is completely depleted — I like to think that he has whole cards yet to be revealed.

*Q: Now to specifically engage your work,* Barack the Barbarian *is one of the funniest books I've read in a while. What was the inspiration for this project? In particular, why the choice of* Conan the Barbarian *when Obama has said he liked other comic book characters like Batman, Spider-Man, and Superman?*

A: The genesis of this project, simply put, was that Josh Blaylock of Devil's Due called me up and said, "We want to put out a comic called 'Obama the Barbarian' and we'd like you to write it." I said, "First off, you should call it 'Barack the Barbarian' instead, and what's the premise?" Josh agreed to the title change and told me that's all they had: the title. I said, "But I just changed it."

*Q: On this topic, are there any satirists you feel significantly influenced by when writing this mini-series?*

A: Harvey Kurtzman, of course. And then there's Henry Beard and Doug Kenney, who wrote *Bored of the Rings*. Satire should be able to stand alone.

*Q: Moving to a more serious topic, there is a long history of racist caricatures in the U.S. linking African Americans to uncivilized behavior and black men to having dangerous sexual interests in white women. In your mini-series you depict Obama as a sword-wielding warrior, and the first issue's cover shows a bikini-clad light-skinned woman wrapping her arms around his thighs. So how do you balance the parody nature of* Barack the Barbarian *with America's racist history?*

A: *Barack the Barbarian* posits a future where cataclysmic climate change, drastic population drop, obliteration of technology, and erasure of national and ethnic identities have rendered these issues superfluous. The mode of the storytelling is that of an oral tradition and legend passed down through generations and getting substantially altered and magnified in the retelling. The extrapolation is that certain societal idiosyncrasies will be as unimaginable in the future as human sacrifice and ritual cannibalism seem to us today.

*Q: I know you said in an interview with Newsarama that you not only voted for Obama, but you also volunteered for his campaign. Do you feel that this is going to affect the story you tell? And if so, how?*

A: Yes, but I made a point of not positioning his election opponents as the main bad guys.

*Q: I've noticed that shows like* Saturday Night Live *have already begun to criticize Obama a bit. Why do you think comic books haven't negatively depicted Obama yet when other forms of media have?*

A: That has more to do with the perceived audience. I think the publishers, even the indies, don't think that the typical Tea Party member is reserving comics at the local shop. I've always thought this was a little strange since it seems like the concept of superheroes is treading close to fascist fantasy — *der Übermensch*. In the end, it is probably (as any cop on the beat can tell you) because at the lowest level, right on the street, be it the South Bronx or Kandahar, what the average person on the block wants is justice — the judicious settling of disputes. The actual form of government is way up there in the clouds to them. Something out of sight and beyond their control. The fantasy of a superior being, who is righteous and fair, and uses his or her powers to solve problems to the satisfaction of all is quite alluring. The negative fantasy of Obama as the foreign-born devil who is out to kill your grandmother doesn't lend itself to a lot of LOL moments, and it's hard to imagine the people who buy into that going into comic shops and browsing — although there are probably a good many who do. I'm still talking about the perceptions of publishers here.

*Q: Given how many comics were produced about Obama and other political figures over the past two years, do you think this represents a watershed moment for how the comic book industry will address elections and politics in the future?*

A: I think the watershed happened twenty-eight years ago when Marvel published *The Life of Pope John Paul II* as a comic.

SECTION FIVE

# News Media and New Media: The Impact of Presidential News Politics and Digital Social Networks

# Change That Couldn't Happen
## News Media's Commitment to Hegemonic Masculinity through Collective Memory in the 2008 Presidential Election

ROBERT E. GUTSCHE JR., JAMES CARVIOU, AND RAUF ARIF

*Introduction — Change That Wasn't Fit to Print*

As Americans called for social change during the 2008 presidential election — after eight years of George W. Bush — Barack Obama promised "hope" and "change" for the U.S. by transforming its place in the world. News media, then, highlighted Obama's new age of that hope and change. They celebrated that as an African American, Obama would challenge the status quo of racial representation in American politics. However, the news media's collective memory of hegemonic masculinity (the negotiation of patriarchal power in society that results in upward mobility, privilege, and dominance) in the political world reinforced the image that U.S. politics is — and shall be — dominated by strong, heterosexual, and masculine men. Obama's skin color didn't change a thing.

In U.S. culture (especially political culture), gender begets power, empowering men to hold political office for centuries. In short, masculinity is a social construct influenced through political practices and culture to develop a social hegemony based on male identity. Connell (1990) calls this "hegemonic masculinity," in which the male identity is directly connected to specifically male stereotypes — such as physical power and competitiveness — resulting in "privileging an idealized masculinity ... to maintain hierarchies of power" (Fahey, 2007, p. 134). The media's narrative connecting masculinity with political power in 2008 election coverage replayed the inherent existence of political power within a candidate's masculinity. News coverage recited memories of President John F. Kennedy as a "prince" and sex symbol, and George W. Bush became — again — a powerful cowboy.

Throughout the campaign, Obama wove the idea of change into his political and new media messages as many Americans became increasingly disenchanted with the U.S.-led wars in Iraq and Afghanistan. This idea of creating change through an Obama administration was not only limited to altering policies regarding U.S.-led wars; rather, the change movement was directed throughout several cultural aspects of society as a whole. In the 2008 election, Obama, as an African American, was to be the anti–Bush, and someone able to break America's racial divide. But as this essay suggests, Obama's promise, his race, and the presence of two high-profile female presidential contenders were still not enough to break the news media's collective memory, their way of retelling stories and constructing reality through media typification — the way reporters categorize stories — and journalistic routines of the past (Robinson, 2006). Men maintained their dominance and role.

Our semiotic analysis of newsmagazines for this essay — a process used to explore symbolic, social and cultural meanings within news (Schwartz, 1998; Kitch, 2005) — suggests that the marriage between sex, power, political involvement, and men in U.S. politics forms a narrative that news media have continued to construct as a representation of the past and as a common theme of U.S. politics today. Analysis of the 2008 primary election from January 2008 to June 2009 in *Time*, *Newsweek*, and *People* magazines provided the data for this study. Stories and photographs of Obama and his male opponents for the White House, we argue, very well fit into categories depicting the candidates as sex symbols, masculine, and powerful.

## *U.S. Presidents and Journalistic Collective Memory*

Following the death of U.S. senator Edward Kennedy in 2009 and then the announcement just months later that his son, Patrick Kennedy, was leaving his seat in Congress, news media turned to the stories they knew the best about the Kennedy family: those of JFK. Within days of Patrick Kennedy's announcement that he would not run for reelection, news media retold the tale of JFK — not as a fallen hero or as a civil rights advocate, but as a sex symbol (Bury & Clarke, 2010). ABC News was among several news outlets releasing information about a forthcoming public auction of love letters between JFK and a much younger woman he met on the French Riviera in the 1950s. Stories of Kennedy as a celebrity, as a masculine figure, as a romantic and sexual personality, as an all–American and as a tragic figure have resonated throughout American media for decades (Kitch, 2005). The Kennedy example is representative of how media depict many men in American politics.

The dominance of male political figures in U.S. political history came clear, once again, in both news coverage and news coverage of popular culture during the 2008 election. *Saturday Night Live*, for instance, did not consistently make the mainstream news over a two-year period only for Tina Fey's version of Sarah Palin, but also for a skit of an elected President Obama calling Hillary Clinton at 3 A.M. over an international crisis. The skit's irony existed only because of the resonance that men usually fill political decision-making roles, not women. But Obama's — and Clinton's — gender roles were also in question: it was Clinton who told a scared Obama to "man up," and that his work is "ball busting." Still, mainstream media covered the male candidates, consistently, as the definite choice, simply because they were men.

Such skits throughout the election — once made viral on the internet — were picked up by mainstream news media and replayed as political satire and fare of popular culture. Though the racial undertone of the *SNL* skit (that a black man must still rely on the power structure of White America) cannot be ignored, neither can the nod to the power structure of the male-dominated Congress and U.S. political structure as a whole. At the time of the 2008 election, the majority of elected officials on Capitol Hill and within the nation's governorships were still men ("United States Congress Quick Facts," 2010; ERGD, 2010). Further, while the Obama phone-call skit parodied a real campaign commercial that had been aired by the Clinton camp — suggesting Clinton was more powerful than Obama in international affairs and diplomacy — the skit became grounded in the media's collective memory of what it's like — and what it takes — to be president.

## Popular Culture and the Making of Men

Audiences, advertisers, and news media are motivated to define news based on what's popular. With capitalism as a driving force behind what's popular, media outlets are led to develop product placement in movies, television shows, and in traditional and entertainment news. What's popular is not decided by audiences, but by marketers, advertising, and TV shows. Reality TV shows such as *Survivor* and *American Idol* pushed the idea of audience power, convergence, cross-promotion, and even the definition of what's news to a new level in the early 2000s (Jenkins, 2006). *Jersey Shore* and *Teen Mom* in 2010 also began to enter popular culture. (At one point, news media needed to know whether Obama knew who Snookie was.)

News channels and outlets that did not even have a direct financial stake in these TV shows (produced by CBS, FOX, and MTV, respectively) turned to news updates and video clips of competing media companies to promote what was popular in an effort to remain useful and legitimate to audiences and advertisers. Indeed, even after reality TV stars from *Survivor, American Idol, Wife Swap, The Apprentice,* and *Jon & Kate Plus Eight* left the shows and went on to appear in other forms of media spotlight, news outlets across the spectrum turned to cover those stars, and ultimately the TV shows from which they emerged.

Such integration today of commercial and news media heightens the involvement of media consumers. News narratives, myth, and stories that broadly resonate with cultures and communities forward dominant social and cultural beliefs, grounding everyday stories in a larger context of meaning and remembrance (Gamson & Modigliani, 1989; Gutsche Jr., 2011; Snow & Benford, 1988; Fahey, 2007). Yet lessons on the cultural meaning of the news reveal that cultural narratives rely on collective memory, the process of turning to past events to tell — or to retell — stories to help readers and journalists recognize, and to make meaning of, contemporary news events (Schudson, 1992; Robinson, 2006). The journalistic processes that contribute to collective memory create "a self-reinforcing process" which "aids in sustaining authority in the present even as the construction of collective memory can only be made legitimate through an act of authority in the present" (Carlson, 2007, p. 168). In short, how we remember things, learn about new things, and try to understand them, is a process unto itself. Collective memory doesn't let us forget. Instead, it influences how we see what's happening today.

Collective memory, then, "is a constant process of reproduction and alteration as authority perpetuates itself through its own narratives that justify that very authority" (Carlson, 2007, p. 168). Indeed, collective memory within the journalism institution lends itself to a sense of nostalgia, which in turn "creates a normative-centered narrative of the past through the strategic activation of particular shared memories (and omission of others). In its construction of an ideal past moment, nostalgia indicts the present as a deviation" (p. 169, parentheses in original). In sum, collective memory fuels coverage of political campaigns, as well as the definition of what a successful political candidate is — at the very least, a powerful male — because it establishes an ideal of what a "real" (male) leader should be and how political figures do or do not match that image.

## *Power, Men, and Politics in the U.S.*

Politics is a power play, even among the most dominant of powerful figures — men. The result is twofold: only men can play politics, and only if they fit into the traditional role of men as being powerful and dominant. Traditionally, hegemonic masculinity has been defined as the representation of men as doers, as those who initiate action in society. Throughout such action, men must remain emotionally distant (Smith, 1974) while appearing highly engaged in setting social standards. Physical power has also been connected to the representation of men and masculinity throughout U.S. culture (Bordo, 1999), linking the image of powerful men with physical strength, not necessarily mental ability. Superman, for example, first emerged in a short story during the 1930s as a villain with mental abilities (Anderegg, 2007, p. 80). Still today a dominant symbol in U.S. mass culture of patriotic power, Superman was recast as a "good guy" five years later and became a hero with superhuman physical strength. His villains, on the other hand, had the brains of the bunch — such as Lex Luthor and Brainiac. Narratives of physical power embedded in this character revealed America's strength in the world. Physical strength could most currently overtake the smartest of super villains. Superman set the standard for what truly was a *super man*.

In the early 1900s, the U.S. was continuing to emerge as a dominant power — led by men — and establishing itself as a place of "doing," rather than a more effeminate thinking space, such as Europe (Anderegg, 2007). Therefore, even today, traditional views of hegemonic masculinity identify the powerful male as heterosexual, able to navigate the ability to be physically strong, aggressive, and even violent while remaining romantic and sexual (Smith, 1974; Cornwall & Lindisfarne, 1994; Neville, 2009).

Hegemonic masculinity has also been defined as the "culturally idealized form of masculine character" (Connell, 1990, p. 83) through which the ideals of masculinity contribute to social scripts that men attempt to follow to meet the perceived standards of what men are, including the use of "acceptable-male" speech, occupation, parenthood, sex, and other social roles (Nye, 2005). Such ideals of masculinity resonate in narratives of how media and communities discuss social issues, describe themselves and others, and focus on the nature and specific aspects of characters in news stories, specifically in how they relate to the predominant cultural ideology of masculinity. Consistently, hegemonic masculinity has been represented with the following five features that are used in this essay to identify symbols of masculinity: (1) physical force and control, (2) occupational achievement, (3) familial patriarchy, (4) frontiersmanship, and (5) heterosexuality (Trujillo, 1991; Connell, 1990; Fahey, 2007).

In the past, these specific features have been used to analyze the role of hegemonic masculinity in the portrayals of sports stars and political figures. In 2007, Fahey explored how the presidential campaign of George W. Bush attributed narratives of "French femininity" to that of presidential contender John Kerry. As the French government opposed international military action of the U.S. following the terrorism attacks of September 11, 2001, the Bush campaign's propaganda capitalized on the political tension between France and the U.S., attempting to undermine Kerry's campaign by seeking "to strip Kerry of the masculine qualities perceived to be necessary to fill the station of president of the United States" (p. 133). This development became a crucial aspect of the 2004 election. "Put simply," Fahey writes, "[t]his Frenchification of Kerry helped both to preserve established hierarchies of power based on gender and to maintain politics in this country and in the world as a patriarchal system. It also feminized and thereby devalued dissent in times of war" (p. 133).

The reproduction of political messages has held a longtime role within U.S. news media (Zelizer, 2004). So, too, has news media been crucial in reproducing cultural and social beliefs — such as hegemonic masculinity — in news coverage of aspects of American culture, especially popular sports (Trujillo, 1991). For example, baseball pitcher Nolan Ryan, through TV news coverage as a pitcher and a product pitchman, was displayed as an athletic and powerful man, a capitalist, the head of his house, a cowboy, and a phallic symbol (Trujillo, 1991). And at a time of increasing celebrity journalism and the availability of news media throughout endless cable channels and Internet sites, hegemonic masculinity also has ample opportunities to be represented in some of America's most prevalent outlets. The concept is easy to find in *Time* and *Newsweek*— two of the self-pronounced national leaders in newsmagazine production — and *People* magazine, which has become an outlet for celebrity news (Kitch, 2005). *People* especially has become a popular source for such news as celebrities enter the political world as activists, and politicians become celebrities (Kamons, 2007). Obama certainly led the powerful pack of politicians with his celebrity status in the 2008 election, for example, but his very presence in the election — and ultimately in the White House — produced opportunities for a media look at the role of men and what men are in U.S. politics, opportunities not fully taken advantage of.

## *Understanding Images as Comments on Society*

Reading images for social meaning is a skill rooted in the practice of examining human behavior and how people think and speak about themselves. Such study within mass communications has a grounded history. Most applicable to this study is the understanding of how to approach symbols of men and power in images. Regarding gender representations in images, Goffman (1979) identifies several aspects of photo composition that demonstrate the power struggle and the cultural placement of men and women in American society (Kolbe & Albanese, 1996). For instance, Goffman recognizes that the relative size of individuals next to each other in an image sets a social tone of importance: the taller of the two holds a dominance and power over the other objects, items, and people. In images that are focused more on parts of the person, the capturing of the "feminine touch" (Goffman, 1979, 29) turns to the use of women's hands to show the submissive aspect of women in U.S. society, whereas images of fists or grasps (often of men) denote power and control.

Goffman's concepts of function rating (the role of the man dominating images through communication or relationships represented in an image) and of the family (in which the man is the leader of the pack) reveal the role of heterosexual, masculine men as being accepted not only by society, but demanded by the public. Goffman (1979) also recognizes the ritualization of subordination, or in other words, the "deference" or "lowering oneself physically in some form or other of prostration" (p. 40), which helps identify in an image the leader, the one with the power.

Decades of evaluating the existence and portrayals of hegemonic masculinity, gender differences, and power within imagery of news media provide a foundation to see how men may be depicted in political news coverage today (Goffman, 1979; Trujillo, 1991; Connell, 1990; Fahey, 2007). Goffman's eye for exploring a message within an image provides a standardized framework for how to analyze images for what messages are — and what messages are not — depicted. Goffman's approach is useful in identifying meanings within images, especially for this project. But why look at just males in this essay? The role of women in politics, despite the entrance of Clinton and Palin, was not questioned as much as the expected masculine behavior of male candidates in the 2008 election. The two women were fulfilling roles that women have played in politics before: either as a vice presidential helper to secure the presidency for a man, such as Geraldine Ferraro in the 1980s, or as a short-running contender, such as Elizabeth Dole's emergence in the 2000 election and Shirley Chisholm in the mid–1900s. All of these women's campaigns and personalities became more of a side conversation in American politics than a campaign-changing influence.

On the other hand, however, the role of African Americans through the introduction, nomination, and legitimization of Obama in the 2008 election provided an avenue for change in how black men are viewed in U.S. society, especially in politics. U.S. blacks in general have had a tumultuous history in how they are involved in the political structure, including how African Americans have been counted in the government census (Omi & Winant, 1994; Snipp, 2003). And while Obama was not the first African American to run for president, he was the first to be nominated by a major political party.

And, indeed, Obama surpassed Clinton — a white woman with a history of political power and name recognition — to represent the Democratic Party in the general election. Therefore, it is the image of the man, the historic political figure, that had the chance to change in the 2008 election as Americans prepared to elect their first African American president, over his contender — the older, white man, John McCain. But this analysis looks deeper than the representations of one man. What follows is an analysis of the degree to which characteristics of hegemonic masculinity appear among the male candidates. Goffman's (1979) approach to reading images helps one explore to what degree the themes of hegemony and masculinity may operate together to represent the candidates as leaders, powerful, sexy — and above all — traditional men.

## *Analyzing the 2008 Presidential Election*

Social forces involved in the 2008 election, in which two women (Hillary Clinton and Sarah Palin) played significant roles in the idea of what gender(s) can play in politics, should have challenged the idea of hegemonic masculinity within mainstream news coverage. Men were no longer alone at the top of potential political power. News media, given the opportunity to broaden their understanding of race relations and gender issues within the U.S. political landscape were allowed an opportunity not only to involve women and the issue of gender in the discussion of a level political playing field of politics, but to reevaluate the role of masculinity in politics. Perhaps there was a true challenge of those stereotypes; this study cannot fully answer that question. We only suggest this: that if there was a challenge (perhaps with multiple political players who openly challenge gender, sex, and race roles during the campaign), it was not strong enough to break the overall hegemonic ideology that seemed to guide the kinds of news coverage we saw surrounding the political players of the 2008 presidential election.

The overall atmosphere of change that dominated the campaign — proposed through slogans and themes of the Obama camp — set a scene for change, even though this essay will suggest that no slogan, message, or even candidate challenged the journalistic collective memory enough to break it. Case in point: following the 2008 election, images of Obama as being "president," indeed the first African American president, overtly changed from him as a candidate to him as being "hot." The May 2009 cover of *Washingtonian* — the regional magazine of the Washington, D.C., area — for instance, showed Obama shirtless on the beach. The image accompanied the second of twenty-six reasons why people should "love" living in the D.C. area. Simply: "Our new neighbor [Obama] is hot" (Baram, 2009). That image — along with others shot earlier in the campaign — easily made way into the collective memory of the exclusive relationship between men and politics. So much so that a 2010 news story about a New Jersey fund-raiser for Haiti reconstruction following a devastating earthquake there included a quote from a comedian at the event who, when commenting on Obama's social policies, discussed not Obama's politics, but his body:

> "The Democrats are not without their faults," he began. "With Obama, the one thing that stands out is the guy works out a lot. He looks a little too good shirtless. Maybe if he spent more time creating jobs instead of working on his abs...," he began, to laughs and applause [Nicholaides, 2010].

If the image of a shirtless Obama had not become popular and evident in mainstream news, presumably such a comment would not resonate with enough of the public to be used so subtly in a general, local news story. But the collective memory of hegemonic masculinity in the United States' male-dominated political world could not be broken.

For this essay to further explore the role of masculinity in how media understand politics, we turned to photographs of male candidates in the 2008 primary election within issues of *Time*, *Newsweek*, and *People* between December 2007 and January 2009. We selected this time period in which the male candidates had been identified in preparation for the primary election on June 3, 2008. Issues of these magazines between December 31, 2007, and June 16, 2008, were then selected to create a more manageable amount of time and content of consistent candidates one week preceding and one week following the primary election day. Candidates involved in the primary election were plentiful compared to the general election as political players vied for the Oval Office. Therefore, turning to the primary election and its candidates provided a wider and deeper understanding of how news media viewed the role of men in the political race in general.

Dozens of images of male candidates that appeared on the magazine cover or that were a part of a larger news story or photographic essay were used. Because of the relevance of opinionated columns in newsmagazines over the past several years, photographs in opinion columns were analyzed; however, headshots, editorial cartoons, illustrations, and other caricatures were not used, despite the value they may have to influence cultural and social understandings of news stories. Larger photographs or those included in news articles and packages reveal aspects of truth or perceptions of realities within society, including the use of gender in the presentation of reality (Newbury, 1999; Goffman, 1979; Huxford, 2001; Kolbe & Albanese, 1996). These larger, more dominant images, then, became the focus for this study.

Images encourage representations of hegemonic masculinity through the stories they tell. Such stories can be considered subjective; however, previous research does help us identify symbolism of masculinity, such as physical force and control, occupational achievement, familial patriarchy, frontiersmanship, and heterosexuality (Trujillo, 1991; Connell, 1990; Fahey, 2007). In many ways, such characteristics of hegemonic masculinity as represented throughout media are similar to Goffman's (1979) characteristics of how gender is represented in news and popular media earlier in the mid– to late 1900s, which aided in the analysis of these images.

Common themes of how media depict gender in mass culture as Goffman suggests are useful in connecting the cultural narratives of hegemony of the past with current-day depictions. These common themes represent the major depictions of male candidates in 2008, suggesting that hegemonic masculinity is ingrained within the journalistic collective memory of U.S. politics and political men. Images that were not included in this study — which did not fit into the themes, but were still large and dominant — were either photos that depicted a candidate in an environment that was unclear, or the nature of the photo was simply to depict the character's face and contained no significant background that was useful in understanding the encoded messages.

News photographs, such as those used in this study from *Time* and *Newsweek*, also tell us stories about society. Photographs, including news photos, are designed to tell objective stories within the frame, the capturing of a moment (Huxford, 2001). Their deeper meanings, however, relate to a larger audience by creating understanding of the socially accepted. Further, news media and popular culture enhance a society's interpretation of reality, as news institutions "are tools that ruling elites use to perpetuate their power, wealth, and status by popularizing their own philosophy, culture, and morality" (Lull, 2003, p. 62), playing a powerful role in the process of hegemony as an enforcer of the dominant ideology. In other words, the wealthy and powerful control the media, use it to their advantage, and send through it their messages to control public opinion and, to some degree, public policy.

Perceptions of what the viewer, user, or reader understands as the dominant messages encoded within media images, text, and symbols (Hall, 1980) sets the stage for how we represent ourselves in everyday life and interpret our sense of reality (Goffman, 1959; Berger & Luckmann, 1966). The image of men as powerful, heterosexual, dominant, violent, and emotionally disconnected, then, influences the daily experience. Men are being made into sexual objects similar to how women have been exploited in advertising and television. For men, this exploitation has become known as "pecsploitation" (Lippert, 1997), the exploitation of powerful and sexualized men used to market and sell products, ideas, and people, such as political candidates. Meanings within images can be deeply engrained in a society. The following, then, attempts to interpret the cultural meanings embedded within news coverage of the 2008 presidential candidates.

## Candidates as Prophets

His figure frames the right side of the image. A woman, her face hidden in the fine shadow created by a flash of light in the center of the picture, reaches to his cheek, cupping it with a delicate touch (*Newsweek*, January 14, 2008, p. 40). Mike Huckabee's face shines. There is a smile. He is the Chosen One.

Such representations of the Jesus narrative — the use of imagery to resemble Christ, Christianity, and traditional Christian values (Milford, 2010; Smith, 1991) — throughout the images of many of the male candidates, reveals a main theme of this study: masculinity among the candidates meant they must measure up to be a Messiah. Hegemonic masculinity emerges through the representation of candidates as religious figures that demand a following. Images of subjects captured outside of traditional religious places, such as a church or mosque, suggest many of the same religious overtones. Such images are presented as though they were shot within a sacred place that is

> explicitly religious, [but] they function in our society to awaken an awareness that is central to religious faith: the stranger, the widow, the orphan, the manual worker, the refugee in Ethiopia is my sister and my brother, and how I respond to these is how I respond to God [Puleo, 1994, p. 5].

Elsewhere throughout the election, photographs cover crowds reaching towards the candidates: one image, for example, shows mobs stretching across the image to touch Obama's hand (*Newsweek*, February 11, 2008, p. 34); and in another, McCain reaches into a crowd of his followers, a low camera angle extends his reach to the viewer herself, asking her to come along (*Newsweek*, June 16, 2008, p. 34). Masculinity is connected to divinity, to ideology, to the role of a prophet or religious leader. Having men in those roles easily resonates with a largely Christian American audience whose historical faith leaders have been men (think Moses, Abraham, and Jesus himself).

The 2008 election was not devoid of more overt religious tones, though. Huckabee was a Christian pastor, and Obama struggled with public and media concerns that he might be Muslim. He also battled controversial statements made by the leader of a church he once attended in Chicago. Following the controversy over Obama's relationship with the divisive Reverend Wright, Obama himself is pictured as a prophet, standing before and beneath a Christian cross (*Newsweek*, May 12, 2008, p. 33). The photograph — either a mockery of his own potential, his religious leanings, or a comment on his "calling" to be president, such an overt connection to religion through imagery — is just one of many images showing him worshiping, "preaching," or praying.

More subtle religious overtones with Obama are just as striking. One example is a *Time* cover image of the back of Obama's head as he presumably speaks to a crowd, while the lighting on his face creates a halo effect (Cormack, 2000; McManners, 2001) around his head (*Time*, March 10, 2008, cover). Obama's back, more than any other candidate in this time period, was shown throughout the three magazines: standing on a plane, talking to a gaggle of reporters, his arms at his hips, shirt sleeves rolled up (*People*, February 25, 2008, pp. 96–97); he is shown from behind walking down a hotel hallway with a rolling cart (*Time*, February 18, 2008, p. 27); his back is to us on a stage at a rally, gesturing to the crowd, shot with a low camera angle as if coming up from behind the stage (*Time*, June 16, 2008, p. 13). In each of these images we appear to be standing with him, standing as though we want to follow. This is the man whom we can trust, who demands to lead — strong and sure.

## *Candidates Leading Us into the Frontier*

It takes more than a glorified man to move into the unknown, to fight into the frontier, however, to lead his people. A frontiersman must also be rugged, prepared, and experienced in leading the charge. To start, he must have already proven that he is the head of his home. Images of the campaign consistently represented its men as the heads of their households, connoting that their leadership of their own domain will easily transfer as they lead the American people. For example, John Edwards (who later was revealed to have had an affair with one of his campaign staff members) was represented throughout a May 18, 2009, *People* magazine spread as a dominant man, in charge of his family. Of all the candidates, Edwards was most shown in jeans, without a tie, with a leather belt, most likely a campaign choice to unveil him to voters as a man's man, and a family man. In the *People* spread, featured in his rustic home, jeans and an open-collar shirt, or driving a John Deere tractor with his young son through the woods, or with his family positioned around him, Edwards was "the man."

Similar posturing for power among the men was replicated in a multitude of settings. On an airplane in a photograph published in *Time* (December 31, 2007, to January 7, 2008, p. 122), Edwards, in his common attire, looks out the airplane door, his posture suggesting that he is looking into the future. His hand is on his hip. He's engaged in taking and leading the charge. In a photograph just below this, Mitt Romney, standing in a New Hampshire ACE hardware store, holds a shopping bag with the store's name on it — possibly inside the sack are his many manly tools with which he will change the country (p. 122).

It's clear the men were portrayed as strong and ready to take charge, having proved themselves worthy by leading their families to prosperity, notoriety, and prominence. A message reinforced in the setting of the photographs themselves, such as within the hardware store, supports their masculinity. While presidential candidates have always trekked across the country during campaigns, the 2008 candidates are often shown embarking on buses, trains, or planes, as if they are riding into the untamed nation. In many images, Obama is shown in silhouette, which hints at his mystique, both as a fairly new national politician and as a black man. One example has Obama silhouetted against a bright sunrise or sunset, his dark image revealing the power that he holds as he walks up the stairs and onto the jet plane (*Time*, May 5, 2008, p. 23).

Other photos representing the candidates as poised or in profile — perfect for Mount Rushmore — also reveal their masculinity. On one magazine cover (*Time*, February 4, 2008) McCain is shown standing with his arms crossed and with a slight smile, uniting the images of prophet and savior with a modern-day bust later in the magazine (p. 33). There, his head is turned for a slight profile, his eyes aimed at the viewer, a solid, stately face. Certainly in Obama's case, the physical power or the primitive power of how African Americans have been portrayed in U.S. history cannot be underplayed (Dates & Barlow, 1990). Yet physical force and control in the shape of fists, strong backs, gestures, and even just sitting within a crowd of soldiers for a photo-op or event — associating oneself to the idea of the military and its power — were quite prevalent in American politics during the period of this study.

In the case of McCain (for example, see *Newsweek*, April 7, 2008, pp. 30–31), he is often shot with reminders of his military past as a war hero after being a prisoner of war in North Vietnam in the 1960s and 1970s (for example, see cover of *Newsweek*, February 11, 2008). In other images, he is placed near the strength of metal and steel, and another example features McCain donning sunglasses, with his tie flying behind him. Dark and thick propellers of an airplane cut into the image, representing a daring, heroic, and wild-ride, movie-star persona fit for a masculine president (*Newsweek*, April 7, 2008, pp. 26–27). Again, even the environment of the photograph — what is around the person — comments on the person himself. Remember, Superman was, after all, "the Man of Steel." And just like a true male, McCain is often shown emotionally distant from his wife next to him. He is a man on a mission, focused on his role as commander (*Newsweek*, February 11, 2008, pp. 26–27).

In one case, a photo caption further distances McCain from his wife: "McCain (with wife Cindy) is many years removed from his rebel days" (February 11, pp. 26–27, parentheses in original). Cindy McCain, in that sentence, is separated from McCain the man, as though "with wife" suggests she is just a second thought. It is the man we care about. She just tags along.

## *Leaders as Straight and Sexy*

Wedding rings mean something. Besides their personal significance for the one wearing it, the researchers of this essay read these rings as a sign of heterosexuality and commitment. As of early 2010, the majority of marriages across the U.S.—acknowledged and legitimized by domestic governments—were between heterosexual couples. And the wedding ring—in the U.S., usually worn on the left ring finger—continued to be a social and cultural symbol of partnerships. Rings, then, for us are symbols of marriage and, therefore, heterosexuality, though not the single symbol. In this case, photograph captions are helpful in how the editors wish to refer to those in the image, such as using the terms "wife" and "husband" to signify a relationship. Yet what was most surprising in our review of these images was the consistent and evident representation of heterosexuality among the men in the photographs. Even in "everyday situations," the wedding ring is pronounced within the image, often shining, almost glowing. More importantly, however, the majority of images in which candidates' rings were more overt were in those images connoting power: the candidate's ring hand was often in a gesture of power, action, in a fist, or pointing. For example, Mike Huckabee, in a forceful conversation with Jay Leno on Leno's TV show set, makes a fist—a sign of power—in making a point. His ring is front and center in the image (*Time*, January 21, 2008, p. 48). The *Time* cover on February 4, 2008, shows McCain in a stoic stance, his arms crossed—a sign of power—his ring reflecting light. John McCain extends his open hand to grab the biceps of someone he meets. The other person is walking into McCain's controlling embrace—McCain's wedding ring in plain view (*Newsweek*, June 16, 2008, p. 33). There is no doubt whether any of these men wished to be shown as straight; wearing a wedding ring is a choice. And there is also no doubt that these men are sexy, or at the very least, sexual.

Yet it is not enough for a male candidate to be sexy, strong, and a proven leader, or even the "chosen" leader. A male candidate must be married, again reinforcing the idea that the proper man and the proper presidential candidate is heterosexual. This view is buttressed by an image of John Edwards standing as the head of his household, taller than his wife, his two children, and his pet dogs (*People*, May 19, 2008, p. 77). They are a family, and John is the boss. Elsewhere, in a more intimate scene, Barack and Michelle Obama cuddle. She leans into him. Their eyes, slightly opened, meet. It's a two-page spread in *Newsweek* (January 14, 2008, pp. 26–27) that reinforces their family and sexual orientations.

And take this photo, in *People* (January 21, 2008, p. 71), to see how marriage makes men be—or stay—in control: McCain and his wife, Cindy, at a rally. She is clapping. He is standing behind her. Both are smiling. It may look as though they are equals. But an inset at the bottom of the image shows an Iraq GI bracelet that McCain wears to remind himself of soldiers fighting for the U.S. The bracelet is also a reminder for the reader about McCain's own battled history and the military power and leadership that came with it. The image sets the record straight: Just as in other images of male candidates for the 2008 election, the man is still in charge.

## *Masculinity, Politics, and the Future*

This essay suggests that men continue to dominate media coverage of U.S. politics and dominate what it means to be in politics. Moreover, we argue that it is only a certain *type* of man—one who is powerful *and* prophetic—that media pay attention to. Even if this outcome may not be surprising, please know that this idea was not the authors' expectation as we entered the study. Nor is that outcome the authors' main argument. Instead, it is argued that masculinity *does not need to be* a function of maintaining a power structure that is predominantly male-oriented and created.

However, it is clearly difficult for the media, both news and entertainment, to change how it views society. First, not only must the messages be altered and accepted by audiences, but news workers themselves must work to alter individual and organizational expectations of political norms in how they cover the news—and the people in it. Second, the concept of collective memory is a powerful and manipulative ideology for news media. While a wonderful avenue to nostalgia, it is not a proper avenue to history. Collective memory is, however, an avenue to understand society through the lens of news workers' own understanding, or, at the very least, their interpretations of selected memories and facts.

## *Conclusions*

To summarize, this essay suggests that the definition of masculinity continues to be limited to power and to the past, as revealed in coverage that connected Obama to JFK's policy and popularity (for example, see Begley, 2008), and also revealed in McCain being consistently linked to his military career. Yet one aspect of how hegemonic masculinity has been defined — through the measure of occupational achievement — does not seem to be as prevalent in the coverage of presidential candidates — their career success. Of course, one does not become a presidential candidate without some career success, yet in such circumstances where career success seems like a given, what's important is whether the media acknowledges that career. Our study suggests this element of manhood was not one that made them more of a man. Instead, their masculinity is defined and celebrated by news media when it is heterosexual and physically powerful.

When evaluating these outcomes and suggestions, it should be noted that the conclusions — while found within a conceptual framework consistent with contemporary literature and methods — could vary based on an individual's background, not to mention gender or sex identification. Despite specific and varying interpretations of this data, this research provides insight for future examinations on this topic: What is masculinity? What is the main influence upon journalists and society that continues to define men, successful men, men in politics, and the office of the president the same way they have for decades? By maintaining such a commitment to hegemonic masculinity as it stands today, media cannot facilitate change. Instead, media outlets remain hostage to cultural and social forces that keep media messages rooted in a limited and defined understanding of masculinity.

## References

Anderegg, David. *Nerds: Who They Are and Why We Need More of Them*. New York: Penguin, 2007.
Baram, Marcus. "Shirtless Obama Makes Washingtonian Cover." *Huffington Post*, April 20, 2009. http://www.huffingtonpost.com/2009/04/20/shirtless-obama-on-cover_n_189283.html (accessed February 21, 2010).
Begley, Sharon. "When It's Head versus Heart, the Heart Wins." *Newsweek*, February 11, 2008, 34–36.
Berger, Peter, and Thomas Luckmann. *The Social Construction of Reality: A Treatise in the Sociology of Knowledge*. New York: Anchor, 1966.
Bordo, Susan. *The Male Body: A Look at Men in Public and in Private*. New York: Farrar, Straus & Giroux, 1999.
Bury, Chris, and Suzan Clarke. "John F. Kennedy Secret Love Letters to Gunilla Von Post — ABC News." ABC News, February 15, 2010. http://abcnews.go.com/GMA/john-kennedy-secret-love-letters-gunilla-von-post/story?id=9836818 (accessed February 16, 2011).
Carlson, Matt. "Making Memories Matter: Journalistic Authority and the Memorializing Discourse around Mary McGrory and David Brinkley." *Journalism* 8, no. 2 (2007): 165–183.
Connell, Raewyn. "An Iron Man: The Body and Some Contradictions of Hegemonic Masculinity." Ed. D. F. Sabo. In *Sport, Men and the Gender Order: Critical Feminist Perspectives*, ed. M. A. Messner, 83–95. Champaign, IL: Human Kinetics, 1990.

Cormack, Robin. *Byzantine Art*. Oxford: Oxford University Press, 2000.
Cornwall, Andrea, and Nancy Lindisfarne. "Dislocating Masculinity: Gender, Power and Ethnography." In *Dislocating Masculinity: Comparative Ethnographies*, 11–47. London: Routledge, 1994.
Dates, Jannette L., and William Barlow. *Split Image: African Americans in the Mass Media*. Washington, DC: Howard University Press, 1990.
ERGD. "Women Who Became Governors," Equal Representation in Government." *Find the Best Domain Names to Register*. ERGD, 2010. Web. 16 Feb. 2010. <http://ergd.org/Governors.htm>.
Fahey, Anna Cornelia. "French and Feminine: Hegemonic Masculinity and the Emasculation of John Kerry in the 2004 Presidential Race." *Critical Studies in Media Communication* 24.2 (2007): 132–150.
Gamson, William A., and Andre Modigliani. "Media Discourse and Public Opinion on Nuclear Power: A Constructionist Approach." *American Journal of Sociology* 95.1 (1989): 1–37.
Goffman, Erving. *Gender Advertisements*, New York: Harper and Row, 1979.
Goffman, Erving. *The Presentation of Self in Everyday Life*. Garden City, NY: Doubleday, 1959.
Gutsche, R. E., Jr. (2011). "Building boundaries: A case study of the use of news photographs and cultural narratives in the coverage of local crime and in the creation of urban space," Visual Communication Quarterly, 18(3).
Hall, Stuart. "Encoding and Decoding in Television Discourse." *Culture, Media, Language: Working Papers in Cultural Studies, 1972–79*. London: Hutchinson, 1980. 128–138.
Huxford, John. "Beyond the Referential: Uses of Visual Symbolism in the Press." *Journalism* 2.1 (2001): 45–71.
Jenkins, Henry. *Convergence Culture: Where Old and New Media Collide*. New York & London: New York University Press, 2006.
Kamons, Andrew. "Of Note: Celebrity and Politics." *SAIS Review* 27.1 (2007): 145–146.
Kitch, Carolyn L. *Pages from the Past: History and Memory in American Magazines*. Chapel Hill: University of North Carolina Press, 2005.
Kolbe, Richard H., and Paul J. Albanese. "Man to Man: A Content Analysis of Sole-Male Images in Male-Audience Magazines." *Journal of Advertising* 25.4 (1996): 1–20.
Lippert, Barbara. *Pecsploitation*. New York: New York, 1997.
Lull, J. "Hegemony." Ed. Gail Dines and Jean McMahon Humez. *Gender, Race, and Class in Media: a Text-reader*. Thousand Oaks, CA: Sage, 1995. 61–66.
McManners, John. *The Oxford Illustrated History of Christianity*. Oxford: Oxford UP, 2001.
Milford, Mike. "Neo-Christ, The Matrix, and secondary allegory as a rhetorical form." *Southern Communication Journal* 75.1 (2010): 17–34.
Neville, Patricia. "Side-splitting Masculinity: Comedy, Mr. Bean and the Representation of Masculinities in Contemporary Society." *Journal of Gender Studies* 18.3 (2009): 231–243.
Newbury, Darren. "Photography and the Visualization of Working Class Lives in Britain." *Visual Anthropology Review* 15.1 (1999): 21–44.
Nicholaides, Kelly. "Haiti Benefit Pulls in Money for Aid." *NorthJersey.com*. 17 Feb. 2010. Web.
Nye, Robert A. "Locating Masculinity: Some Recent Work on Men." *Signs* 30.3 (2005): 1937–1962.
Omi, Michael, & Winant, Howard. *Racial Formation in the United States*. New York: Routledge, 1994.
Puleo, Mev. "The prophetic act of bearing witness" *Arts Magazine* 01 July 1994: 1–6.
Robinson, Sue. "Reporting through the Lens of the Past: From Challenger to Columbia." In Jill Edy & Miglena Daradanova. *Journalism* 7.2 (2006): 131–151.
Schudson, Michael. *Watergate in American Memory*. New York: Basic Books, 1992.
Schwartz, Barry. "Frame Images: Towards a Semiotics of Collective Memory." *Semiotica* 121.5 (1998): 1–40.
Smith, Craig R. "The persona of Jesus in the Gospel According to St. Matthew." *The Journal of Communication and Religion* (1991): 57–70.
Smith, Dorothy E. "Women's Perspectives as a Radical Critique of Sociology." In Sandra Hard-

ing, ed. 1987. *Feminism and Methodology*. Bloomington, USA/Milton Keynes, UK: Indiana University Press and Open University Press (1974): 69–76.

Snipp, C. Matthew. "Racial Measurement in the American Census: Past Practices and Implications for the Future." *Annual Review of Sociology* 29 (2003): 563–588.

Snow, David A., and Benford, Robert D. (1988). "Ideology, Frame Resonance, and Participant Mobilization." In Bert Klandermans, Hanspeter Kriesi, and Sidney Tarrow, eds., *From Structure to Action: Social Movement Participation Across Cultures*. Greenwich, CT: JAL. (1988): 197–217.

"United States Congress Quick Facts." *ThisNation.com* (2010). Web. (Inactive URL/Unable to Locate Source).

Trujillo, Nick. "Hegemonic Masculinity on the Mound: Media Representations of Nolan Ryan and American Sports Culture." *Critical Studies in Mass Communication* 8 (1991): 290–308.

Zelizer, Barbie. *Taking Journalism Seriously: News and the Academy*. Thousand Oaks, CA: Sage, 2004.

# The President Speaks to America's Schoolchildren
## Outline of a Brouhaha
JOHN T. "JACK" BECKER

*Introduction: A Tempest in a Teapot*

On August 26, 2009, the White House and Department of Education announced that President Barack Obama planned to talk to America's schoolchildren on the eighth of September. The White House announcement stated that the president would speak on the importance of students "taking responsibility for their success in school." The "address" would take place at 12:00 noon EDT at Wakefield High School in Arlington, Virginia. The speech would be broadcast live via C-SPAN and www.WhiteHouse.gov. However, the contents of the proposed speech were not released. The speech followed in the footsteps of other presidential remarks to schoolchildren, most recently Presidents Reagan in 1988 and George H.W. Bush in 1991, both delivered in public school settings. Many other presidents in the past addressed schoolchildren, but not in a live broadcast or from a public school as President Obama planned to do. The announcement stated that the planned speech would be similar to his predecessors', emphasizing that "a good education depends on hard work and personal responsibility for learning and achievement" (White House, September 2, 2009).

One would assume that a pep talk to schoolchildren would be nonpartisan and uncontroversial, especially one touted as a speech encouraging "educational success." One critic called a speech to schoolchildren as American as apple pie and mom (Gillman, September 3, 2009). However, this assumption did not take into account the political climate pervading the country at the time, where seemingly everything the president did or said became political fodder. The object of this essay is to outline the events immediately preceding, during, and after the president's speech in order to explain why the "tone" quickly became so rancorous. I've divided the media studied into two camps. The first, traditional media, is in reference to newspapers, and new media references radio talk shows, blogs and other Internet media outlets. Several "academic" explanations will be examined including that of "media experts."

## *The Tempest Begins*

A large part of the reaction to the president's speech did not center on the speech itself, although criticism of the president's speech started before a word of it was actually known. After it became common knowledge that the speech would be a "pep talk" and not partisan, attacks turned to the lesson plans prepared by the Department of Education, which officials at the Education Department stated were prepared to aid teachers (Haag, September 3, 2009). Education officials hoped teachers would show the president's speech and then build lessons around the speech using the suggested lesson plans. The lesson plans (titled "Menu of Classroom Activities" by the Department of Education) included two sets of plans, one for Pre-K through sixth graders and the other for grades seven through twelve (Department of Education, September 8, 2009). Officials hoped the suggestions would help "engage students and stimulate discussion." Both menus included suggestions for activities to do before the speech, during it, and afterward. Activities included guided listening, brainstorming, and a discussion of the speech's main points.

Owing to the temper of the times, conservative Republicans began their attack on the speech before the date of the president's remarks (September 8, 2009). Attacks began when the state chairman of the Florida Republican Party, Jim Greer, denounced the speech on September 1, 2009. In a statement released via the Internet, Greer condemned the president for "his socialist agenda and socialist ideology" (Republican Party of Florida, 2009).

Increasingly the Internet is used to release statements, or opinions, often anonymously. The statement, repeated in the blog *Tampabay.com*, went on to state that the president was "using taxpayer dollars to indoctrinate America's children to his socialist agenda. The idea that schoolchildren across our nation will be forced to watch the president justify his plans for government-run health care, auto companies, and bank bailouts [is] ... an invasive abuse of power" (Holan, 2009). Greer concluded that, "now that school is back in session, President Obama has turned to America's children to spread his liberal lies, indoctrinating America's youngest children before they have a chance to decide for themselves" (Republican Party of Florida, 2009). Greer's remarks included a link to "learn more about the president's speech," which connected readers to a U.S. Department of Education website. Upon review of the link, no mention of the controversial issues was found, let alone any attempt to indoctrinate students in socialism.

The materials emphasized citizenship, personal responsibility, goals, and persistence (Holan, September 2, 2009). On September 2, 2009, bowing to media pressure, the White House announced that it would release on the following Monday, September 7, 2009 (Labor Day), the contents of the speech. Since the study materials were not an issue at this time, no mention of them was made in the press release (White House, September 2, 2009). On September 3, 2009, conservative blogger and radio talk show host Dana Loesch continued the attack on the president's planned address, but she turned her attack to the lesson plans, not the speech itself. She attacked the use of the lesson plans on two points: chastising Secretary of Education Arne Duncan for sending the materials directly to principals and teachers (not elected school board officials) and "wasting" students' time on a message they hear "all the time." She then proceeded to launch a campaign urging parents to keep their children home on the day of the speech (Loesch, September 3, 2009).

On the same day, conservative commentator, blogger, and author Michelle Malkin went on the offensive as well. She claimed that schools, and by association the Obama administration, have "used students as little lobbyists on everything from illegal immigration, to gay marriage, to anti-war activism, and most recently, census collection." She concluded by asking, "Will Obama be able to resist issuing a call to arms to the youth [of America] to marshal help in passing his legislative agenda" (Bookman, September 3, 2009)?

Following Malkin's attack, columnist and deputy editorial page editor of the *Atlanta Journal Constitution*, Jay Bookman, noted in his blog that the president had no intention of doing what Greer, Loesch, and Malkin claimed. Bookman quoted Education Secretary Arne Duncan: "In this special address, the president will speak directly to the nation's children and youth about persisting and succeeding in school. The president will challenge students to work hard and set educational goals" (Bookman, September 3, 2009). On the same day the conservative *Washington Times* jumped into the fray with an article written by Matthew Mosk. Echoing the conservatism of its owner Sun Myung Moon, founder of the Unification Church, also known as the Moonies, the article "White House Flunks Civics Exam: Obama Lesson Called Political" Mosk stated that the address erupted into controversy, "forcing" the White House to pull out its eraser and rewrite a government recommendation that teachers "help the president." The article continued, basically reiterating the hysterics of Malkin.

Presidential aides acknowledged that the White House helped the Education Department craft the proposal, which met with "fierce criticism from

Republicans and conservative organizations" (PolitiFact.com, September 1, 2009). Conservatives and Republicans objected to younger students "writ[ing] letters about what they can do to help the president." Another proposal in the lesson plan recommended that students "engage in a discussion about what the president wants us to do" immediately after listening to the speech (Mosk, September 3, 2009). By Wednesday evening, September 2, 2009, the offending sentence in the menu of activities, which asked children to think about how they could "help the president," had been replaced. Obama officials changed "help the president" to "write themselves a letter about how they can achieve their long and short term educational goals" (Haag, September 3, 2009). But the "revision" to the "menu of activities" did not appear soon enough in the day to head off the rapid-fire reaction that spread the rest of the day on conservative talk radio and websites. "Critics of the president [repeatedly] argued that some of the messages included in the 'menu of classroom activities' strayed dangerously close to politicizing the classroom" (Mosk, September 3, 2009).

The idea of adding a lesson plan or menu of options to the package of materials sent to schoolteachers was hatched during a meeting between White House and Department of Education officials. The lessons were developed by educators during the meeting, and some of the lessons were developed without knowing the context of the speech (LoBianco, 8). The package of lesson plans went out electronically with a letter on August 26 from Secretary Arne Duncan. In the letter he encouraged school administrators to air the president's broadcast, which coincided with the start of school in many parts of the country (Haag & Kim, September 3, 2009).

## *The Tempest—Texas Style*

Meanwhile in Texas the furor ignited a rapid response from ultra-conservatives in the Dallas–Fort Worth metro area. According to an article in the September 3, 2009, *Dallas Morning News*, "Obama's Plan to Speak to Schoolchildren Ignites Furor in Dallas Area," "A groundswell of parent opposition may force many North Texas school districts to question whether to air it [the president's speech] live in classrooms" (Haag & Kim, September 3, 2009). The article went on to say, "The president announced the speech weeks ago, but opposition and concerns spread rapidly Wednesday morning, September 2, 2009, through conservative social networking Web sites and radio talk shows." By midday, local school districts were inundated with hundreds of phone calls from parents urging them to not show Obama's speech at school, and some parents threatened to keep their children home. "We had no idea that there would be a public outcry," said Laura Jobe, a Mesquite Independent School District (ISD) spokeswoman. "It caught us by surprise." Another area spokesperson said, "We rarely hear of parents pulling children out of classes" (Haag & Kim, September 3, 2009).

Dallas area school districts responded to the conservative backlash in many ways. Wylie ISD spokeswoman, Susan Dacus, said, "All parents I have talked to have been very negative," and not surprisingly school officials decided against showing the speech as a district-wide activity. Teachers were given the option as to how they would incorporate the president's speech into their day's lesson. Other districts, including Carrollton–Farmers Branch and Mesquite, stated they would probably do the same. McKinney ISD spokesman stated they would make viewing the video optional, but stated, "It's a unique opportunity." But Allen ISD administrators encouraged teachers to show the video, and officials spent time Wednesday urging parents not to withhold their children the day of the speech. Officials in Allen, McKinney and other districts said the absences wouldn't be excused. Yet some parents continued to plan on taking their children out of class. The sentiments they expressed were the same: "We do not want the government intruding in our lives. It's dangerous ground for a president to ask students to advocate his policies for reform, and that is exactly what he is doing" (Haag, September 3, 2009).

Barb Walters, president of the Texas Democratic Women of Collin County, contended that the outrage was mostly manufactured. "Emotions are running so high in politics," she said. "People are just shoving signs and fists into other people's faces. Whatever happened to civil discourse?" Fred Moses, chairman of the Collin County Republican Party, said he had not heard anyone who was concerned about the speech. "As long as the president is not talking about his agenda or policies, we all need to encourage our kids to do better" (Kim & Haag, September 3, 2009). Before the president gave the speech, Larry J. Sabato, director of the Center for Politics, University of Virginia, said that he doubted Obama would risk criticism by giving a political speech. "If this is simply a pep talk by the President of the United States to school kids," Sabato said, "to me that is in the category of mother and apple pie." Curtis Gans, director of the Center for the Study of the American Electorate American University, stated that George H.W. Bush, in 1991, did not stir up the same visceral reaction when he delivered his speech to schoolchildren. "There was no virulent hatred of George H.W. Bush. Sometime between Bork [the senate hearing on the Bork nomination for the Supreme Court] and [the Clinton] impeachment ... it [the tone] became progressively less civil." Bush didn't stir up the same reaction as the foes of Obama, who is portrayed as peddling socialism. The difference is the presence of "Facebook and other social networking sites used ... to spread alarm about Obama's speech" (Gillman, September 3, 2009).

On September 4, 2009, responding to more complaints, the White House reiterated it would release advance copies of the speech and revise the language in the lesson plans. As it turned out, only one line was changed in the lesson plans by the Obama administration. The changes came as more Dallas–Fort Worth school districts decided not to show the speech, even districts that had promised earlier in the week to do so. They reneged on their promises in an effort to placate vocal conservative parents. Some districts opted to play a recording of the speech after school (Haag, September 3, 2009).

Even after the changes, school officials (in Texas and elsewhere) continued to receive hundreds of calls and e-mails from parents who demanded that the speech not be mandatory for students to watch, and many callers accused the president of injecting politics into the classroom, thus echoing what they had heard on conservative radio talk shows or read in blogs. Dallas school officials decided to not require students to watch the speech and allowed teachers and principals to decide whether to view the speech or not. Highland Park ISD did the same. Richardson ISD recorded the speech and showed it a day later, but only to those kids who had permission from their parents to watch it (permission slips). No class time was spent discussing it. Allen school officials scratched plans to have some students view the speech live, saying they would record and review it, and then possibly replay it the following week. Carrollton–Farmers Branch ISD did the same. Mesquite ISD officials said they debated the issue but decided against it since it interfered with some lunch periods. Lovejoy ISD also decided not to show the speech, in part because the district does not have the bandwidth to support live Web video on whitehouse.gov (Haag, September 3, 2009).

In a *New York Times* article "Obama's Plan for School Talk Ignites a Revolt," James C. McKinley Jr. and Sam Dillion wrote that the uproar over the speech, in which the president intended to urge students to work hard and stay in school, had been particularly acute in Texas, where several school districts, under pressure from parents, made plans to let children opt out of "lending the president an ear" (McKinley & Dillon, September 4, 2009). Some parents were quoted as saying they were concerned because the speech had not been screened for political content. Another parent did not like the idea of the president having direct access to her child (McKinley & Dillion, September 4, 2009). The *Dallas Morning News*, on the same day, carried a story by Todd J. Gillman stating that the uproar in the Dallas area prompted hundreds of complaints for a school sick out. Gillman reported, "The sick out was called by parents to 'avoid left-wing indoctrination,' during the speech" (Gillman, September 3, 2009).

The *Times* article continued by stating that Mark Steyn, a Canadian author and political commentator, speaking on the Rush Limbaugh show on Wednesday, had turned up the volume of the attacks by accusing Mr. Obama of trying to create a cult of personality, comparing him to Saddam Hussein and Kim Jong Il. The *Times* article reported that parents in not only Texas, but California, Colorado, Connecticut, Georgia, Illinois, South Carolina and Utah called school officials. But one Houston parent of two school-aged children, Phyllis Griffin Epps, had a different view, saying that telling children they should not hear the president of the United States, even if the parents disagree with his policies, sends the wrong message to children. Epps stated "It's difficult for me to understand how listening to the president, the commander in chief, is damaging to the youth of today" (McKinley & Dillon, September 3, 2009).

In an effort to explain the furor, Curtis Gans, director of the Center for the Study of the American Electorate at American University, said that the conservative right is in a take-no-prisoners strategy because they did not get back into the White House. "Facebook and other social networking sites [were] used to spread the alarm. In this case, to spread alarm about the president's speech." The rules for public discourse are much harsher now. Professor Gans agreed with several of his colleagues, "Sometime between Bork and impeachment ... it became progressively less civil" (Gillman, September 3, 2009).

Another *Dallas Morning News* reporter, James Ragland, entered the fray when he wondered in his column, "A Few Loudmouths Turn Obama's Positive Message into Frenzy," how the discourse in America had fallen so far. He wrote that it is in a "pathetic point where a few crackpots can smear and demonize the president.... These fringe lunatics are cleverly bending minds and hearts." He claimed that "toxic" radio talk show hosts and scatterbrained social networking websites were whipping parents and school officials into a "McCarthy-era frenzy." He called the frenzy real "tinfoil-hat stuff" (Ragland, September 3, 2009).

## *The Tempest Changes Direction*

International opinion began in earnest on September 9, 2009, when *The Guardian* printed a rather subdued article in its international edition by Ewen MacAskill. MacAskill wrote that Republicans and conservatives like Glenn Beck, buoyed by their success in opposing health-care reforms, led the attack on Obama's speech to schoolchildren (MacAskill, September 5, 2009). In the *Weekend Australian*, Brad Norington wrote "Obama's Classroom Speech

Backfires" and reported that many school districts will not show the speech (Norington, September 5, 2009).

On September 6, the *Lubbock Avalanche-Journal* reported on the furor and the effect it was having on West Texas schools. In the article, "LISD Head Says Technology, Not Politics, the Reason Broadcast Stopped," Lubbock Independent School District (LISD) officials claimed that technical problems, not political considerations, were the reason the school district would record the president's speech rather than showing it live. "Our primary reason for not airing it live was the bandwidth," said Superintendent Karen Garza. Terry Driscoll, the LISD executive director for technology, stated that the school district's bandwidth only supports forty to fifty computers in a live feed. The decision was made Wednesday to transfer the president's message from the live feed to DVDs. School officials did not address the issue that the president's speech would simultaneously be broadcast on CNN and would not cause a bandwidth problem. Apparently showing the president's speech on CNN was not an option for LISD students. Garza went on to opine that most of the controversy concerned the materials developed by the Department of Education, not the speech itself. But although the controversy changed from the contents of the speech to the wording of the menu of options, LISD continued with its plan to not air live the president's speech (Gulick, September 6, 2009).

But after the contents of the speech were read, the tide finally turned in favor of the speech. The *New York Times* reported in its late edition of September 8 that officials of Guilford County Schools in North Carolina had decided to air the president's speech after reading the transcript of the speech posted on the White House's website. The *New York Times* quoted Nora K. Carr, chief of staff to the superintendent of Guilford County Schools: "It is refreshing, frankly, to see a leader talk about the need for students to take personal responsibility. It makes you wonder what all the fuss was all about." The week before, many Guilford County parents had called schools in anger, many after hearing conservative radio attacks on the planned speech. But opinion changed by week's end as other parents called expressing anger over the district's decision to allow students to "opt out." But in many school districts, watching the speech remained optional. Although the superintendent of the Los Angeles Unified School District called the president's speech an "extraordinary opportunity to engage in a teachable moment," it was only shown to students who desired to see it. School districts in New York took a similar stand — showing it to students who expressed a desire to see it. Officials in Loudoun County, Virginia, schools stated that students would be too busy to watch (Dillon, September 6, 2009).

On the day the speech was made public (Monday, September 9, 2009) via the White House website, *The Times* (London) printed an upbeat article by Giles Whittell in which he called the speech motivational and said that parents who thought his remarks would be "uninvited" or at worst socialist indoctrination can now read it for themselves. *The Times* article continued, calling Obama's speech "uplifting and at times deeply personal." He repeated the theme that helped propel him to the White House: "Where you are now doesn't have to determine where you'll end up. In America you write your own destiny" (Whittell, September 7, 2009).

The article stated that the planned speech provoked a storm of protest, even before it was made public. Parents deluged schools with calls asking whether watching it was mandatory. One mother, it was reported, wept during a CNN interview at the thought her children might be exposed to a speech she had not personally vetted (Whittell, September 7, 2009).

## *The Aftermath and Cleanup*

National and international newspapers printed positive responses to the event. The *St. Petersburg Times* (Florida) reported that few children opted out of the speech. Tony Marrero reported the speech was a big hit with the 22,000 schoolchildren of the Hernando (Florida) school district (Nohlgren, September 8, 2009). Opt-outs varied widely between schools and were between 1 and 15 percent, officials said. Teachers responded positively to the speech as well. Jason Glitsky said the brouhaha over the address was "absolutely ridiculous." "I don't see where the problems are and why the party lines had to be drawn. There are lessons here that transcend social studies," the subject Mr. Glitsky teaches. "This whole episode is a good example of group behavior" (Nohlgren, September 8, 2009).

In the state where the brouhaha reached its loudest, Texas, support of the speech was attentive and upbeat. An editorial in the *Beaumont Enterprise*, "President's Speech Did Not Cause Turmoil," began, "The speech was given and the Republic survived, despite scaremongers who tried to drum up hysteria beforehand." They (the scaremongers) promised parents the speech would be a politicized affair that would "taint the younger generation and turn them into Obama robots." Instead, the nation's students heard a neutral speech that encouraged them to study hard, overcome barriers and stay in school. Most people agreed with everything the president said. "This pep talk was just a pep talk" (Anonymous *Beaumont Enterprise* editorial, September 9, 2009). An article by Tawnell Hobbs in the *Dallas Morning News* reported that Dallas high school students gave the president a standing ovation. Afterward, many called the president's words inspiring. About four hundred students watched the speech at Booker T. Washington High School. The speech was followed by a Q&A session, which lasted about twenty minutes.

A few students questioned why the talk was not shown in every school, considering how motivational it was. Students were genuinely impressed that the president decided to speak directly to them. Coming from the president, it made a big impact. But in the end, not all Texas schools showed the speech live. Former Dallas mayor Ron Kirk said he was befuddled about the opposition to a highly non-partisan speech. "[This was one of the] few moments in my life when I'm embarrassed to say I am from Texas" (Hobbs, September 9, 2009).

Meanwhile columnist James Ragland, *The Dallas News*, editorialized in his September 9, 2009, column that apologies were due Obama for the ado over his talk, saying that the premature reaction was a "farcical" affront to the Oval Office and "was tantamount to spitting on the flag." He compared it to theater of the absurd. Dallas, he noted, had its own role in the mess, since local talk show hosts urged parents to boycott schools and worked parents into believing their kids would be "indoctrinated." "What once was laughable is now frightening with so many everyday folk jumping without thinking" (Ragland, September 9, 2009).

In shades of a massive generation gap, students saw the speech quite differently than parents. Students who saw the speech were generally inspired by the President's suggestions on how to succeed and his personal story. Comments included, "I learned a lot about his [President Obama's] early life and struggles." Another student from Texas stated, "My family did not talk about the uproar surrounding the speech all that much; we liked the idea of the president talking directly to schoolchildren. Many parents should just 'let it go.'" The *Houston Chronicle* reported in "Obama Speech Hits Home for Some..." that several Houston-area schools opted to show the lunchtime address, with few opt-outs (parents requesting their children not watch the speech). At Frost Elementary, third and fourth graders watched the president's speech in the school library. No parents opted out their children in the working-class-neighborhood school. A student commented, "It was exciting to hear. He encouraged us to stay in school." Another commented, "They [Michelle Obama and her parents] worked hard." The principal of Frost Elementary said she liked the president's message: "We work hard [at Frost Elementary] to create a college-bound culture. It's wonderful to have our president set the standard" (Mellon, September 9, 2009). Not all Houston-area schools saw the speech live; some recorded the speech to show later. But even so, few parents opted out their children. In most districts, less than 1 percent of students opted out. In one high school, Westside High, a private school, about 300 of the 3,000 students (or 10 percent) opted out of watching the president (Mellon, September 9, 2009).

International opinion about the speech, expressed in newspapers, was forthcoming on the ninth of September. It included an opinion piece from the *International Herald Tribune*, written by Sam Dillon. Even Jim Greer, the article stated, alluding to the Florida state Republican chair, did not find anything to criticize in Obama's speech and allowed his children to watch it. The article warned that Republicans stand the chance of being seen (in America) as just attacking anything Mr. Obama proposes. It was unclear, the paper reported, just how many of the 50 million school kids in the United States actually saw the speech live. What is clear is that it is increasingly difficult to find common ground in the United States (Dillon, September 9, 2009). The *Straits Times* (Singapore) wrote in "Obama School Speech Quells Outcry" that the speech was little more than a "fatherly pep talk on the virtues of staying in school.... The outbursts [against the speech] were little more than a storm in a teacup" and laid bare the bitterness that divides the United States (Garekar, September 9, 2009).

Two Australian papers, *The Advertiser* and the *Daily Telegraph*, reported that Obama won the school talk in a speech about real-life lessons. Both articles summarized the events leading up to the speech and mentioned some radio talk show hosts, like Tammy Bruce who compared the president to a shady lawyer from Chicago (Crawford, September 9, 2009). An article by Lara Marlowe in the *Irish Times* reported that mainstream Republicans shied away from the debate [concerning the speech] and the president even got support from Newt Gingrich and former first lady Laura Bush, who said, "There is a place for the president to talk to schoolchildren and encourage them" (Marlowe, September 9, 2009).

## *The Backlash*

Beginning on September 12, 2009, the backlash in the United States started, with protests, rowdy school-board meetings, and letters to the editor in newspapers. At the Lewisville, Texas, school-board meeting, citizens criticized the superintendent of schools, Dr. Jerry Roy, for his decision not to air the president's speech and for his explanation that it was logistically difficult to broadcast it to the 50,000 students of the district. One person complained, "You reinforced the stereotype that the South and Texas is hopelessly backward." Roy claimed that he provided a link to the speech that would allow teachers to use the speech as a "teaching tool," if they get a permission slip from parents (Hundley, September 12, 2009). Several hundred people packed a school-board meeting at the East Pike Elementary School in Indiana to speak out against the district's decision to not televise the speech.

At the meeting it was learned that the decision was not made by the board but by the superintendent of schools, Dr. Deborah Clawson, on the Friday before Labor Day. Clawson claimed the district made provisions to show the speech at a later time, but one person who spoke at the meeting, Cookie Moretti, said, "There is no substitute for the live event. We [the school district] have showed live the inauguration of several presidents, the tragic events during 9-11, and the Steelers Super Bowl victory parade." "History," she said, "is not an event delayed." Moretti continued that the school district has a policy that elected officials can come and speak to students during school hours. One of the main purposes of public education is to expose students to a diversity of thoughts and ideas, to encourage decision making. An official of the local chapter of the NAACP spoke at the school-board meeting as well; Edwina Vold stated that not showing the speech sends the wrong message to white as well as African American children. Another speaker called the decision a slap in the face to the United States and its two party system (Stout, September 12, 2009).

In Texas, the backlash continued as well, but in much more muted tones. Arlington ISD superintendent Jerry McCullough apologized for his mishandling of the speech. Arlington did not show the speech live, but it did bus twenty-eight fifth graders to Cowboy Stadium to hear ex-president George W. Bush and First Lady Laura Bush speak. Several Arlington civic leaders accused the school district of hypocrisy. McCullough noted that the speech was recorded by the district, and teachers had access to it. He sincerely regretted that "this chain of events occurred and brought negative attention to the district" (Mosier, September 12, 2009). Denton ISD superintendent, Ray Brawell, found himself apologizing as well. He stated he should have gotten more parental input before canceling the live showing of the speech. The backlash continued throughout the U.S. until mid–October, when black leaders spoke in favor of dismissing Valdosta City Schools superintendent Bill Cason. The leaders claimed the decision to not show the speech was racially motivated. Others expressed their unhappiness that the majority of the school's administration is (still) white, while 80 percent of the students are black (Anonymous, October 13, 2009).

## *The New World Order of Viral Politics*

An article by *Washington Post* staff writer Ann Gerhart summed up the relationship of modern politics with modern communication technology most succinctly when she wrote, "In today's viral world, who keeps a civil tongue?" The nation's political discourse seems sour, angry, and even dangerous; it's "uglier than it has ever been." But rousing political speech has been around for a long time. Presidents as far back as Thomas Jefferson had to tolerate vicious personal attacks. But Mark Potok of the Southern Poverty Law Center explained the difference between past political discourse and that of today when he said,

> Completely false allegations incubate in the fringe [on the Internet] and jump within days to the mainstream [media], distorting any debate or progress we can have as a society. What's different is that a great deal of this is [generated by] real fear and frustration with a very real demographic and cultural change [Gerhart, October 11, 2009].

Professor Danielle Allen, a Fellow at the Institute for Advanced Study stated that the spread of Internet usage in the mid–1990s, the rise of conservative talk radio, and twenty-four-hour cable news have added a new dimension to the political debate. The Institute for Advanced Study is a private independent research center established in 1930 at Princeton University. It encourages theoretical research and intellectual inquiry in the sciences and social sciences. Albert Einstein, J. Robert Oppenheimer and George Kennan were all fellows at the Institute. Professor Allen goes on to say the real change came from the Internet, giving everybody the opportunity to be a great communicator (for about fifteen minutes). In a 2009 online interview with the *Washington Post*, she stated that e-mail has the ability to take two facts and make a false story out of them. She related the story that Obama was a Muslim and how it started on the Internet; at the time of the story she did not think it mattered much, until she heard that many people in the Ohio and Texas primaries quoted the story as the truth. As a political scientist, she was concerned about the fact that so many people were acting on and "voting out of a falsehood." She mused how a democracy can counter falsehoods (Allen, January 16, 2009).

Allen has studied and written about this Internet phenomena and its impact on democracy and has come up with the following observations. She found that many splinter groups (fringe groups) use the Internet effectively. Members of these groups are often scattered widely across the United States and do not reach a "critical mass" in any one area. Through the use of the Internet they can form a critical mass, communicate with each other, and begin to believe and act like they are more numerous and powerful than they really are. Many of these groups are, in Allen's words, nativist groups and reflect a growing unease in the country. (The growing Tea Party would certainly be considered the latest incarnation of a nativist group, although Allen did not specifically mention them.) In the past, nativist groups distrusted immigrants, non–Protestants, and non-whites. Not surprisingly they favor limiting immigration, stricter security of the borders, lower taxes, and smaller government generally, and they make effective use of the Internet.

The use of the Internet allows fringe groups to remain autonomous (and in many cases anonymous) and yet play a part in a larger effort. Allen found out that one person can start a lie, such as Obama's supposed Muslim affiliation, and another can spread the lie. The first person cannot be blamed for spreading the lie, while the latter cannot be blamed for starting it (Allen, January 16, 2009).

In the past, presidents spoke without the rancor President Obama's speech created. Franklin Roosevelt gave hope to the American people during his "fireside chats." Live coverage of man's first walk on the moon and President Reagan's speech after the *Challenger* tragedy helped give meaning to a tragic event. Coverage of the 9-11 disaster helped the country determine what the response would be to the senseless acts of violence on that day. But in a comparatively short time the mood in the country has gotten overly political and highly toxic. Professor Allen may have it correct; people don't talk to each other anymore, especially from different backgrounds or points of view. People are afraid to interact, which she says is an essential act of a democracy. An informed electorate makes a democracy work.

Not too long ago most Americans lived in smaller towns or in rural areas. Before mass media, people met regularly at meetings, church, or even at social events like bowling. At these events and meetings, people met with their friends and neighbors and talked about the issues face to face. Allen believes that discourse was more civil because it was face to face and with people you knew well or met with on a regular basis. Although small-town life is considered stifling by many and is not noted for its creativity, small-town life was and is noted for its friendliness and civility. Since the Internet allows communities to form based on specific political interests, people are able to avoid significantly interacting with others who have different opinions. Due to this, people stopped talking to each other, and opinion making came from other sources. Talk radio and fringe blogs filled the void, much to the detriment of our democratic society. Allen says that people need to overcome their fears of the "ideological other" and engage fact-checked information sources that may challenge what they know and how they perceive the world so that citizens may exchange ideas and form a consensus through the free flow of ideas.

## References

Allen, Danielle. Institute for Advanced Study. January 16, 2009. http://www.ias.edu/people/faculty-and-emeriti/allen (accessed November 12, 2009).

Allen, Danielle. Interview with Matt Mosk. *Washington Post*, January 16, 2009.
Anonymous. "Dallas County GOP stuck in reverse." *Dallas Morning News*, October 30, 2009, 2W6.
Anonymous. "President's speech did not cause turmoil." (Editorial). *Beaumont Enterprise* (Beaumont, TX), September 9, 2009, 4.
Anonymous. "Residents demand resignation from superintendent." *Valdosta Daily Times*, October 13, 2009, 1.
Anonymous editorial. "Irrational Obama protesters speak poorly to youth." *Dallas Morning News*, September 3, 2009, 30.
Bookman, Jay. "Even an Obama speech to children sets off partisan outrage." September 3, 2009. http://blogs.ajc.com/jay-bookman-blog (accessed October 10, 2009).
Cabluck, Harry. "Three districts say they will not show Obama's speech live." *Austin American-Statesman*, September 4, 2009, B1.
Crawford, Carly. "Obama gives kids a real life lesson." *Daily Telegraph* (Australia), September 9, 2009, 16.
_____. "Obama wins talk to schools." *The Advertiser* (Australia), September 9, 2009, 33.
Department of Education. "Menu of classroom activities." September 8, 2009. http://www2.ed.gov/admins/lead-/academic/bts.html.
Dillon, Sam. "After reading president's speech to students, critics cool off." *International Herald Times*, September 9, 2009, 9.
_____. "Work hard and dream big, Obama." *New York Times*, September 8, 2009, 14.
Drago, Mike. "Obama's address to school kids prompts right-wing calls for 'sickout.'" *Dallas Morning News*, September 2, 2009, 3.
Edgecomb, Kathleen. "NS students finally get to watch Obama." *Day* (New London, CT), September 12, 2009, 9.
Fish, Stanley. "The Obama show." *International Herald Tribune*, September 26, 2009, 8.
Frist, Bill, and Richard Riley. "America can do better on education." *Politico*, November 13, 2009.
Garekar, Bhagyashree. "Obama's school speech quells outcry; address turns out to be fatherly pep talk as 'socialist' directive is modified." *The Straits Times* (Singapore), September 9, 2009, 14.
Gerhart, Ann. "In today's viral world, who keeps a civil tongue?" *Washington Post*, October 11, 2009, A1.
Gillman, Todd J. "Uproar over Obama's planned speech to students reflects polarized country." *Dallas Morning News*, September 3, 2009, 5.
_____. "Why the fuss over Obama's speech to students?" *Dallas Morning News*, September 4, 2009, 2W.
Gulick, Joe. "LISD head says technology, not politics, the reason broadcast stopped." *Lubbock Avalanche Journal*, September 6, 2009, 3.
Haag, Matthew. "More Dallas–Fort Worth schools say no to Obama's speech despite changes." *Dallas Morning News*, September 4, 2009, 3.
_____. "White House revises proposed lesson plan on Obama speech." *Dallas Morning News*, September 3, 2009, 2W.
Haag, Matthew, and Theodore Kim. "Obama plan to speak to schoolchildren ignites furor in Dallas area." *Dallas Morning News*, September 3, 2009, 5.
Hamburger, Tom. "President to echo age-old advice; will tell students to stay in school." *Boston Globe*, September 8, 2009, 10.
Hobbs, Tawnell D. "Dallas students ignore controversy, applaud Obama speech." *Dallas Morning News*, September 8, 2009, 11.
Holan, Angie Drobnic. "Republican Party of Florida says Obama will 'indoctrinate' schoolchildren with 'socialist ideology.'" *St. Petersburg Times* (Florida), September 3, 2009, 4.
Hundley, Wendy. "Parents criticize Lewisville ISD decision not to air Obama." *Dallas Morning News*, September 16, 2009, 6.
LoBianco, Tom. "Obama speech furor called 'silly.'" *Washington Post*, September 7, 2009, 8.

Loesch, Dana. "Dana Loesch has launched a campaign." Askville.com, September 3, 2009.
Lupica, Mike. "Time for the loons to shut up and listen." *Daily News* (New York), September 7, 2009, 4.
MacAskill, Ewen. "Obama tones down his appeal to pupils after indoctrination claims." *The Guardian* (London), September 5, 2009, 19.
Marlowe, Lara. "President sets out to motivate children despite partisan row." *Irish Times*, September 9, 2009, 10.
Marrero, Tony. "Obama speech without hitch." *St. Petersburg Times* (Florida), September 9, 2009, 1.
McKinley, James C., and Dillon, Sam. "Obama's plan for school talk ignites a revolt." *New York Times*, September 4, 2009, 1.
———. "Parents see sinister goals in Obama's school speech; Texas at heart of uproar, as president is accused of planning to push socialism." *International Herald Tribune*, September 5, 2009, 8.
Mellon, Ericka. "Obama speech hits home for some, not for others." *Houston Chronicle*, September 9, 2009, 1.
Mosier, Jeff. "Arlington schools superintendent apologizes for Obama speech controversy." *Dallas Morning News*, September 12, 2009, 14.
Mosk, Matthew. "White House flunks civics exam; Obama lesson plan called political." *Washington Times*, September 3, 2009, 2W6.
Nohlgren, Stephen. "Obama speech exhorts kids." *St. Petersburg Times* (Florida), September 8, 2009, 1A.
Norington, Brad. "Obama's classroom speech backfires." *Weekend Australian*, September 5, 2009, 17.
PolitiFact.com. "Pants on fire." September 1, 2009.
Ragland, James. "A few loudmouths turn Obama's positive message into poison." *Dallas Morning News*, September 4, 2009, 2(w).
———. "Apologies due for ado over Obama talk." *Dallas Morning News*, September 9, 2009, 4.
Republican Party of Florida. "Republican Party of Florida says Obama will 'indoctrinate' schoolchildren with 'socialist ideology.'" September 1, 2009.
Stout, Jared. "Indiana area blasted for 'no show' policy on Obama speech." *Blairsville Dispatch* (Blairsville, PA), September 18, 2009, 2.
White House. "President Obama to speak directly to students in National address on education Success." *The White House Blog*, September 2, 2009.
———. "The President's School Speech — Student Reactions." *The White House Blog*, September 14, 2009. http://whitehouse.gov/blog/The-Presidents-School-Speech-Student-Reactions (accessed October 10, 2009).
Whittel, Giles. "Back to school with a word to the wise from Obama." *The Times* (London), September 8, 2009.
Williamson, Elizabeth, and Merrick Amy. "School choice: To air Obama or not?" *Wall Street Journal*, September 5, 2009, A3.

# Obama Jungle Fever
## Interracial Desire on the Campaign Trail
CAROLINE A. STREETER

What they're going to try to do is make you scared of me.
— *Barack Obama*

Nobody in this section of the country believes the old threadbare lie that Negro men rape white women. If Southern white men are not careful, they will over-reach themselves and public sentiment will have a reaction; a conclusion will then be reached which will be very damaging to the moral reputation of their women.
— *Ida B. Wells-Barnett*

## *Introduction*

This essay analyzes Barack Obama's ascendance to presidency of the United States as a dizzying and dazzling example of the power of intersection — of identities, of technologies, and, palpably, of race (Crenshaw, 1992). Barack Obama is the child of an interracial union and is thus himself a person of mixed race. Like most biracial Americans of black and white descent, Obama identifies as black (Schermo, 2000). Simultaneously, from the time he gave his pivotal keynote speech at the 2004 Democratic National Convention, Obama emphasized the ways his heritage overlapped with white American identity. There we first heard his humorous self-description: "a skinny kid with a funny name," the son of an immigrant father from Kenya and a mother from Kansas, America's "Heartland."

This essay argues the president's campaign generated two competing narratives about interracial relationships between white women and black men. These cultural texts consisted of, first, a charged historical taboo: white women's desire for black men. The second, while sacred and timeless, is also historically "new" in American culture: relationships between white mothers and their black sons. These contradictory concepts of interracial intimacy were also expressed in different media. This essay argues that overlapping narratives of interracial desire emerged in a contemporary media also characterized by a compelling intersection of old and new. Twenty-first-century media technologies are divided into two types: the old mode of print and broadcast television, and the new mode of the Internet. This essay demonstrates that media about Barack Obama powerfully conjured competing, yet overlapping, narratives of interracial desire in modes of technology both competitive and deeply intersectional.

Explicit prohibitions of interracial marriage are anachronisms Americans would rather forget; many are surprised to learn that interracial marriage was forbidden in numerous states as late as 1967 (U.S. Supreme Court, 1967). Fewer still are familiar with the term *miscegenation,* concocted in 1863 by anti-abolitionist Democrats attempting to discredit President Abraham Lincoln's Republican Party. In an anonymous pamphlet, they claimed his administration advocated "interbreeding" of whites and blacks until the races were indistinguishably mixed. "Miscegenation" grafted two Latin words: "miscere" — to mix, and "genus" — race. Unlike the prior term for race mixing — *amalgamation* — miscegenation did not derive from scientific observation. Nevertheless miscegenation acquired pseudo-scientific status and became incorporated in vocabularies of political debate and jurisprudence (wordiq.com, 2010).

In contrast, the twenty-first century's currency of the term *jungle fever,* a coarse description of interracial sexual desire, demonstrates that social attitudes regarding cultural taboos do not always take the form of a progressive trajectory — from prejudice to enlightenment, from racial violence to racial harmony. In this essay, I show that interracial relationships between white women and black men, however normalized in American society, retain the charge of the forbidden.

Interestingly, however, provocative images of interracial sexuality did not damage Obama's candidacy. His warning to supporters in Missouri at a rally in summer 2008, "[W]hat they're going to try to do is make you scared of me," referred to a different discourse of mixing and threat (Herbert, 2008). Obama's Republican opponents constructed a formidable apparatus characterizing him as a terrorist threat of multiple dimensions. The right-wing media was critical in capitalizing on the American public's post–9/11 fear of Muslims and tapped into historical fears of anti-government groups such as communists and black nationalists. In view of this, one might argue that contemporary Americans have turned a corner with respect to disapproval of interracial sexuality between black men and white women. One might be mistaken. This essay concludes with an analysis of former congressman Harold Ford Jr.'s unsuccessful bid, in 2006, to become the Democratic Party's candidate for

Senate in Tennessee. Ford's campaign was apparently derailed by the infamous "Call me, Harold" ad — a television spot funded by GOP supporters of his rival Bob Corker. "Call me" suggested that access to sexy white women was part of Ford's corrupt agenda. As in 1863, accusations of race mixing can be potent political weapons.

## Historical Repression of Interracial Desire

In an 1892 editorial that appeared in her newspaper *The Free Speech* (published in Memphis, Tennessee), journalist and political activist Ida B. Wells-Barnett challenged prevailing images of white women falling victim to "black brutes," declaring that interracial sex took place between consenting adults:

> In numerous instances where colored men have have [*sic*] been lynched on the charge of rape, it was positively known at the time of lynching, and indisputably proven after the victim's death, that the relationship sustained between the man and woman was voluntary and clandestine, and that in no court of law could even the charge of assault have been successfully maintained [Wells-Barnett, 1991].

This blistering critique was part of Wells-Barnett's response to the lynching of three friends: Thomas Moss, Calvin McDowell, and Henry Stewart, owners of the People's Grocery Company in Memphis. W.R. Barrett, a white grocer, "threatened by the new, black owned operation used the pretext of a falling-out among some boys in the neighborhood to stir up ill will against blacks" (Dray, 2003). Subsequently, a confrontation between Barrett and Calvin McDowell escalated to the familiar pattern of black men being imprisoned, next captured by a mob storming the prison, and finally lynched. Wells-Barnett's passionate rejection of racist orthodoxy was the last time her voice emerged from the South. Forced to flee Memphis by white men enraged by the editorial, she "became an exile; her property destroyed and her return to her home forbidden under penalty of death" (Wells-Barnett, 1991).

Whether derived from actual events or intentional parodies of social life, the contemporary examples in this essay are part of a narrative thread about interracial sexuality, disputing the stereotype of black brutes and virtuous white victims. The historical knot at the beginning of the thread was identified by Wells-Barnett as the lie used to justify lynching. At the turn of the century, Wells-Barnett argued that lynching was a weapon of racial terror with roots in the post–Reconstruction period. The Ku Klux Klan, founded in Tennessee following the Confederacy's surrender in 1866, capitalized on the withdrawal of Federal troops from the South in 1877. The KKK was instrumental in the backlash against former slaves, focused on dismantling their economic and political gains. Emancipation created a social world in which skin color was one of the only substantive characteristics distinguishing the majority of white southerners — small farmers decimated by the war — from the ex-slaves. White supremacy was the discourse that soothed the defeat of the Confederacy. White male privilege facilitated the re-creation of the Southern belle, although this incarnation differed considerably from the Scarlett O'Hara prototype. No longer protected by affable Uncle Toms and wealthy white planters, this Southern belle was under the constant threat of rape by black men, who viewed sexual possession of her as ultimate confirmation of their masculinity. Ordinary white men used this convoluted logic as justification for lynching. Ida B. Wells-Barnett redefined lynching as a violent crime, and she held white men accountable for their hypocrisy.

Wells-Barnett captured the core hypocrisy driving lynching: that racial violence was imperative to protect white female virtue. Her unusual juxtaposition of two phrases — "positively known" and "voluntary and clandestine" — adds significant nuance to how we comprehend the day-to-day status of interracial liaisons in the post–Reconstruction South. Ida B. Wells-Barnett asserted that lynching used ordinary relationships to inflame otherwise tolerant communities. In her research, Wells-Barnett gave numerous examples, from various towns, of white women known to engage in sexual relations with black men, often in the context of employer and employee. According to Wells-Barnett's editorial, local whites knew about such consensual relationships in their towns, knew that they were clandestine, and tolerated the open secret in their midst (Horowitz and Peiss 1996). Given everyday experience, "nobody believed the thread-bare lie that Negro men rape white women." Rather, as Wells-Barnett warned southern men, escalating accusations of rape only impugned the white female virtue they claimed to protect.

## *A Face-Off of Gender and Race: (White) Women versus Black (Men and Women)*

In November 2004, a satirical portrait of Barack Obama — then Democratic candidate for Senate in Illinois — appeared on the cover of the *Washington Monthly* under the heading, "The Great Black Hope: What's Riding on Barack Obama?" (Wallace-Wells, 2004). The goofy rendition of the "skinny kid with a funny name" standing knock-kneed in a boxing ring could not be more different from its historical referent, boxing legend Joe Louis (1914–1981), the "Brown Bomber" — also known as the Great Black Hope (Bak, 1998). In 1938, Louis "[became] the symbol of American freedom over Nazi totalitarianism" when he defeated German boxer Max Schmeling in a rematch, inspiring whites, for the first time, to root for a black American boxer (Public Broadcasting System, 2004). Joe Louis's management tried to mold him into the opposite of his predecessor, Jack Johnson (1878–1946), a gifted boxer notorious for regularly flouting the color line: at one point he married a white woman. Joe Louis's managers groomed him to cultivate white approval by strictly adhering to certain rules of deportment: key among these, do not be photographed with white women.

Journalist Benjamin Wallace-Wells's story for the *Washington Monthly* began in Boston, at the 2004 Democratic National Convention, site of Obama's now-famous address. Wallace-Wells led off with an anecdote about Corey Booker — "(the) young, handsome African-American Rhodes Scholar.... The party's kingmakers and talent scouts ... were thrilled to see him, and eager to game out with him how Booker might win his next run [for Mayor of Newark, New Jersey]." (Subsequently Booker won the mayoral election and is currently serving a second term.) "Approached by *two more excited white women* [my emphasis], mouths open, and ready to gush ... Booker leaned back and smiled his big, easy smile ... and one of the women stuck out her hand.... 'I just wanted to congratulate you on your speech she said. It was so *stirring* — Mr. Obama.'" (Wallace-Wells, 2004).

Barack Obama's status as an object of desire for white women constituted a running subtext during the primaries. Despite early evidence of this infatuation with Obama, throughout the primary campaign, pundits predicted a vast divide separating (tacitly white) women expected to vote for Hillary Rodham Clinton and African Americans (a tacitly gender-inclusive group) expected to vote for Barack Obama. Mainstream media pitched a continuous narrative about competing social interests and the influence of identity on politics. The early primaries facilitated the notion of Obama and Clinton as polar candidates, with victories plotted on a national pendulum. Obama stunned the nation when he won the Iowa Caucus on January 4, 2008 (*Time*, 2008). Clinton, who was at that time the clear front-runner, quickly recovered by winning the New Hampshire primary just days later (MSNBC, 2008).

The Clinton campaign's juggernaut notwithstanding, it became evident in early 2008 that another current ran through mainstream representations of the primaries: conventional media had its own "crush on Obama" (Ettinger, 2010). Although Clinton performed brilliantly in debates, prominent talking heads such as Jorge Ramos, George Stephanopoulos and the late Tim Russert treated Clinton with mild disdain, clearly drawn in by Obama's charisma. A starry-eyed Stephanopoulos was particularly enchanted: "You are so cool.... Do you think that is a function of your race?" (Obama, *The Daily Show*, 2008) The campaign complied with the public's passion for Obama by consenting to the seemingly countless invitations to appear on magazine covers, many of them featuring the candidate's very appealing countenance, especially when illuminated with his megawatt smile.

The campaign did not address evidence of these numerous crushes on Obama, least of all satirical media on television and posted on YouTube, which fearlessly mined the salacious aspects of interracial sexuality. Late-night television sketch comedies *MADtv* and *Saturday Night Live* were brilliantly attuned to the ways ubiquitous visual representations of Obama and Clinton recalled the historical dread of race mixing. On November 24, 2007, recently canceled *MADtv* broadcast the sketch "Under Barack Obama," a rather daring parody of the music video for the mega-hit *Umbrella*, recorded by pop artist Rihanna (*MADtv*, 2007). Much of the video mimics *Umbrella*, including an over-the-top, apparently nude segment with Clinton and Obama painted head to toe in silver (Rihanna, 2007). The video's depiction of "Mandingo love," Clinton and Obama rutting in bed, was a particularly funny parody of cultural representation. Although the two mime sexual intercourse, the interracial sex is not the erotic spectacle of hyper-sexual black man and nymphomaniac white woman. Instead, they are dressed as a conventional non-descript couple: Clinton in a girdle and Obama in briefs, T-shirt and socks.

On February 23, 2008, long-running sketch comedy *Saturday Night Live* broadcast a sketch that, like *MADtv*, enacted a layered cultural critique: parodies of representation and its subtexts (*Saturday Night Live*, 2008). The setting of a debate between Clinton and Obama, moderated by John King and Tim Russert, ratcheted up the media's real-life coolness toward Clinton and worship of Obama to an absurd degree. The male journalists' fawning was a telling comment on how the president's magnetism disarmed across gender lines. *SNL* was unambiguous about white female lust for Obama, raising admiration of the candidate's storied "eloquence" to an orgasmic response on the part of commentator Campbell Brown. *SNL*'s sketch incorporated an effective intersection of old and new media by including Internet sensation Amber Lee Ettinger's persona Obama Girl singing "I Got a Crush on Obama."

In a subsequent real-life debate between the candidates, Hillary Rodham Clinton chastised journalists by invoking *SNL*'s spot-on depiction of the media bias toward Obama. Her comment illuminated the porous boundaries between the real and its representation. This example crystallized the primary campaign's unique function as a territory of cultural intersection of potent discourses of race and sex, along with the critical role of Obama as the ideal locus for these numerous crossings.

## White Mothers and Black Sons

Extensive media coverage of Obama's relationship with his mother constituted the competing narrative about interracial intimacy that emerged during the primary campaign. Old media made clear the late Ann Dunham Sutoro was the most important white woman in Obama's life (Ripley, 2008). She seems to have embodied both flower-power optimism and second-wave feminist autonomy, qualities evident in many white American women whose children scholars define as the "biracial baby boom" (Root, 1992). The slow erosion of white male (and traditional cultural) prerogatives to protect "their" women was a key factor; facilitating their move toward economic, social and sexual independence (Jones 1990). The marriage between Barack Obama's parents was an example of the revision of the traumatic history of race mixing in the United States, repudiating white male sexual entitlement and dispossession of mulatto children.

Still, the general social acceptance of interracial marriage belies the tendency among bi/multi-racial African Americans to identify as black (Schermo, 2000). This is a logical development of historical circumstances: white society's censure of interracial marriage and categorization of blacks according to the so-called one-drop rule (Davis, 2001). Historically, the distinction drawn between whites and blacks in the United States rested on the notion of white blood purity (Saks, 2000). Inheritance of any so-called traceable amount of black blood — one drop — made one racially impure, and hence black. Eventually, African Americans adopted this imposed racial classification and transformed it into a shared cultural identity. The imperative for African Americans to constitute as a group based on an illogical blood rule were reclaimed, reshaped, and over time independently crafted black identities and communities across boundaries of blood, color and so on.

In a fashion similar to attestations in memoirs by and interviews with numerous biracial Americans of black and white descent, Obama's close relationship with his white parent did not conflict with his African American identity (Cross, 2006; Funderberg, 1994; McBride, 1996). Notwithstanding deep affective ties with his mother and her parents, along with a boyhood in multi-cultural Hawaii, Barack Obama craved guidance in how to become a black man, an aspiration he pursued on basketball courts in Hawaii, and eventually realized in black Chicago's barbershops and churches (Obama, *Dreams from My Father: A Story of Race and Inheritance*, 1995).

However, Sutoro's idiosyncratic choices — unions with Obama's Kenyan father and her second child's Indonesian father — made Obama's mixed-race heritage anomalous vis-à-vis most American children of interracial marriage. Despite representations of him as a racial exotic, in many ways his background conformed to the normative model of a white "native." The "skinny kid with a funny name" grew up resembling Americans of, for example, Irish and Italian descent. Obama grew up aware of his unique ethnic and national heritage, but it had little role in shaping his core identity as an American (Waters, 1990). His unusual name was, at least until young adulthood, the only tangible sign of a tenuous connection to African ethnicity. His adoption of the Anglicized "Barry" in early life reflected a generations-old immigrant practice (Obama, 1995). In his star-making debut on the national stage in 2004, Obama articulated a biography likely to appeal to white Americans because it reiterated what made him just like them. The 2008 Democratic National Convention (where Obama formally accepted his party's nomination for president) featured a biographical film, which, as my analysis will show, represents a critical paradigm shift with regard to mixed-race people and identity. Throughout the primaries, Obama had the unique problem of continually being challenged as to his authentic American identity. For example, his opponents exploited the naïveté of many Americans by challenging Obama's citizenship. His birthplace, Hawaii, was exotic and distant enough to be characterized as a hazy site of national identity. Repeated requests for Obama's birth certificate persisted long after the document was made available. Obama's given middle name of "Hussein" cast suspicion on his claims to be Christian. Finally, elisions between the name "Osama" and "Obama" occurred in media on numerous occasions, further facilitating the casting of a terrorist pall by displacing Barack Obama with America's worst enemy Osama Bin Laden, self-proclaimed mastermind of the 9/11 attacks.

The film screened at the 2008 Democratic National Convention framed Obama, potentially our first black president, as a favored son of America's Heartland — a definitively white site of the national identity. This response to the multi-pronged campaign to demonize Obama — to "make you scared of (him)" — was a striking move designed to bring to life the skinny kid with a funny name, the persona offered to white Americans as a figure of shared identity. The film depicted Obama's African relatives far less than his white family, in particular his grandparents, with whom he lived for most of his youth. Emphasizing Obama's roots in Kansas has the rhetorical advantage of invoking a heartland particularly resonant for Americans, for whom the film *The Wizard of Oz* is a cultural touchstone. Dorothy's timeless chant, "There's no place like home," invokes a particularly American longing for rural, small-town life. (The gay community's signifying revision, "Dorothy, we're not in Kansas anymore," could describe the recurrent paranoia that gripped some white people fearful of an end to "White America" [Hsu, 2009]). Obama's noted address, "A More Perfect Union" (colloquially known as his "Race Speech), of March 18, 2008, traced the trajectory of a United States whose perfectibility he grounded in rectifying racial asymmetries (*Huffington Post*, 2008). The 2008 DNC film showed his campaign's awareness that securing victory pivoted on support from America's white voting majority. Barack Obama's American identity had to be grounded in traceable white blood. In this way his campaign strategy displaced the one-drop rule, which, while originated to protect white blood purity, has become virtually unknown to contemporary white Americans, and implicitly natural to black Americans.

## What Keeps Obama Black?

At President Obama's inauguration on January 20, 2009, the Rev. Joseph Lowery closed his remarks with a play on a familiar African American adage:

> Lord, in the memory of all the saints who from their labors rest, and in the joy of a new beginning, we ask you to help us work for that day when black will not be asked to get back, when brown can stick around, when yellow will be mellow, when the red man can get ahead, man, and when white will embrace what is right.

Lowery's words revised a folk saying virtually every African American has heard:

> If you're white, you're all right,
> If you're brown, stick around,
> If you're black, get back!

This humorous calculus of skin color is not entirely understood by people unfamiliar with black cultural history. The relative advantage of lighter skin color among African Americans is a historical phenomenon, which has over time become an individual rather than a group privilege.

In the decades following the Civil War, Southern states rolled back the rights of ex-slaves and free people of color by instituting the system of segregation that came to be known as "Jim Crow." The pivotal legal challenge to the segregation of public facilities, *Plessy v. Ferguson*, instituted the notorious "separate but equal" convention (U.S. Supreme Court, 1896). The case involved the light-skinned Homer Plessy occupying a seat in the "white" car of a Louisiana train. He was forcibly removed from the train when he refused to move to the "colored" coach. Plessy, described in the Court's ruling as "seven-eighths Caucasian and one-eighth African blood," was from a prominent family among Louisiana's mulatto aristocracy in a city characterized by a three-part racial hierarchy rather than the racial dualism prevalent in the United States as a whole (Williamson, 1995). *Plessy* is important because it challenged the logic of racial distinctions. Homer Plessy's mixed-race background and white (hence "all right") appearance showed that racial prejudice was the effect of unjust social practices rather than genuine difference. If Plessy was black, what made white people racially distinctive (Davis 2001)? Thus, seven years before W.E.B. DuBois declared, in 1903, that the color line was the twentieth century's definitive challenge, *Plessy* exposed the status of race as conceptual rather than visually evident (DuBois, 2005). Contemporary theorists have gone on to refine *Plessy*'s insight by theorizing that race is a function of social narrative and political power—a process of racial formation—rather than intrinsic difference (Omi and Winant, 2004).

In the context of this essay, *Plessy*'s relevance is the analogous position between African Americans whose mixed-race background is the result of historical relations among whites and blacks (and Native Americans), and biracial African Americans with a white parent. The dictionary definitions of *mulatto* clearly demonstrate the overlap between these categories—one being "the first-generation offspring of a black person and a white person" and two "a person of mixed white and black ancestry" (*Merriam-Webster Dictionary*, 2010). Barack Obama, our nation's first so-called black president, fits the first definition. Obama relates, in his autobiography, "I ceased to advertise my mother's race at the age of twelve or thirteen, when I began to suspect that by doing so I was ingratiating myself to whites" (Obama, *Dreams from My Father: A Story of Race and Inheritance*, 1995, ix). As we have seen, however, his campaign skillfully deployed his biracial heritage. His ease in relating to white people and his light-skinned appearance cemented his desirability as a political candidate. He was an exemplary black man and to many, as Joseph Biden opined, "the first mainstream African-American [presidential candidate] who is articulate and bright and clean and a nice-looking guy, ... I mean, that's a storybook, man" (CNN, 2007).

## *On the Campaign Trail: Marketing Miscegenation in the Twenty-First Century*

The sexual revolution and the feminist movement were important precursors to the evolution of sexual liaisons between black men and white women to open relationships and legal marriages (Klein, 2008; Bai 2008). Notwithstanding the race and sex of the plaintiffs in *Loving v. Virginia*—Richard Loving, who was white, and Mildred Jeter, who was black (and Native American)—the significant majority of these interracial marriages take place between black men and white women (DaCosta, 2007). This pattern puts the nail in the coffin of the stereotype of threatening black brutes and virtuous white victims. However, proving the erroneous nature of this social construction does not rob it of power. This image, however enmeshed with a history of violence, also contains the potent erotic charge embodied by cultural taboo. Unsurprisingly, cultural images of dread and fear projected onto interracial sex mask an inversion: a desire transforming this social taboo into an erotic object of fascination.

In our twenty-first century, sexual liaisons between black men and white women have come to assume a different position in American culture — exploited in a capitalist economy that uses sex to sell. On the campaign trail, Barack Obama's charm was legendary, yet consistently chaste. His wife, Michelle — beautiful, intelligent, articulate, along with attractive and appealing daughters Sasha and Malia — seemed a made-to-order first black first family. Obama's embodiment of ideal husband and father put him above reproach without dimming his sex appeal. The erotic charge of interracial sexual desire on the campaign trail shifted instead to images of white women.

Interestingly, the suggestive display of white woman's bodies crossed the boundary between representation of the real (photographs of voters) and representation in the mode of consumer objects (photographs gracing items for sale). This proximity of the real and representation is a powerful mode of intersection. Two examples in 2009 spoke to a particularly resonant erotic image of women — a close-fitting T-shirt stretched over the large breasts of a blonde. In an article about young Obama supporters published in June, *Newsweek* magazine cropped a photograph to feature a youthful, voluptuous, blonde woman in a snug T-shirt bearing Obama's face and the phrase "Obama for Change" (*Newsweek*, 2009). The example of consumer products is a birthday greeting card I purchased at a California Target store in April 2009. It depicted a tanned, curvy white woman — anonymous because the top of the photograph stopped at her chin, but evidently blond from the fringe of hair on her shoulders — in an even tighter T-shirt, knotted above her waist, and emblazoned with just one word: "Obama." Inside the card reads the inscription: "Now That I've Got Your Attention, Happy Birthday!" (Tomato Cards, 2008). Unlike the photograph in *Newsweek*, the greeting card draws an unambiguous connection between interracial sexuality and Obama. The card's message can be expanded: now that one has been arrested by the spectacle of a sexy white woman "branded" with the name of an attractive and charismatic black man ... at this point the birthday message seems beside the point, but then again, the card itself is beside the point. The card's most important function is the circulation of an image that jolts consumers into spending money.

The Internet produces a strange twist on representation and temporality: it is at once ephemeral and permanent. Andy Warhol's prediction of an ecumenical "fifteen minutes of fame" has been exploded by technology. No matter how deeply "cached," to post online is to post forever. "Obama Girl," the Internet persona created by Amber Lee Ettinger, was a signal example of how the viral environment of sites such as YouTube can upend the conventional media hierarchy. Obama Girl was a post-feminist invention grafting the sexual revolution to a new form of exhibitionism and voyeurism. The video "I Got a Crush on Obama" blended teenage idol worship, the pinup aesthetic, and reality television in a kind of cultural mash-up. The transformation of Obama Girl from wacky Internet posting to a figure representative of the zeitgeist is a powerful example of this technology, and of how a white woman used Obama's candidacy to create a personal brand as interracial sex kitten.

## *Harold Ford Jr.: A Candidacy Gone Awry*

To look at Barack Obama's political career alongside that of Harold Ford Jr. is to be plunged into a crash course in the politics of black racial authenticity in America — its vagaries, contradictions, and the virtually unfathomable calculus used to determine just what it takes to succeed as a black representative in American politics. This essay concludes with a return to Memphis, Tennessee, to analyze the derailment of a political campaign tarred, if you will, by the brush of interracial sex. In Benjamin Wallace-Wells *Washington Monthly* article "The Great Black Hope," he identified Obama as one of the "few black politicians for whom their race isn't a ball-and-chain, but a jet engine — the feature that launches them into stardom" (Wallace-Wells, 2004). In this group, Wallace-Wells included Harold Ford Jr., scion of an illustrious political family and at the time a five-term congressman from Tennessee. His father, Harold Ford Sr., "served eleven terms in the U.S. House of Representatives from 1974 to 1996 ... the first African American elected from the state of Tennessee to serve in Washington" (Brennan, 2006). In 2006, Ford Jr. campaigned "to be the South's first black senator since Reconstruction" (Darman & Romano, 2006). After a promising start, his bid for the Senate was stalled by a Republican attack advertisement on television. Among other claims, the spot used suggestive imagery to imply that interracial sex was part of Ford's corrupt agenda.

Few may recall that just a decade ago, Harold Ford Jr. was poised to become the "articulate, bright and clean" candidate to break the color barrier at the higher echelons of the political hierarchy. At the Democratic National Convention of 2000, Ford — at the time just thirty years old — delivered the keynote speech. Unlike Barack Obama, Ford's message was grounded in a traditional black American identity, one marked by the struggle for civil rights. Ford addressed the audience: "I stand here tonight because of the brave men and women, no older than I am today ... who were willing to stand up, and in many cases sit down, to create a more perfect union" (*New York Times*,

2000). At the time, Ford's political profile seemed ideal; he was young, "an African American who represents diversity [and] a moderate" (*New York Times*, 2000). Still, Harold Ford Jr. failed to generate the excitement that greeted Barack Obama's keynote speech of 2004. According to the *New York Times*, "Mr. Ford did not get the usual exposure of the top-billed speaker. He did not take the stage until nearly 11 P.M. E.D.T. when the major networks ended their coverage" (*New York Times*, 2000). In retrospect, it seems evident that the Obama team was far more aggressive in paving the way for his rise; they had the advantage of a compelling candidate, but they were also brilliant media strategists.

Unlike his lukewarm reception at the 2000 DNC, Ford's bid for the Senate in 2006 was greeted with a measured enthusiasm. The midterm elections seemed to favor Ford, a so-called "Blue Dog" Democrat, conservative enough to appeal to right-of-center party constituents, yet potentially able to deliver a crucial seat in the Senate (Darman, 2006). Ford's fortunes turned when late in the campaign, as reported by *Newsweek*, the "GOP sponsored an ad featuring a blonde cooing, 'Call me, Harold' (in reference to Ford's appearance at a Super Bowl party for *Playboy*) (*Newsweek*, 2006). The television advertisement spot supporting Ford's Republican opponent Bob Corker featured with the tagline, "Harold Ford. He's just not right." The footage included a series of talking heads, a diverse group making brief statements:

A black woman: "He looks nice. Isn't that enough?"

A white woman: "Terrorists need their privacy."

An older white woman: "I want to pay more marriage taxes."

A white man: "So what if we take money from porn movie producers? Doesn't everyone?"

An older white couple: "I want to pay taxes after I'm dead."

A white man dressed in hunting clothes: "I have enough guns."

And finally, a young white blonde woman, shown bare shouldered (and thus seemingly unclothed): "I met Harold at the Playboy Party!" Subsequently she mouths the words "Call me, Harold," one hand to her ear, and winks.

The so-called "Call me" ad generated a flurry of responses, most expressing dismay about the inflammatory content. The media quickly reached consensus that the GOP were willing to appeal to latent fears of miscegenation to motivate southern voters.

Although "Call me" shamelessly trolled the questionable waters of historical narratives of miscegenation, I maintain that the overall effect, on the level of cultural representations, was more kitschy than pointedly dangerous. But the critical peril in "Call me" is precisely its source: Ford's opposition. The sheer expense of running a television advertisement is a strong argument that intimations of miscegenation were, at least in the minds of some Bob

Corker supporters, effective weapons against an African American candidate. The threat here is the possibility — however slight — that such messages could motivate deadly violence.

## *Conclusion*

In this essay, I proposed that President Barack Obama's candidacy generated two contradictory, yet overlapping, discourses about interracial intimacy between black men and white women. The first consisted of interracial sexuality, the second, relationships between mothers and sons. I also argued that old and new media came into play during the campaign, creating a complex environment also characterized by difference and overlap. I argued that Barack Obama was a powerful figure of intersection, mediating historical taboos and the ever-evolving viral world of new media.

Barack Obama's appeal included being conceptualized as an object of desire by and for white women. However, although some entertainment media lampooned historical representations of "jungle fever," interracial sexuality did not cast a pall on his campaign. Rather, the media's various "crushes on Obama" seemed only to increase his attractive aura. Critically, more graphic sexual representations of interracial desire were displaced onto the bodies of white women. Obama's status as an exemplary black candidate, "articulate, bright and clean," was supplemented by his image as devoted husband and father. In the mainstream media, Obama's relationship with white women was crystallized as the deep bond he shared with his mother. Unlike the vast majority of biracial people, Obama, the son of a Kenyan father, had to establish his identity as a genuine American through his mother. This is an unusual mode of identity for African Americans, whose racial classification has been determined by the one-drop rule.

The example of Harold Ford Jr.'s unsuccessful Senate campaign shows that intimations of miscegenation can be used to instill fear and loathing, especially in southern states, where interracial sexuality has been strongly resisted. The discourses of threat used to demonize Barack Obama were, instead, focused on fears of terrorist threats from within: a different type of miscegenation. Still, inflammatory language during the campaign recalled the chilling atmosphere of the late nineteenth century, when black men and women were subject to what Ida B. Wells-Barnett called mob rule. In May 2007, the secretary of the Department of Homeland Security, Michael Chertoff, "authorized ... protection for [Obama]" — it was "the earliest the Secret Service [had] ever issued a security detail to a [presidential] candidate" (Zeleny, 2007). On February 19, 2008, Fox News pundit Bill O'Reilly, replying to a caller on his show, claimed he "didn't want to go on a lynching party against Michelle Obama" (Media Matters, 2008). The currency of such language shows how troubled the relationship between history and the present time can be. These points of intersection point us toward dazzling possibilities, even as they remind us of the vast unfinished business of race relations in America.

## REFERENCES

Adler, Ben. "Newsflash: Democrats in New York Overwhelmingly Pro-choice." *Newsweek*, January 8, 2010 (accessed July 21, 2010).
Bai, Matt. "Is Obama the End of Black Politics?" *New York Times Magazine*, August 6, 2008. www.nytimes.com/2008/10/magazine/10politics-t.html.
Bak, Richard. *Joe Louis: The Great Black Hope*. Dallas: Da Capo, 1998.
Begley, Sharon. "How Your Brain Looks at Race." *Newsweek*, February 23, 2008. http://www.newsweek.com/2008/02/23/how-your-brain-looks-at-race.html (accessed September 14, 2010).
Belton, Danielle. "The Black Snob." *Blacksnob*, April 23, 2008. Blacksnob.blogspot.com (accessed 2010).
Berke, Richard L. "The Democrats: The Overview: Led by Pack of Kennedys from Stage Left, Liberal Wing Takes Center Stage." *New York Times*, August 16, 2000. www.nytimes/2000/08/16/us/democrats-overview-led-pack-kennedys (accessed August 26, 2010).
Brennan, Carol. "Black Biography." Answers.com, Gale Group. 2006. www.answers.com/topic/erria-ford-sr (accessed September 13, 2010).
Chang, Jeff. "'Ladies and Gentlemen, (Is This) the Next President of the United States?'" *Vibe* magazine, September 2007, 181.
CNN. "Biden's Description of Obama Draws Scrutiny." CNN.com, February 9, 2007. cnn.com/2007/POLITICS/01/31/biden/obama (accessed 2010).
Crenshaw, Kimberle Williams. "Whose Story Is It, Anyway? Feminist and Antiracist Appropriations of Anita Hill." In *Race-ing Justice, Engender-ing Power: Essays on Clarence Thomas, Anita Hills and the Nature of Social Reality*, by Toni Morrison, 391–402. New York: Pantheon, 1992.
Cross, June. *Secret Daughter: A Mixed Race Daughter and the White Mother Who Gave Her Away*. New York: Viking, 2006.
DaCosta, Kimberly McClain. *Making Multiracials: State, Family and Market in the Redrawing of the Color Line*. Berkeley, CA: Stanford University Press, 2007.
Darman, Jonathan. "The Path to Power." Politics on MSNBC.com, October 30, 2006. http://www.msnbc.msn.com/id/15366095/site/newsweek (accessed September 14, 2010).
Darman, Jonathan, and Andrew Romano. *Newsweek*, August 14, 2006 (accessed July 15, 2010).
Davis, F. James. *Who Is Black? One Nation's Definition*. University Park: Pennsylvania State University Press, 2001.
Dray, Philip. *At the Hands of Persons Unknown: The Lynching of Black America*. New York: Modern Library, 2003.
DuBois, W.E.B. *The Souls of Black Folk*. Enriched Classics Series. New York: Simon & Schuster, 2005.
Ettinger, Amber Lee. "Crush on Obama." Obama Girl. Video created by Ben Relles. 2010. http://obamagirl.com (accessed August 1, 2010).
Funderberg, Lise. *Black, White, Other: Biracial Americans Talk about Race and Identity*. New York: Morrow, 1994.
Herbert, Bob. "Running While Black." *New York Times*, August 2, 2008.
Horowitz, Helen Lefkowitz, and Kathy Peiss. *Love across the Color Line: The Letters of Alice Hanely to Channing Lewis*. Amherst: University of Massachusetts Press, 1996.

Hsu, Hua. "The End of White America?" *Atlantic Monthly*, January/February 2009.
Huffington Post. "Obama Race Speech." March 18, 2008. www.huffingtonpost.com/2008/03/18/obama-race-speech-read-th_n_92077.html (accessed September 14, 2010).
*Jon Stewart Show.* Television. Directed by Comedy Channel Television Network. Performed by Jon Stewart. 2008.
Jones, Hettie. *How I Became Hettie Jones.* New York: Grove, 1990.
Kelley, Raina. "Let's Talk About Race." *Newsweek*, December 4, 2006. http://www.newsweek.com/search.html?time=any&order=date&start=20&q=HAROLD+FORD (accessed September 14, 2010).
Klein, Joe. "Obama's Historic Victory." *Time*, January 4, 2008. http://www.time.com/time/politics/article/0,8599,1700132,00.html (accessed 2010).
*Loving v. Virginia.* 388 U.S. 1 (U.S. Supreme Court, June 12, 1967).
*MADtv.* "Under Barack Obama." Season 13, episode 1308. Performed by *MADtv*. November 24, 2007.
McBride, James. *The Color of Water: A Black Man's Tribute to His White Mother.* New York: Riverhead Books, 1996.
Media Matters. "Research: O'Reilly: 'I Don't Want to Go on a Lynching Party against Michelle Obama.'" Media Matters for America, February 20, 2008. http://mediamatters.org/research/200802200001 (accessed September 14, 2010).
*Merriam-Webster's Dictionary.* "Mulatto." 2010. http://www.merriam-webster.com (accessed August 24, 2010).
Moran, Rachel. *Interracial Intimacy: The Regulation of Race and Romance.* Chicago: Chicago University Press, 2003.
MSNBC. "Stunner in N.H.: Clinton Defeats Obama." MSNBC.com, January 9, 2008. msnbc.msn.com/id/22551718 (accessed May 1, 2010).
*Newsweek.* "Is America Ready?" December 25, 2006. http://www.newsweek.com/search.html?time=any&order=date&start=20&q=HAROLD+FORD (accessed September 14, 2010).
———. "Younger Voters Have Gone Obama's Way." June 2, 2009.
*New York Times.* "Democrats Overview." August 16, 2000. www.nytimes.com (accessed September 13, 2010).
Obama, Barack. *Dreams from My Father: A Story of Race and Inheritance.* New York: Times Books, 1995.
———. "Interview by George Clip." *The Daily Show*, Comedy Central. May 13, 2008.
Omi, Michael, and Howard Winant. *Racial Formation in the United States from the 1960s to the 1990s.* 2 vols. New York: Routledge, 1994.
*Plessy v. Ferguson.* 163 U.S. 537 (U.S. Supreme Court, May 18, 1896).
Public Broadcasting System. "American Experience: Black Boxers and the Idea of a 'Great Black Hope.'" Public Broadcasting System, September 22, 2004. www.pbs.org/wghb/amex/fight/peopleevents/e_race.html (accessed 2010).
Rihanna. *Umbrella Music Video.* Directed by Chris Applebaum. Accessed on YouTube, August 2010. Performed by Rihanna, featuring Jay-Z. 2007.
Ripley, Amanda. "Raising Obama: A Mother's Story." *Time*, April 28, 2008, 42–36.
Romano, Renee C. *Race Mixing: Black-White Marriage in Postwar America.* Boston: Harvard University Press, 2003.
Root, Maria P.P. "Introduction." In *Racially Mixed People in America*, by Maria P.P. Root. Newbury Park, CA: Sage, 1992.
Saks, Eva. "Representing Miscegenation Law." In *Interracialism: Black-White Intermarriage in American History, Literature and Law*, ed. Werner Sollors, 61–80. New York: Oxford University Press, 2000.
*Saturday Night Live.* Season 33, episode 5. Performed by Saturday Night Live. 2008.
Schermo, Diana. "Despite Options on Census, Many to Check 'Black' Only." *New York Times*, February 12, 2000.
Tomato Cards. "Obama Birthday Card." Recycled Paper Greetings. DCI Studios.com, Redtree Studios.com, 2008.

Wallace-Wells, Benjamin. "The Great Black Hope: What's Riding on Barack Obama." *Washington Monthly*, November 2004, 32–38.
Washington Associated Press. "Breitbart News by Email." June 3, 2008. www.breitbart.com/article.php?id=D912O5FG0&show article=1 (accessed July 21, 2010).
Waters, Mary. *Ethnic Options: Choosing Ethnic Identities in America*. Berkeley: University of California Press, 1990.
Wells-Barnett, Ida B. *The Selected Works of Ida B. Wells-Barnett*. Schomburg Library of Nineteen-Century Black Women Writers. New York: Oxford University Press, 1991.
Williamson, Joel. *New People: Miscegenation and Mulattoes in the United States*. Baton Rouge: Louisiana State University Press, 1995.
Wordiq.com. "Miscegenation." 2010. http://www.wordiq.com (accessed August 17, 2010).
YouTube. "Lyrics to Under Barack Obama." LyricsMania, November 24, 2007. www.lyricsmania.com/under_barack_obama_lyrics_youtube.html (accessed 2010).
Zeleny, Jeff. "Obama Placed Under Secret Service Protection." *New York Times*, May 3, 2007. www.nytimes.com/2007/05/03/us/politics/04Obamacnd.html (accessed July 21, 2010).

# How to Understand Obama's Election News Coverage
## An Interview with Daniel Berkowitz

NICHOLAS A. YANES, WITH DERRAIS CARTER AND ROBERT E. GUTSCHE JR.

Daniel Berkowitz is a professor in the School of Journalism and Mass Communication, and an associate dean at the University of Iowa. He has won several awards from the Radio-Television, Media Ethics and Public Relations Divisions of the Association for Education in Journalism and Mass Communication. Berkowitz has also edited two foundational texts: *Social Meaning of News: A Text-Reader* and *Cultural Meanings of News*.

Q: *When discussing how journalists cover presidential candidates, what are some of the common narratives that continuously appear? In particular, what are some of the characteristics that are layered onto the categories of Republicans and Democrats, and U.S. politics in general, by news outlets?*

A: To start off, it is important to define the notion of narrative and its related concept, mythical narrative. A narrative is a story told through a familiar plot and a standard set of story actors. The "Cinderella story" would be an example of a common narrative — an ironic tale where a plain young woman is treated badly by her stepmother and stepsisters, yet ends up marrying a prince after a chance meeting with him. Along the way, she receives help from a fairy godmother and others. This basic story emerges in a variety of settings and with a variety of specific characters in books, plays and films. When a story form is also built upon enduring cultural values, it can be considered as a mythical narrative — myth contains not only a standard plot and actors, but also restates a society's key meanings. Both narrative and mythical narrative go beyond simple characteristics and categories.

With news coverage of presidents, I do see a few mythical narratives repeating themselves over time. These narratives also come in the inverse of a common form. For example, the narrative of the heroic quest represents an idealized form for a presidential narrative — the character takes on a daring journey for society's salvation, facing a valiant struggle at great personal sacrifice. Ultimately, the character succeeds and all is well, although the hero suffers or dies in the end. The story of Franklin D. Roosevelt would be one example; John F. Kennedy would be another.

Another presidential narrative involves a character born of humble roots, who perseveres to improve his lot in life, eventually rising to become a great leader while never forgetting where he began life. The stories of Abraham Lincoln and Barack Obama both fit this mold.

Clearly, the hero narrative has an inverse — the leader who never does anything unless it is self-serving. Likewise, the self-made man narrative has an inverse, too — a leader who is born with silver spoon in mouth, reaching the presidency despite his liabilities and weaknesses. I think that the story of George W. Bush would fit into both of these inverse narratives.

I prefer this conceptual orientation rather than "characteristics" or "categories," where we lose a lot of the cultural meanings that lurk below the surface. Those labels limit understanding of presidential news coverage to simple stereotypes, including the Republican-Democrat dichotomy. In essence, categories call only for basic schematic thinking. It is cultural meanings that are most important to news.

*Q: Many have claimed that Obama's campaign was a departure from how other previous candidates ran for president, mainly because of his use of social networking technology. Do you think Obama's use of popular communication technologies like social networking sites and cell phones had a significant impact on how elections will be covered by the press from now on?*

A: One of the clearest indicators of how social networking technologies shifted the election's outcome was the groundswell of support from younger voters — those most attuned to the newer forms of communication. Only a niche segment of middle-aged and older voters would be using social media to the same degree.

I imagine that popular communication technologies will take their place in the mix of election coverage tools and channels. But there is a gap between these technologies as information sources for media audiences and reporting tools to be used by journalists.

Overall, I see communication technologies such as Facebook and Twitter as more of a benefit to campaign organizations than for journalists. In essence, they provide a channel of self-interested information from candidates to journalists that journalists have to sort through. I do see the possibility of evolving forms of blogging growing in utility, though, because they take a longer form, and journalists can connect them to their other duties.

*Q: With Obama's campaign being so driven by grassroots tactics, would you say Obama's campaign simultaneously used and subverted mainstream media's ability to construct him as a candidate?*

A: I think that it was not the grassroots tactics, but the Obama campaign's ability to capitalize on the mainstream media's need to capture abstract, unconventional stories in a resonant form. Essentially, by casting Obama into the narratives of Lincoln, Kennedy and FDR, the mainstream media had a chance to tell the stories about our society and its icons that we love to hear. This was also important because Obama did not fit the usual candidate mold and was more difficult to report on.

*Q: A significant difference between Obama and everyone else running for president in 2008 was that he is African American. How did his ethnicity affect how journalists reported on him?*

A: This was the "elephant in the middle of the room." Although the Obama campaign drew on narratives of America's revered leaders, they were rarely willing to invoke race and avoided connections between Obama and Martin Luther King Jr. To play up race would encourage divisiveness about voters. Obama was already different than the typical elite presidential candidates because he came from a single-parent family, had spent part of his youth living outside the U.S., was multi-racial, and came from Hawaii.

Race did not really become a part of Obama's news coverage until his inauguration, when becoming the first African American president added a "gee whiz" factor to the story, while also allowing the mainstream media to tell a variation of the rags-to-riches story — especially for African Americans.

*Q: Almost all popular entertainment outlets commentated about the election; popular examples of this are shows like* The View, The Daily Show *and* Saturday Night Live. *How did these types of non-news outlets affect the narratives presented by journalists?*

A: What makes these popular parodies work is how they highlight the unspoken but obvious, while also providing caricatures that concisely define the candidate. Because the shows draw a large audience, their portrayals build audience expectations for future news about the candidates.

One stream of communication research refers to "second-level agenda setting," where the media highlight and emphasize the *characteristics* of people, issues and events that have joined the first-level agenda of topics to be covered in the news. By definition, a good satirical portrayal would end up in a second-level agenda-setting role. To appear resonant to audiences, news media would then need to present narratives that coincide with popular portrayals.

*Q: One thing that Obama arguably did better than any other candidate is how well he "branded" himself. Could you briefly discuss the Obama brand and how it impacted media coverage of Obama?*

A: What was the Obama brand? I think it was a mix of (a) "Yes we can" turn things around, (b) fresh but not naive, and (c) a candidate who had the charisma and drive to get things done.

Fortunately, there was a good alignment between what Obama was "selling" and what he was delivering. A worst case scenario would have been to hearken to comparisons of JFK, but to come across as somebody like Dan Quayle or George W. Bush. Because of the alignment, media coverage became much more manageable — after all, Obama didn't match the typical candidate's elite profile, and the election came at a time when change was much needed.

In all, Obama's brand came at a time when American society was fragmented and unsure of itself. Its promise of a better future — a return to the good years in the past — brought favorable news coverage of a hopeful tomorrow without much questioning.

*Q: On October 29 of 2008, Obama aired a thirty-minute commercial, titled "American Stories, American Solutions," that focused on health care, taxation, other key components of his campaign and was watched by close to 30 million viewers. What are your thoughts on "American Stories, American Solutions"? Specifically, do these types of extended political ads capitalize on or complicate the stories news outlets produce?*

A: Sorry, but I don't think I was one of the 30 million who saw this. However, I would expect that an important goal would have been to reset parts of the issue agenda and highlight aspects of those agenda items that would be most salient. That said, it would have been difficult to create a massive shift in public understanding of the Obama campaign through this program — the strategy for messages would need to offer a subtle shift in emphasis.

We know that the outcomes of attempting to influence public opinion are rarely predictable and that reinforcing and strengthening existing attitudes is an easier task than trying to *change* public opinion. By bringing out an issue attribute or opinion more strongly, this kind of ad could work toward this kind of reinforcement. If an issue were cast in a different light to the existing public opinion frameworks, the challenge would be more difficult and perhaps bring some risk of backfiring.

*Q: Finally, do you think some of the implications of studying the 2008 election will influence how scholars understand presidential news coverage? Additionally, how do you think this election will alter how professors teach students about political news coverage?*

A: I think one of the key lessons of the 2008 election is to consider the context of the times and how candidates position themselves in relation to society's pressing needs from a new administration.

In 2008, we were facing extremely low confidence in leadership, a flailing economy, and an ongoing war. John McCain came across as a nice guy who wasn't taking the nation anywhere in particular. Combining this with Sarah Palin as his running mate — a candidate with little experience and even less common sense — we knew she would be unpredictable at best.

On the other hand, Obama's call for unity and change did resonate with the sentiment of the times, building the nation's support for a relative newcomer with a short track record — context made the difference. That's what I see as the key lesson from the 2008 election.

# New Media's Impact on Elections
## An Interview with Obama Girl Creator Ben Relles

JAMES CARVIOU

Ben Relles attended UW–Madison for college and then moved to Philadelphia after graduating. He was a founder of the marketing company Market Vision Inc., where he served as president from 1997 to 2002. He attended the Wharton School of Business from 2002 to 2004 where he graduated with a degree in marketing. From there he went on to create the video production company known as Barely Political. This company's first product was the music video "I Got a Crush on Obama," starring Amber Lee Ettinger. The video became an overnight sensation and helped fuel the demand for similar products. The Obama Girl franchise and other videos would allow Relles and Barely Political to be established as a significant new media production company.

The goal of this interview is to shed light on what inspired Relles to create Obama Girl, how he feels it influenced the interaction between popular media and popular culture, and how it established a new model for profiting off of the political system.

*Q: What was it about candidate Barack Obama that inspired you to create Obama Girl and launch Barely Political? Did his race or age play a factor in your choice?*

A: There was a lot of media attention about how young people were infatuated with Barack Obama, so I thought it would be funny to exaggerate that and create a character that had an actual crush on him. He had qualities women look for in men — power, honesty, looks. And I thought it'd be humorous if what she liked about him were his political policies. Race and age didn't play a factor in the choice.

*Q: If race and age didn't play a factor in choosing Obama, why has his popularity been credited to his mainstream presence in popular culture?*

A: I'm not saying his coolness isn't linked to his race or age. I'm saying *we* didn't choose to do a video about him because of those things.

I would not say his popularity has been linked to his mainstream presence in pop culture in any kind of conclusive way. I think his popularity came from what he said, what he promised, what he represented.

*Q: After Obama Girl there were other attempts to mimic your creation, none mirroring its success. What do you believe these other political pop-culture endorsements lacked?*

A: There's always something to being first, so to some extent from a publicity standpoint, the Obama Girl video had that going for it. But I also thought it was based in something real — that young people were crazy about him as a candidate. So that made the video emblematic of the Obama campaign. Our Obama Girl videos were seen over 100 million times, but there were dozens of parodies out there with tens of thousands of views, so those were fun to track.

*Q: In an interview, Amber Lee Ettinger mentions that few people knew who Obama was while the video was being made. What do you think of the relationship between Obama Girl's and Obama's increase in popularity after the video came out? Do you believe the video, or the resulting media frenzy, had anything to do with Obama's political rise?*

A: I like to think it was part of the initial wave of interest and excitement around him as a candidate. I'm sure the impact was very minimal, but I like that it represented something very real — that with YouTube, individuals had an opportunity never available before the 2008 election. They could create a video for a few hundred dollars and have it seen by potentially millions of people. It does help democratize the election process to some degree. It gives people a way to comment on candidates, whether that's using remixing, satire, commentary, or other methods. Ultimately more people remember the YouTube videos about Obama than his own TV advertising, so I do believe they had some impact.

*Q: There is a history of popular media hyper-sexualizing minorities in a negative fashion. In particular, African American men have often been portrayed as sexual threats to white women. How do you think Obama Girl's acknowledgement of Obama's attractive physique reflects or intervenes in this dynamic?*

A: I'd like to think for younger generations race doesn't enter their minds when they watch a video like the Obama Girl one. The short answer to the question is, "It doesn't."

*Q: How are youth today able to distinguish from contemporary controversies that surround race, like for example the Birthers and other groups that concentrate on skin color for their political motivations?*

A: I suppose as time passes people become increasingly more tolerant for a myriad of reasons. Not my area of expertise though. Are young people more aware that hating people because of their race is idiotic?

It's just not an area I've studied or am well versed in. How youth today see race through a different lens is complicated. Every generation this century, I think society has become more tolerant.

*Q: The 2008 presidential election marked the first major political race since the launch of YouTube. What do you think made YouTube an ideal platform for Obama Girl? Moreover, how do you think YouTube changed how campaigns were and will be directed?*

A: YouTube probably does change the way campaigns are run. Candidates think about their own YouTube channels. They think about how what they say can possibly be taken out of context (or in context) to become huge YouTube videos. And they think about how they can empower their supporters to create YouTube videos.

*Q: Given Newt Gingrich's lackluster announcement that he will be running for office, what is it about YouTube that some politicians get and others don't? Is there a particular profile of a candidate that would be successful utilizing YouTube as a promotional resource?*

A: I'd say some get that it is a new medium and can be used to show a side of them that mainstream media can't. Some don't and treat it the same.

No, there is no one profile. I think many different types of candidates could be successful utilizing YouTube.

*Q: In addition to YouTube, how do you think social networking and other new media platforms will influence elections? For instance, do you believe Twitter will affect the rhetoric politicians use?*

A: Yes, twitter will affect it. Facebook will affect it. Tumblr will affect it. Any social platform used by millions of people has the power to affect the election by giving people a voice they may not have previously had.

*Q: Are people benefiting from social networking in the political process?*

A: Yes. People are using social networks to communicate directly with a loyal and dedicated audience.

*Q: There is usually a distinct set of criteria for choosing appropriate spokespeople to represent public figures, especially the president (I say this knowing that Obama Girl had no official affiliation with the campaign). What were the criteria employed for selecting Amber Lee Ettinger?*

A: Looking for someone attractive, funny, and willing to go along with the joke if it became a national media story.

*Q: Did you find perspectives through web searches? What was the website where you stumbled upon Amber? What criteria sparked the final decision?*

A: I found her on her website. She was the third person I met for the part, and she did not audition. We just had coffee. I found Amber on Howard Stern's website where she was their girl of the month, and then that led me to her website. Since she was funny and willing to act goofy on camera I thought she made a good fit for the part.

*Q: Explain how you reacted to Obama's public response to Obama Girl. Was it what you expected? How do you think Obama Girl influenced Obama's mainstream/pop-culture brand identity?*

A: I was excited he acknowledged us. It was not what I expected, but fun to see him comment on us a few times. I think Obama Girl slightly brought to the forefront the idea that people were infatuated with Obama. The positive side of that (young people being excited about politics) and the negative (perhaps supporting candidates for the wrong reasons).

*Q: Can you take a moment to describe how the popularity of Obama Girl has brought you success? In addition to professional and financial success, how has this video created other opportunities for you to pursue?*

A: When the video became really popular, my website was acquired by the company Next New Networks. Later Next New Networks (and Barely Political) was acquired by YouTube, where I now work. The Barely Political channel has now been viewed over 1 billion times and is viewed over 40 million times per month.

Outside professional success, the video allowed me to attend a lot of political events like political conventions and debates. It was really gratifying to be a part of the story of how YouTube affected the election.

*Q: Obama Girl was a huge financial success for you and Barely Political. How do you think new media has influenced the way commercial interests profit off of political campaigns and figures?*

A: I suppose social networks influence fund-raising a lot, and it has created an industry of "social media gurus" who will charge campaigns a lot of money.

*Q: Besides "social media gurus" making money by teaching candidates about social networks, do you think there will be more people that will follow your example by capitalizing on the potential to make money off the persona of a particular candidate while not being affiliated directly with their campaign? How will people take advantage of the fresh political platform of social networks for profit? Are there any upcoming initiatives in the works through YouTube for the 2012 election?*

A: Yes. (Not sure.)

*Q: With the 2012 election approaching, what are your plans for Obama Girl? Given that his base has been unexcited about his performance as president, how do you feel this might affect the Obama Girl brand in the 2012 election?*

A: Not sure yet. We did the video four years ago this month, so it's probably about time we start thinking about whether there's something funny to be done for the 2012 election.

*Q: Though Obama Girl was popular and well liked, do you think these types of videos promote or undermine civic engagement in politics? Why or why not? Any examples of other videos besides Obama Girl?*

A: Some do undermine it, and some don't. It'd be impossible to generalize I think. But yes, it is a platform for the next generation of voters for sure.

I'm biased, but Obama Girl I thought promoted civic engagement to some extent because it reached a younger demo and helped show how many people could be reached by a YouTube video. Other examples that promote civic engagement: Hillary 1984, will.i.am, James Kotecki's show, the JibJab videos, Alphacats videos, the Young Turks.

## SECTION SIX

# INTERNATIONAL RESPONSES: OBAMA'S POPULARITY GOES GLOBAL

# Obama for Obama
## Barack Obama in Japanese Popular Culture
YUYA KIUCHI

## *Introduction*

During his presidential campaign, Barack Obama did not only have avid supporters in the South Side of Chicago where he had worked as a community organizer, or in Mombasa, Kenya, where his paternal heritage existed. A small city in Fukui Prefecture, Japan, incidentally named the City of Obama, with only slightly over 30,000 residents, was a center of international media attention for its enthusiastic Barack Obama fan club, Obama for Obama (City of Obama, 4). Ironically, the city was located only two hours away from Fukui City, the hometown of Masunaga Optical Manufacturing, the eyeglass maker for Sarah Palin. The launching and development of the fan club by those with no political power or voting rights in the American presidential election and for a candidate whose policy was little known to most Obama residents at the time epitomizes a unique phenomenon between Japanese popular culture and then-presidential candidate Barack Obama. The unprecedented level of popularity that Barack Obama gained in Obama City reflected the aspirational nature of his image in a trans–Pacific context and how the Japanese willingly imported, consumed, and oftentimes produced that very image. Simultaneously, this social phenomenon that started in February 2008 and continued until the end of the year showcases the local community's well-planned use of Barack Obama for its municipal revitalization efforts. Barack Obama as an iconic brand in Japanese popular culture significantly helped the city revitalize its economy, showcasing one of the practical roles that popular culture often plays.

Barack Obama had no association to any activities of Obama for Obama. The presidential candidate knew little about the existence of the City of Obama and its fan club. In early March 2008, when a journalist asked him if he knew about the city, he simply answered, "Yes, a nice town" ("Obama Shi wo Nice Town"). Barack Obama's emergence as a popular-culture brand and icon in Japan was independent from any of his political and non-political organizations or activities. The fan club is a voluntary organization with no political agenda. Its members simply wished to have a good time cheering for Obama and to help the city regain its economic and social vitality in the midst of its sluggish economy and continuous outflow of residents. Despite this separation between President Obama and Obama for Obama, it is nevertheless important to remember that residents and fan club members felt that they were a part of the "movement for change" that Obama as a candidate had advocated. This idea of change was not something foreign in the city of Obama. Residents had long sought a way to bring change to the city so that they could one day revitalize the community. This was why they held numerous events including public viewings of election results on CNN and other major American media channels.

Those who watched reports during these public viewings in the city of Obama could have very easily thought they were somewhere in the United States. Seeing residents' enthusiasm, they would have had difficulty believing that the people who had gathered to cheer for the candidate and chanted "Obama! Obama!" lived on the other side of the Pacific with no political interests in the United States. Examining how the city of Obama turned Barack Obama into a local popular-culture icon and the enthusiasm of the movement for Obama's candidacy reveals the way in which the city's residents used Obama's aspirational image to strengthen their community and revitalize its economy. Their support being so passionate, a journalist in Washington, D.C., jokingly asked Junichiro Keimura, a journalist from the *Asahi Shimbun*, how many delegates the city of Obama had (Keimura).

## *Origin*

The origin of the fan club, Obama for Obama, goes farther back than February 4, 2008. This day marked not only Super Tuesday, but also the birthday of the club. Some residents in the city of Obama, however, had supported Obama since December 2006, before he officially announced his candidacy for president. A TV program that aired at the end of 2006 introduced an anecdote from Obama's previous trip to Japan, recounted by Obama himself. The story goes that an immigration officer who greeted then–Senator Obama mentioned to him that he was from the city of Obama. Senator Obama answered that he had heard of the city. Although a column published on March 7, 2008, in the *Fukui Shimbun* questioned the validity of the story, the story was widely shared and discussed in various media ("Kansha"; "Route"). After learning about this conversation on the TV program, Shouryu Tamagawa, a Buddhist priest of the Haga Temple in Obama City, suggested to then–Mayor Toshio Murakami that he should send a letter to Barack Obama as a sign of friendship (Tanaka). Mayor Murakami sent a letter and a set of locally produced lacquer chopsticks to Obama in January 2007. Although the city did not receive a response back from the senator, Murakami sent another local specialty, a good luck doll, to him in February 2008. A month later, Mayor Murakami received a letter from Obama postmarked February 21, who was by then a presidential candidate. He signed the letter "Anata no Yuujin" (Your friend). About thirty media staff correspondents including non–Japanese outlets such as CNN and the Associated Press gathered at city hall in Obama for a press conference with the mayor expressing his surprise and gratefulness for receiving the letter. He commented, "I am surprised that we heard back from him. It almost felt we had known each other for a long time.... I imagine he is busy with his election but he does not talk about it much. I can sense his gracefulness and sincerity." He further continued, "If our city could become sister cities with Honolulu, maybe Mr. Obama, if he becomes the president, will visit Obama during his future stay in Japan." Pictures of the smiling mayor with the letter in his hands appeared in more than twenty national and local newspapers in Japan. Although a few residents had continued to follow then–Senator Obama and his aspiration for the presidency, it would be over a year after most residents had first heard the anecdote that the fan club could would be established ("Obama Shi e"; "Obama Shi no"; Takahashi, "Yori Ai wo Komete"; Takahashi, "Obama Shi kara"; "Obama e Obama Shi"; "Obama Shi kara Itenshin"; "Obama Giin"; "Obama Shi kara Obama shi"; "Obama Gets Letter"; "Obama Sends"; "Kouryu").

Before Obama for Obama started gaining attention, the City of Obama had seldom been featured in international media. It was a very small town not well known even to many Japanese people. It was a major change for the city to welcome journalists from the U.S., France, the UK, Germany, Switzerland, Australia, Brazil, and Spain, and many other countries. Journalists from Al Jazeera traveled from Qatar to feature the enthusiastic support by Obama residents for the presidential candidate. As a result, following the public viewing event, for a short time the city was listed number two on the American Yahoo! Search ranking ("Fujui Obama shi"). Although this newly established global presence of the city changed the city in several ways, the city itself had been one of the very traditional areas in Japan. Known for its traditional arts and crafts, Obama City relies on its fisheries and cultural and historical tourism. One of the residents who were interviewed by a non–Japanese press mentioned that she had never even heard English in real life ("Obama ni Kugiduke").

The story of a popular morning television soap opera in 2007 and 2008, *Chiritoten*, also attests to the conservative life in Obama. The story took place in Obama, focusing on the importance of the preservation of tradition. The location for the story was selected because Obama was a city where traditional industries and values had been respected and passed down to its residents even today. The city also experienced the stagnation of the local economy and the outflow of population since the late 1980s that many other municipalities had. The statistical review published by the municipal office reveals this problem clearly. While the population under fifteen years old has declined by over 1,000 over the last fifteen years, the population over sixty-five has increased by approximately 1,500 (City of Obama, 7). The closing of the Wakasa Matsushita Denki Corporation undermined the local economy, leaving over five hundred employees at least temporarily unemployed in 2000 (Tosa). The trans–Pacific awareness that developed among the residents of Obama City, therefore, was something new to Obama. It was an optimal opportunity to revitalize the ailing city.

Obama residents' enthusiasm manifested particularly in two ways: various types of public events and diverse kinds of products, both of which used Barack Obama as a popular cultural icon. From public viewing of CNN to the performance both in Japan and in the U.S. of a local Hawaiian dance group, "Obama Girls," various events planned by Obama for Obama turned the American presidential election into a series of festivals where they consumed Senator Obama as an aspirational brand that advocated the "change" and "hope" that many residents hoped existed in the Japanese society. Similarly, the merchandizing efforts by the fan club and the local businesses that resulted in Obama burgers, Obama T-shirts, Obama chopsticks, Obama-buns with bean paste, and many other products exemplified grassroots efforts to revitalize the local economy. It was not a coincidence that this very idea of bottom-up social movement was a significant part of presidential candidate Obama's political ideal, at least in the mind of many residents of the city.

Obama for Obama started with a realistic objective to revitalize the city while holding fun and entertaining events, and with a "half-joking" objective to support the presidential candidate (Fujihara). Obama's residents believed that active participation alone would have a positive impact on the economically ailing city. It was evident to anyone's eye that their activities would not help Obama in his race in any way. The founding members of the club, however, felt that it would be a fun idea that could eventually establish a base for a long-lasting social mechanism to keep the city's economy afloat (Ono). FBC, a local cable television channel, reported that four residents of Obama City gathered at a local bar on February 4, 2008, while the world media talked about the latest developments of Super Tuesday. Those who were present were

Seiji Fujihara, the president of a local hotel; Yasunori Maeno, an owner of a sewing company; Yuko Oe, a worker at a local paper store; and Shouryu Tamagawa, the aforementioned Buddhist priest. Well rooted in their local community, they agreed to launch a fan club, conduct public relations efforts, manufacture merchandise, and encourage residents' participation in events simply to have a good time regardless of their age or occupation.

Although the very origin of the fan club existed in an anecdote at an airport in Tokyo, Hisao Akao, an executive member of the club explains that this now-famous episode was just a reason to learn more about Barack Obama, but not the reason to support him. Their support for Obama was founded upon the idea of change. Akao states that the call for change "not only attracted empathy from Americans but has been shared and has helped young leaders in the City of Obama who try to actively engage themselves in the events in the city and to revitalize their home town." Additionally, Obama's first autobiography was considered "the bible for community formation and revitalization" that the organizers in Obama modeled after. Akao continues to explain that the change for local communities that Obama had promoted was not based on the destruction of the old but on preservation of the past and cherishing of the good. This idea of change was particularly appealing to the many tradition-valuing residents in Obama (Akao, "Obama Kouho," 1–2).

The outline of the group further stipulated the objectives of the organization. Referring to the Arabic meaning of the word "Barack," or "the blessed," Obama for Obama recognized that "Barack Obama" could mean "the blessed City of Obama." The document also pointed out that the philosophy of the local high school well matched the values that Barack Obama represented: work hard, eliminate discrimination, and enrich the body and mind. The excitement and fun that many residents of Obama felt about the candidate were not manifested because of a simplistic objective of pursuing entertainment. Rather, such feelings were meant to nurture motivation in the city and allow the city residents to feel, "I know little about politics or community building, but I think people just like me are being a part of Obama for Obama." In the organization's words, its purpose was to "create future" that is beneficial to the city (Obama for Obama).

## Events and Merchandise

One of the first events was at the Omizuokuri festival, a festival with over 1,200 years of history, on March 2, 2008, sponsored by the Jingu Dera Temple. The fan club contributed one of the fourteen flaming torches and carried it around the city. The belief of the festival is that a wish will come true if it is written on a torch and burnt during the event. Seiji Fujihara commented that he hoped that this tradition of Obama would bring a positive result in the preliminary voting that was scheduled in Texas, Ohio and other states over the following two days ("Obama shi Gorieki"; Katsura). This was one of the very first events in which Obama for Obama was successful in achieving the pragmatic objectives of bringing local residents together on a day of traditional festivity and of initiating a series of events using their support for Barack Obama as a means for local revitalization. One city hall worker explained that even those who had initially opposed Fujihara's idea began to accept Barack Obama once they learned that the candidate had a sincere personality which corresponded with the city's traditional values (Tosa).

One of the participants of the festival was the city's first African American English teacher, Ms. Wilson. She was an English language teacher at local Wakasa Higashi High School. Ms. Wilson moved from Newark, New Jersey, where she worked at a municipal office for two years, to Obama in the summer of 2007 and had been a supporter of Senator Obama. Witnessing various events in the city and carrying the lighted torch herself, she made a documentary to record the residents' support for Obama. She explains, "It [Obama for Obama] all began as a joke that the city and the candidate had the same name. But it became a big issue because people talked about it. Obama's popularity is based on grassroots support. I am interested in the commonality between the two activities" ("Obama to Bei").

At noon local time on March 5, 2008, the first primary election poll viewing event took place at the Food and Culture Center. Approximately three hundred residents dressed in "I Love Obama" T-shirts sat in front of five flat-screen televisions showing CNN live. As what Fujihara described as "a surprise," approximately 150 journalists both from inside and outside of Japan, including CNN, Agence France-Presse, and the Associated Press, also gathered. Apart from the unexpected number of journalists, the event was a well planned one. It was not just an occasion for residents to get together during their lunch break and watch CNN. Fujihara and other executive members of Obama for Obama made sure that the enthusiasm that had begun to surface all over the city over the past few weeks would last as long as possible. While the large flat screens showed the developments at the polls, a group of musicians from Osaka performed an upbeat fan song for Obama. About twenty female dancers who learned the hula at a local dance school demonstrated their performance on the stage. Visitors were served buns with bean paste inside with Obama's caricature branding, Obama burgers, sushi rolls with deep-fried pork (deep fried pork is called "*katsu*" in Japanese, which also means "victory") and other food samples. The synergy between event planning and product merchandizing developed very early in the fan club's community revitalization efforts ("Obama Shi Ouen"; "Hisshou Obama Atsui"; "Zembeini"; Takahashi, "Obama Shi Katte"; "Backing Barack"; Tosa).

Obama for Obama offered the City of Obama a rare but enriching international experience at its gatherings. At the public viewing on March 5, 2008, a Kenyan worker at a travel agency in Tokyo who identified himself as "Daniel" joined the event. He explained that when he first heard about the fan club, he did not understand why there was a support group in Japan. Nevertheless, in *Zoom-In Super*, he enthusiastically stated, "I felt I needed to cheer for Mr. Obama with people in Japan." Holding a Kenyan flag and an "I Love Obama" T-shirt in his hands, he commented, "If Senator Obama wins, the youth in Kenya will feel that they can achieve as much as he has and the world is equal." Although he was not from Obama, he was welcomed at the event (Ito).

Participants' hope to raise the sense of community through the presidential election on the other side of the Pacific was apparent among the hula-dancing Obama Girls. Shitsuko Nakamura, the oldest member of the group at sixty-four years old, had prepared for this day for two weeks. She commented that if Barack Obama won the election, she would like to forge a community tie not only within the City of Obama but also with Hawaii. Yuko Oe, a founding member of Obama for Obama and the leader of the Obama Girls, also emphasized, "We are yet to have enough skills to perform in front of many people. But we just wanted to bring people together across age and occupational differences" (Ito). Those who came to see the performance agreed with the dancers. Naoko Kasuya, a college student from Fukui Prefectural University, also underlined the relationship between the election and the city's revitalization by explaining, "I decided to help out to make the city a more cheerful place" ("Obama Shi e Shiminra"). Similarly, a local liquor shop owner commented that he hoped that a chance would come to the City of Obama so that its economy would be revitalized and its community reinforced ("Hisshou Obama Shi").

Obama residents' attempt to reinvigorate the sense of community did not only take place within the city. In April 2008, the Obama Girls announced that in June they would attend the twenty-ninth Matsuri [festival] in Hawaii, an annual cultural exchange event focusing on dancing and singing. Ms. Oe, the leader of the group, explained that the trip was organized to enhance the sense of community pride and to establish an inter-community tie with Honolulu. Earlier in the month, the city had already sent an official mayoral letter to Mayor Mufi Hannemann of Honolulu expressing its wish to become sister cities ("Honolulu"). Mayor Murakami expressed his wish by stating, "I hope we will be able to let the city and the idea of education through good eating habits be known widely in the world" ("Etsuzanjakusui"). Obama for Obama's plans to involve Hawaii in its activities, as well as to forge relations with other cities and tourist locations within Japan that bore the name "Obama," were manifestations of their strategy to revitalize the city. While the group seemed to simply cheer for the presidential candidate, analyzing the types of activities that it engaged in and examining what its members sought to achieve reveals that their support of the political campaign was far from the primary drive of their enthusiasm.

It was not only Honolulu with which Obama tried or was able to establish a friendly tie. (Mr. Lynn Caldwell, a former principal of Eckstein Middle School in Seattle, Washington, sent a letter to the City of Obama in March 2008. The middle school and Otoku Middle School in a neighboring prefecture of Ishikawa had been sister schools since the early 1990s and had promoted mutual exchange programs for over fifteen years. Hearing about the Obama for Obama activities, Mr. Caldwell decided to ask his friend in Japan to forward him the letter that expressed his gratitude in promoting international understanding at a local level ("Kanazawa no Doi San ni"; "Bei kara"; "Bei Seattle"; "Kanazawa no Doi San").

The promotional effect of the Obama for Obama movement was immense. Within two months of the founding of the fan club, over 150 media outlets had visited the city to interview members of the club and city residents and to feature programs and articles on the local support of Obama. Between February 4 and March 9, 2008, news programs on six major domestic television channels in Tokyo alone featured Obama for Obama for over four hours and twenty-five minutes. The number was exponentially larger when the analysis included non-news programs, programs aired outside of Tokyo, and channels available via cable or satellite. Based on the price charged by each broadcasting company for a fifteen-second commercial, Nihon Monitor, a research firm specializing in television audience surveys, estimated that the advertisement impact for those thirty-five days in Tokyo alone was at least 4 billion yen. The number for all television appearances was estimated to be worth at least 8 billion yen ("Obama Shi Koukoku"). The then mayor of the city, Mr. Murakami, told the Agence France-Presse that Barack Obama had "an excellent advertisement effect" ("Kaigai").

Merchandizing was also a major part of the City of Obama's promotional efforts via the iconic role of Barack Obama. But such an idea of using the American presidential candidate's name to promote its products was nothing new. Chikusui Canycom, a Japanese manufacturer of agricultural tractors, had named its products after several major political figures. One of their bush trimmer models is called "Bush Cutter George" and another "Bush Cutter George Jr." Chikusui's wheeled carrier is called "Hillary." The City of Obama emulated this promotional strategy. Its residents witnessed various types of

Obama merchandise. Obama for Obama designed a logo that was shared — sometimes for free and other times for purchase — with members of the club as well as with residents of and visitors to the city. For this image, the fan club underwent an elaborate process of obtaining the rights to reproduce and of controlling the rights to use the logo that featured the caricature. The immediate purpose of the use of the Obama caricatures was promotion of the products. Concurrently, there continued to exist an undercurrent of residents' hope to revitalize their city's economy by reinvigorating small-scale stores that were the backbone of the city's business economy.

Much of the Obama merchandise features local food specialties. *Obama Kaiseki*, or the Obama dinner menu, includes crab meat, mackerel, and other locally fished seafood. The dinner was packaged with an overnight stay at the Sekumiya Hotel, Mr. Fujihara's property, for 12,000 yen (Sekumiya). Obama Sea Foods Corporation developed Obama Burgers featuring mackerel and sea bream meat sandwiched with lettuce between buns. Executive Den Matsumiya states, "We have made fish burgers using horse mackerel and sardines. Now it is time to make burgers with more selective fish." On a public viewing event day, Kouyouan, one of the most traditional and valued pastry shops that have supplied the Japanese imperial family with sweets, donated three hundred buns with bean-paste filling with Obama's profile branded on them. For such a prestigious store to pursue a product portfolio including what could be considered a spur-of-the-moment merchandise was a rarity. Once these buns were featured on various national and international media outlets, however, Kouyouan began to receive an unprecedented number of orders. Hideyuki Kafuku, a customer at the store, notes, "The store owner was smiling when he said, 'We did this only because we wanted to help our small city recover from its hard times'" (Kawahara; Kafuku). Shiboju, another very traditional pastry shop, launched their "Good Luck Obama Rolls" in February 2008. The cocoa-flavored rolled cake has sugar-coated chestnuts inside. The store clerks explain that the name for sugar-coated chestnuts, *kurikinton*, sounds similar to "Clinton." Cocoa-flavored dark brown cake symbolizing Obama wrapping around *kurikinton*, or Clinton, were to show Obama's victory over Hillary Clinton. The Obama roll sold three times more than regular rolls, Shiboju explained. Its president, Masahiko Shimuzu, launched a victory cake with bean paste inside. The top of the cake has a heart branded with the Japanese word for "victory" (Kawahara; Kimura).

Some of the most popular non-food items with the Obama caricature were Obama T-shirts sold for 2,000 yen, and *happi* coats. For image rights reasons, the original version of the T-shirt had the drawing of the back of the head of "someone who looks like Obama." Only fan club members were able to obtain a T-shirt with Obama's profile printed on it, after they paid 1,500 yen for their membership. Within the first ten days of sales, about 250 had been sold. A part of the revenue was saved for the downtown revitalization fund. T-shirts with Obama's front profile were given for free to Obama for Obama members as recognition of their membership. The fan club, launched by four local residents with sixteen members, had grown to over five hundred, including those who lived outside of Fukui Prefecture and even outside of Japan, by the end of March 2008 ("T-Shirts"). The original *happi* coats were distributed only to the club's executive members. Danna Goodyear of the *New Yorker* reported that Mr. Fujihara made an appointment one day to offer a *happi* coat to the city's newly elected mayor at the time, Kouji Matsuzaki (Goodyear).

In addition to these T-shirts and traditional coats, Obama City had a large portfolio of Obama merchandise that promoted the city. These examples show that merchandizing efforts did not only aim to generate profit from sales but to create a sense of community and forge closer ties among residents and those who visited or were interested in the events happening in the city. On the one hand, having products to wear allowed the sense of community or group to be forged. At public viewing events or any other fan club hosted events, dozens if not hundreds of residents and non-residents gathered dressed in the same attire. On the other hand, promoting chopsticks, fish, and other products indigenous to Obama enabled local industries to promote themselves through Obama for Obama. Although the initial intention of the club was to have fun, it nevertheless reflected the city's serious concerns about its future, which the fan club successfully addressed through its activities.

## *Discontents and Reaffirmation of City Identity*

While many supported the fan club's activities, others voiced their concerns or dissatisfaction about Obama for Obama's "infatuation" with the presidential candidate. Disagreement was heard both inside and outside of the city. Some argued that members of the fan club did not know enough to be able to support Obama as a candidate for the American presidency. Some others claimed that the pursuit of fun contradicted the traditional values preserved in the city. Others simply did not share the fan club's excitement. Following the public viewing event on March 5, 2008, city hall received over fifty phone calls and e-mails, in addition to ten letters the following week. City officials explained that half of the correspondences were supportive whereas the other half were critical ("Shi e Sampi"). Yoshikazu Takagi, a seventy-three-year-old resident of Kyoto, wrote,

I understand that many municipalities seek various ways to activate their economy in the midst of economic downturns. I also understand that some cities are desperate. But isn't it too much to promote a city by taking advantage of the presidential election? It was not just residents of the city but even the Mayor of Obama was elated when he received a letter back from him [Takagi].

Criticism against Obama for Obama in general questioned the appropriateness of using the presidential election, an event whose outcome would doubtlessly affect Japan heavily. Mariko Takahashi, a fifty-six-year-old resident of Nagoya, wrote, "I feel [people in Obama] are overly and simplistically celebrating [Obama's candidacy] without acknowledging our life and happiness could be affected by who becomes the president" (Takahashi, "Koe").

Hisao Akao, however, was confident that Obama for Obama activities were meaningful. On the one hand, he acknowledged that "[since we have not lived in the U.S.] we have never experienced great history and environment and problems that the country has. We are not able to identify ourselves with the problems that American people are experiencing.... We have not had enough time to educate ourselves to support or not support other presidential candidates." On the other hand, he explained, "just as you would be touched when you read a book or meet someone, we empathized with Mr. Obama as a model leader of our grassroots work and decided to support him." Akao refutes that it is just an infatuation.

> By watching news programs and reading books, we have empathized and been impressed with Mr. Obama's achievements and struggles as a community organizer and a community leader. Now that our supporting activities have become well known, many of you might feel we are just having a good time. But "to have fun" and "to be jovial" are significantly motivating when it comes to establishing communities. While we value our forums where we can sincerely discuss what to do with our community, we also cherish the passion that Americans have displayed during this election season [Akao, "Obama Kouho," 3].

Similarly, Mr. Fujihara commented, "I think what we offer is something that you can smile just by looking at. I hope this will allow the City of Obama to be well known in Japan" ("Ouen Moeru"). Obama for Obama represented the inner voice and passion of the residents of the city. Its policy document explains that its activities did not force, drive, or encourage the people of Obama to express themselves at the public viewing on Super Tuesday or at other events. It claims that the organization simply offers a place where the repressed feelings of residents explode by finding a figure who can connect their passions for change and for tradition. The document concludes that this apolitical movement is to connect the city to the world and the world to the city in hopes that residents of Obama will feel their hometown to be their true home (Obama for Obama).

Kazumi Akao, a clay doll designer living in Kanagaza Prefecture, south of Tokyo, epitomizes such sentiments. She attended the second public viewing event which took place on April 23, 2008. Traveling from Kanagawa, she brought a Barack Obama doll that featured a big smile and a thumb-up. To a journalist from a local newspaper agency, she commented, "I seldom come back to Obama. But this time, I felt I had to come back and cheer with others in the city" (Shiroyama).

Obama for Obama indeed had a positive impact on the city's economy. Without doubt it immediately raised general interests in the City of Obama. Its official municipal website, which had usually received about 20,000 visitors a month, had over 50,000 visitors in February 2008. Mr. Fujihara explained, "By using the internet, we can share information with many people." The website of the fan club which contains a link to the municipal website received as many as 3,000 visitors in early 2008 ("Ouen Moeru"). Ken Hirai, a local store owner, notes that there are more people near the Obama train station. Seiwa, a major lacquer chopstick store, now limits the number of chopsticks that each customer can purchase to meet the demands of as many customers as possible. Its president mentioned that demand exceeded the maximum production capacity of the company (Murakoshi). At the end of March, a new store, Wakasaya, opened in the city's shopping district. Although it is open only from Friday to Monday, many tourists stop by to purchase Obama merchandise and other local specialties. From Obama T-shirts to "I Love Obama" headbands, to *happi* coats, the store is an example of the local revitalization process and of the attempt to sustain the growth. In its new branch location, chopsticks with a printed Obama logo, Obama burgers, and other products will be sold. On some days, as many as fifty sets of chopsticks are sold at the branch location. It will also serve as the main office for the fan club where new members can register themselves and receive their member T-shirts ("Obama Miyage"; Takahashi, "Wakasaya"). Both stores opened in empty spaces in a shopping district. Although there remain about ninety stores in the district, the number of empty storefronts continues to increase, due mostly to the lack of a younger generation to carry on the businesses. The main store was located in an old cell phone store. The branch location was in an empty lot in Tsubaki Kairo, a commercial building that is a part of the city redevelopment project. Hiroaki Kinoshita, the president of the local merchants' organization stated, "I hope these stores will help tourists feel welcomed and also help the downtown area be stimulated" ("Aki Tempo").

These examples show that despite numerous cases of resistance and doubt concerning the activities of Obama for Obama, the fan club was able to achieve its goal and attract wide support. Mr. Fujihara was quoted in an interview on *Real Time* on February 5, 2008, as saying, "I hope Mr. Obama will do well for the City of Obama." Observing the trend in tourism in Obama, he later commented to Takebayashi that since March 2008, there was a 15 percent increase in the number of tourists visiting the city (Fujihara to Takebayashi). Events have brought together local community members and successfully welcomed visitors and journalists both from Japan and from abroad.

## Conclusion: The Future

The victory of Obama at the end of the election in November 2008 was a major shift for Obama for Obama. Residents of Obama and media totaling approximately two hundred people marked the election on November 4. They gathered at the community center at noon on November 5 to watch the election outcome together as they had done before. Later on the same day, Obama for Obama hosted a celebration gathering with around four hundred participants, including the Kenyan ambassador to Japan, Denis Awoli. The gathering was titled "A Big Party Regardless of the Election Outcome!" This name alone suggests that celebration of victory was not necessarily the main purpose of the gathering. It was to commemorate the over half-a-year-long process of community organizing and development. It was an event where, one of the residents commented, "the task was how to turn our enthusiasm about President-Elect into the stimulation of our city" (Iwamoto; "Itsuka").

The end of the elections signaled a major shift in the raison d'être of Obama for Obama, from an organization supporting a presidential candidate to one supporting a leader whose idealism the group members shared. With approximately 1,800 club members, Obama for Obama continued to cheer for Obama but also continued to pay attention to global peace, friendship across the Pacific, cultural understanding, and other grassroots community activities. In his letter addressed to Mr. Fujihara and Mr. Tamagawa, Mr. Akao stated, "Now that we know Mr. Obama will be the president, we must clearly restate the purpose of our organization. What should we do next?" (Akao to Fujihara).

On January 20, 2009, Obama City once again became the locus of international understanding through President Obama. Although Obama for Obama members initially planned to attend the inauguration in Washington, D.C., they decided to postpone their trip due to security concerns. Instead, they held an event that involved all the temples, shrines, churches, and other religious and faith-based organizations. Over one hundred media representatives from fifty agencies reported in total on nine temples and churches ringing their bells seven times, the number of oceans on the earth, wishing for global peace across oceans. At Haga Temple, where one of the core members of the group Mr. Tamagawa works, over two hundred residents gathered late in the evening to participate in the event. Mr. Fujihara greeted Obama residents by saying, "In Obama, we have a long history of welcoming and understanding differences. The new American President also shares the same value. I hope he will realize a more peaceful world and we will at the same time work hard for the same objective" (Ikegami; "Daibutai"). Although an official recognition by President Obama did not happen until November 14, 2009, during his visit to Tokyo in which he stated, "I could not have come here without sending my greetings and gratitude to the citizens of Obama," it was evident to Fujihara and his group's activities that residents saw a similar sense of values in Obama and tried to revitalize their city by emulating the new president (White House).

## References

Akao, Hisao. Letter to Seiji Fujihara and Shouryu Tamagawa. January 14, 2009.
_____. "Obama Kouho wo Katte ni Ouen suru Kai [Obama for Obama]." The City of Obama.
"Aki Tempo ni Miyagemono Ten [Souvenir Shops in Empty Store Space]." *Yomiuri Shimbun* April 9, 2008.
"Backing Barack." *The Daily Yomiuri*, March 6, 2008.
"Bei kara [From the United States]." *Nikkan Kenmin Fukui*, March 11, 2008.
"Bei Seattle [From Seattle, U.S.]." *Hokuriku Chunichi Shimbun*, March 11, 2008.
City of Obama. Obama Shi Toukei Sho [City of Obama Statistical Report]. Obama, Fukui, 2007.
"Daibutai [A Big Event]." *Fukui Shimbun*, January 21, 2009.
"Etsuzanjakusui." *Fukui Shimbun*, March 2, 2008.
Fujihara, Seiji. Letter to Akira Takebayashi. Nov. 15, 2008
_____. "Re: Obama Daitouryou Kouho ni Tsuite [Regarding Presidential Candidate Obama]." E-mail to Yuya Kiuchi, March 11, 2008.
"Fukui no Jimoto [Local Community in Fukui]." *News Real Time*. NTV, Tokyo. February 5, 2008.
"Fukui Obama Shi ni Shuzai ga Sattou [Influx of Media in the City of Obama, Fukui]." *Nikkei Shimbun*, February 15, 2008.
Goodyear, Dana. "Postcard from Japan: Campaign '08 Abroad." *New Yorker*, October 20, 2008, 32–33.
"Hawai'i de Obama PR [Promoting Obama in Hawai'i]." *Fukui Shimbun*, April 19, 2008.
"Hinkaku to Seizitsusa Kanjiru [I Sensed His Gracefulness and Sincerity]." *Sankei Shimbun*, March 5, 2008.
"Hisshou Obama Atsui Kouru [Passionate Message for the Victory of Obama]." *Asahi Shimbun*, March 6, 2008.
"Hisshou Obama Shi [For Mr. Obama's Victory]." *Asahi Shimbun*, March 5, 2008, evening ed.
"Honolulu Shi ni Shinsho [Letter to the City of Honolulu]." *Fukui Shimbun*, April 12, 2008.
Ikegami, Hiroyuki. "Heiwa Rinen [Peace Principle]." *Fukui Chunichi Shimbun*, January 12, 2009.
Ito, Ryuhei. "Ouen no Wa DonDon [Expanding Circle of Support]." *Nikkan Kenmin Fukui*, March 6, 2008.
"Itsuka Kennai Houmon wo [One Day We Hope He Will Visit Us]." *Yomiuri Shimbun*, November 6, 2008.

Iwamoto, Asato. "Obama ni Yes We Can [Yes We Can in Obama]." *Yomiuri Shimbun*, November, 6 2008.
Kafuku, Hideyuki. "Obama Manju [Obama Buns]." *Kouyouan*. http://www4.ocn.ne.jp/~kou youan/obaman-nankun-5.html (accessed October 5, 2009).
"Kaigai Media Zokuzoku [Many Foreign Media]." *Asahi Shimbun*, February 16, 2008.
"Kanazawa no Doi San [Mr. Doi from Kanazawa]." *Hokkoku Shimbun*, March 11, 2008.
"Kanazawa no Doi San ni [To Mr. Doi in Kanazawa]." *Hokkoku Shimbun*, March 10, 2008.
"Kansha Shiteimasu [We Are Grateful to You]." *Yomiuri Shimbun*, March 16, 2008.
Katsura, Bunchin. "Hanamizake wa Kanbai [Liquor for Cherry Blossom Watching Is Sold Out]." *Kobe Shimbun*, March 19, 2008, evening ed.
Kawahara, Kazuo. "Obama to Obama [Obama and Obama]." *Aimikku* 28, no. 3 (2008): 13.
Keimura, Junichiro. "Obama Shi e no Tegami [Letter to Obama City]." *Asahi Shimbun*, March 7, 2008, evening ed.
Kimura, Keiko. "Obama wa Choushi ni Norisugi? [Excessive Playfulness in Obama?]" *Aera*, March 17, 2008, 70.
"Kouryu ni Obama Shichou Egao [Smiling Mayor for Interaction]." *Yomiuri Shimbun*, March 5, 2008.
Murakoshi, Yasuji. "Nuribashi Nado Kouka [Impact on Lacquer Chopsticks and Other Products]." *Nihon Keizai Shimbun*, March 29, 2008.
"Obama e Obama Shi Reijou [Reply from Obama to Obama]." *Mainichi Shimbun*, March 4, 2008, evening ed.
Obama for Obama. *Kiyaku [Policy]*. The City of Obama, 2008.
"Obama Gets Letter from Obama." *Daily Yomiuri*, March 5, 2008
"Obama Giin Obama Shi e Reijou [Thank You Letter from Senator Obama to Obama City]." *Hokuriku Chunichi Shimbun*, March 4, 2008, evening ed.
"Obama Miyage Matomete Hasshin [All Obama Souvenirs Can Be Found Here]." *Fukui Shimbun*, March 29, 2008.
"Obama ni Kugiduke [Nailed to Obama]." *Sankei Shimbun*, March 20, 2008.
"Obama Sends Thank-You Letter to Obama (City)." *Herald Tribune Asahi*, March 5, 2008.
"Obama Shi e Shiminra Atsui Seien [Residents' Enthusiastic Support for Obama]." *Naigai Times*, March 3, 2008.
"Obama Shi Gorieki Kitai Shite [You Will Have Good Luck, Mr. Obama]." *Fukui Shimbun*, March 4, 2008.
"Obama Shi Haiboku [Loss of Mr. Obama]." *Zoom-In Super*. NTV, Tokyo. March 10, 2008.
"Obama Shi kara Henshin Todoita [Answer Came Back from Mr. Obama]." *Asahi Shimbun*, March 4, 2008, evening ed.
"Obama Shi kara Obama Shi e Tegami [A Letter from Mr. Obama to Obama City]." *Yomiuri Shimbun*, March 5, 2008.
"Obama Shi Koukoku Kouka 40 Oku Yen [Mr. Obama's Advertisement Effect Is 4 Billion Yen]." *Asahi Shimbun*, April 3, 2008.
"Obama Shi no Obama Shi Ouen [Obama City's Cheering for Mr. Obama]." *Yomiuri Shimbun*, March 2, 2008.
"Obama Shi no Ouen Arigatou [Thank You for Your Support from Obama City]." *Tokyo Shimbun*, March 4, 2008, evening ed.
"Obama Shi Ouen Obama Shi wo Sekai Chukei [Live in the World: Obama City Supporting Mr. Obama]." *Yomiuri Shimbun*, March 5, 2008, evening ed.
"Obama Shi wo Nice Town [Obama City Is a Nice Town]." *Sports Houchi*, March 4, 2008.
"Obama to Bei Kouryu Hirogatte [Expansion of Interaction between Obama and the U.S.]." *Yomiuri Shimbun*, February 22, 2008.
*Ojamattere*. FBC, Fukui. July 5, 2008.
Ono, Takaaki. "Fukui Dayori [A Note from Fukui]." *Yomiuri Shimbun*, April 21, 2008.
"Ouen Moeru [Heated Cheering]." *Nikkan Kenmin Fukui*, March 4, 2008.
"Route." *Fukui Shimbun*, March 7, 2008.
Sekumiya. "Obama Kaiseki Plan [Obama Menu Plan]." https://asp.hotel-story.ne.jp/ver3d/

ASPP0200.asp?hidSELECTPLAN=63559&hidSELECTCOD1=20010&hidSELECTCOD2=001 (accessed October 5, 2009).

"Shi e Sampi Ryouron [Various Responses]." *Fukui Shimbun*, March 13, 2008.

Shiroyama, Izumi. "Moeagaru Obama Netsu [Heated up Passion for Obama]." *Nikkan Kenmin Fukui*, April 24, 2008.

Takagi, Yoshikazu. "Letter to the Editor." *Mainichi Shimbun*, March 26, 2008.

Takahashi, Mariko. "Koe [Voice]." *Asahi Shimbun*, March 12, 2008.

Takahashi, Takayuki. "Obama Shi kara Henrei [Reply from Mr. Obama]." *Mainichi Shimbun*, March 4, 2008, evening ed.

———. "Obama Shi Katte ni Atsuku [Heated Obama City]." *Mainichi Shimbun*, March 5, 2008, evening ed.

———. "Wakasaya Aitsugi Open [Wakasaya Stores Are Opening]." *Mainichi Shimbun*, April 9, 2008.

———. "Yori Ai wo Komete [With More Love]." *Mainichi Shimbun*, March 4, 2008, evening ed.

Tanaka, Yoshihiro, and Taro Yamazaki. "OBAMA Futtouchu [Boiling OBAMA]." *Mainichi Shimbun*, March 2, 2008.

Tosa, Naohiko, Kouji Kise, and Takuya Sumikawa. "Bei Daitouryou Sen Ayakari Rettou [How the Archipelago Is Taking Advantage of the U.S. Presidential Election]." *Asahi Shimbun*, March 5, 2008.

"T-Shirts Ninki [Popular T-Shirt]." *Yomiuri Shimbun*, March 24, 2008.

White House. "Remarks by President Barack Obama at Suntory Hall." White House. November 14, 2009.

"Zembei ni Obama no Nekki [Obama Passion Reported in the U.S.]." *Sankei Shimbun*, March 5, 2008, evening ed.

# Obama-Mania in Turkey
## Popular Culture and the Forty-Fourth President of the United States in a Secular Muslim Nation

ZAFER PARLAK AND TANFER EMIN TUNC

As a secular Muslim nation "that eludes categorization — part of Europe and Asia, but somehow not comfortable with the socially constructed label 'Eurasian'; bordered by the Mediterranean Sea, but somehow not 'Mediterranean'; contiguous with the Middle East, but not 'Middle Eastern'"— Turkey is currently engaging in its own identity negotiation. Occupying a liminal space "between their Eastern heritage and the elusive/alluring 'modernity' of the West," Turks have, for the past century, looked to the United States for both political guidance and cultural inspiration (Tunc, 131–132). Consequently, U.S. presidential elections have been of great interest to Turks. The tone of an American presidency can have a substantial impact on both the way Turkey is perceived globally and on how it assesses itself domestically. Turks' perception of the United States, on the other hand, is intimately linked to popular cultural representations of presidents, and their administrations, in the Turkish media. Turks adored Kennedy and his glamorous image, and they disliked Nixon immensely due to his inextricable identification with Vietnam. They bought into the global characterization of Reagan as an "American cowboy" who would rid the world of evil Communists, and relished Clinton for his charm, wit, and sex appeal.

During George W. Bush's administration, however, Turkey became decidedly anti–American due to disagreements over U.S. policy in Iraq. Bush's name became the equivalent of a swear word in daily parlance, and America was demonized in both the media and in popular culture (Turks even wrote novels that referred to a hypothetical future Turkish-American war). Turkish newspapers were overwrought with anti–Bush political cartoons, and some

Turks also composed anti–American protest songs — an activity which, during the golden age of Turkish-American relations in the 1950s, would have been enough to ensure years in a prison cell. As in many other countries, Obama's election to the presidency was hailed in Turkey, and almost overnight reversed negative political and cultural representations of America. Obama marked a fresh beginning in the long history of Turkish-American relations — one which, interestingly enough, transcended every socio-economic class in the country. While the political elite celebrated Obama's victory at the U.S. embassy, peasants in eastern Turkey sacrificed forty-four sheep to celebrate the election of the forty-fourth president of the United States, and even decorated their villages with Obama posters. Moreover, Turkish popular culture, which had once identified America (as represented by George W. Bush) as the source of all global problems, began looking to the United States (as represented by Barack Obama) as the potential source for a new global peace.

Turkish admiration for Obama reached a fevered pitch during his April 2009 visit to Turkey. *MediaCat*, "a Turkish media magazine, placed Obama on its front cover and even compared him to Mustafa Kemal Ataturk (1881–1938) — the founder and first president of the Republic of Turkey — in terms of his leadership and vision" (Parlak, 378; *MediaCat*, no. 17). Other outlets of popular culture also participated in the glorification of Obama. Turkish pop singer Mustafa Topaloglu composed a song entitled "Obama" (2009), whose music video was broadcast on both Turkish and American television channels (it was even shown on *Jimmy Kimmel Live*).[1] At the height of its popularity, Topaloglu performed this song, which adapts aspects of American Blues music, in front of projected images of a crying child, a missile, a world map, and a rotating globe — all suggesting America's world domination. As Topaloglu's lyrics express, Turks not only expect hope from the new president but, ambitiously, world peace.

Numerous Obama humor blogs, photomontage sites, comic strips, and countless examples of parodies, impersonators, and imitators have also flooded Turkish popular culture. Such explicit adoration and pro–American sentiment was unthinkable during the George W. Bush presidency, suggesting that Obama has been able to replace the image of the "ugly American" with an idealistic American "superhero" of African-Muslim descent who has the power to correct the ills that the Bush administration imposed on the world.[2]

Barack Obama's visit to Turkey in April 2009, which was his first trip to a predominantly Muslim country as president, was a public relations victory. The visit was so positive that newspapers allotted several pages to the story for what seemed to be weeks; at least five widely circulated humor magazines (*Uykusuz*, no. 84; *Leman*, no. 909; *Girgir*, no. 14; *Penguen*, no. 342; *Cafcaf*, no. 23) and two newsmagazines (*Turkiye Newsweek*, no. 24, and *Aksiyon*, no.

748) placed Obama on their cover pages, and several television channels broadcast the visit live. For the first time, an American president's ethnic and religious background became an obsession in the Turkish media. Newspaper headlines referred to Obama by his Muslim middle name, "Huseyin" (as it is spelled in Turkish), and endearingly called him "Our Huseyin" (Parlak, 379; "Huseyin'i Cok Sevdik," 1; "Ben Barack Huseyin Obama"). They even speculated that he secretly practices Islam ("Secret Muslim," 17; "He Is a Muslim," 7).

While countless popular-culture references to Obama exist in the United States and Europe, as this essay will illustrate, what makes the Turkish context so compelling is that the majority of the material being produced — whether in comic books, on television, in humor magazines, or in newspapers — is from a distinctly secular, Muslim, pro–Western stance, which represents a dramatic shift away from the anti–Americanism of the George W. Bush years. While the portrayals themselves range from an overt deification of Obama to depictions that speculate about the future of Turkish-American relations, they all have one aspect in common: they have inspired Turks to reassess the American Dream — both personally and politically — in light of Obama's ascendancy to the presidency. Obama's decision to come to Turkey, his speech to the Turkish Parliament, and the meeting between Obama and the Turkish prime minister Recep Tayyip Erdogan in December 2009 merely reaffirm this thesis. As Obama has repeatedly emphasized, and many Turks have taken to heart, "The United States has been enriched by Muslim Americans. Many Americans have Muslims in their family, or have lived in a Muslim-majority country — I know, because I am one of them" (Parlak, 379).[3] Turks, as a result, have embraced Obama and his message of change and mutual acceptance, and have used numerous popular culture outlets to reframe him as "one of their own."

## *Pre-Obama Turkish-American Relations: A Brief Overview*

Turkey possesses a unique global socio-cultural position due to its special geo-strategic and geo-political location, which connects not only continents but also faiths. It has a population of 73 million and boasts the seventeenth largest economy in the world. As a Western-oriented, secular, Muslim-majority country (99 percent of Turks are Muslims), Turkey's unique position as an East–West bridge endows it with the utmost importance in terms of global security, international trade and inter-cultural and inter-faith dialogue. However, Turkey is socially important not just because of its military and economic position in the world; it also plays a significant role in American foreign relations and the international reception of American culture, especially in the Middle East. As Zafer Parlak elucidates, "Turks have had over two hundred years of contact with America; first as Ottomans, and later as citizens of the Republic of Turkey. Throughout this period ... their perception of America has shifted numerous times" (359). Cold War Turkey was one of the most pro–American countries in the world, whereas today, it is, at least according to public opinion polls, one of the most anti–American. The roots of this current friction lie in the American invasion of Iraq and its outcome. With Obama's election to the presidency and his recent visit to Turkey, however, a new honeymoon era seems to have begun.

After World War II, Turkish-American relations underwent a period of rapid development as Turkey sought the United States' political and economic assistance to fight off communism. Threatened by Soviet claims on Turkey's eastern provinces and the Bosphorus region, Turkey entered the "Western camp" and played a crucial role in the containment of the Soviet Union. Turkey's inclusion in the Truman Doctrine and the Marshall Plan tied the Turkish economy to the United States. Meanwhile, the Turkish definition of patriotism also transformed from a distinct allegiance to the new republic to a pro–Americanism that was equated with anti-communism. This honeymoon era, however, resulted in Turkey's partial alienation from the Muslim world and its Arab neighbors, where leftist and anti–American tendencies were on the rise. An alliance with the U.S. also led to political and economic reform in Turkey and the institutionalization of a multi-party parliamentary system with free elections, a free market system, and the liberalization of the economy. Turkey had (and still has) the second-largest military presence in NATO, which reinforced its position in the U.S.-led Western struggle against Soviet expansionism.

What ended the Turkish-American honeymoon of the 1950s and early 1960s was America's "indifference" to the growing Cypriot question:

> Turks started to view Americans as unreliable allies, especially after the discovery of President Johnson's June 1964 letter to Turkish Prime Minister Ismet Inonu. The letter effectively blocked Turkey's ability to intervene in Cyprus as a guarantor to stop the unrest between Turkish and Greek Cypriots. Still referred to as a diplomatic atomic bomb, the letter warned Turkey not to employ American weapons in Cyprus and stated that if it did so, NATO would not protect Turkey in case of Soviet attack. When the news was leaked to the national print media, Turks became furious at what they interpreted as political blackmail, and launched anti–American protests in major cities. They started to question the wisdom of pursuing an extreme pro–American policy; thus, anti–Americanism began to take root in Turkey [Parlak 369].

Soviet anti–American propaganda and the rise of leftist movements only added fuel to Turkish anti–American sentiments, which in the 1960s and 1970s, took the form of anti–U.S. protests, songs, literature, and other expressions of popular culture such as comic books (Parlak, 369–372). However, some Turkish conservatives, nationalists and religious groups, who self-identified as patriots and friends of America, were able to resist this anti–American sentiment, mostly because they labeled those who questioned pro–Americanism as leftists and traitors who "sold out to communism."

The military coup of September 12, 1980, initiated a second honeymoon in Turkish-American relations. This honeymoon reached its peak during the Turgut Ozal era (1983–1993). Ozal, both as prime minister and as president of Turkey, adopted a stricter version of the American capitalist free enterprise system with the hope of further liberalizing the Turkish economy. Just like the Menderes administration that had sent Turkish soldiers to Korea in 1950, President Ozal gave immediate support to American troops in Operation Desert Storm (1991). The extreme pro–Americanism of Ozal was reinforced by frequent meetings with and phone calls to President George H. W. Bush, and their depiction — at least in the Turkish media — as a "couple" (one famous 1991 photograph features Bush and Ozal, both in casual attire, outside the Blue Mosque in Istanbul). After the collapse of the Soviet Union in the 1990s, Turkish popular culture reacted by portraying the U.S. as an engine of globalization and a champion of human rights, freedom, and democracy. Turkey's pro–American stance continued into the 1990s, despite allegations that the U.S. gave covert support to the PKK (the separatist Kurdish terrorist organization) for the formation of an independent Kurdish state within and around the borders of Turkey (Parlak, 372–373).

The capture of PKK leader Abdullah Ocalan in Kenya in February 1999, through alleged American help, once again made the U.S. the focus of Turkish media praise. Moreover, "President Clinton's visit to Turkish earthquake sites in October 1999 further increased America's popularity. Headlines of Turkish newspapers referred to Clinton as 'one of us' or 'like a Turk'" (Parlak, 373). Despite the sex scandal surrounding President Clinton, the Turkish media, which tends to guide popular culture, continued to portray him as a sympathetic and charismatic leader. Numerous comedy programs parodied Clinton; however, there was almost no negative portrayal of America through the persona of the president. *Hayatim*, the Turkish translation of Clinton's life story (*My Life*, 2005), which recounted his rise from poverty to the U.S. presidency, remained on the Turkish best-sellers list for weeks. "Even though the cover of the Turkish humor magazine *Leman* teased Turks who treated members of the Clinton family like deities, many younger Turks displayed a genuine reverence for the United States" (Parlak, 373–374; *Leman*, vol. 419, 1). Moreover, the children of the thousands of anti–American protesters who had shunned the U.S. in the 1960s and 1970s after the Johnson letter now regarded the nation as the "land of freedom, and sought to study and/or obtain permanent residence in America. Turkey became especially proud of being an American strategic partner in matters concerning Central Asia and the Middle East" (Parlak, 374).

During the first decade of the new millennium, Turkish-American relations became a veritable "roller-coaster ride":

> Despite its concerns about alleged American support of the PKK, Turkey entered the [2000s] as a pro–American country. As victims of terrorism themselves for more than three decades, Turks shunned the 9/11 terrorist attacks. Turkish newspapers [featured] headlines [such] as "We are all Americans." Turkey even deployed soldiers in Afghanistan to remove Al Qaeda and oust the Taliban regime. However, Turkish support in Iraq did not materialize when, on March 1, 2003, the Turkish Parliament refused the US request for permission to allow American forces to use southeastern Anatolia as a second front in the war against Iraq.... For the Bush Administration, this was proof that Turkey was an unreliable ally seeking its own material interests in Iraq.... Some Turks even [came to believe] that the [George W.] Bush Administration exploited the 9/11 attacks and the concepts of democracy and freedom [in order] to secure America's global interests in the Middle East, North Africa and Central Asia [Parlak, 375–376].

President George W. Bush's speech at the NATO summit in Istanbul in June 2004 attempted to assuage these sentiments and included the message that the U.S. was not at war with Islam. To emphasize his point, he spoke in front of Ortakoy mosque on the Bosphorus. However, his statements concerning peace, tolerance and "dialogue between civilizations" went unheard amid anti-NATO and anti–American protests all around Turkey.

During the George W. Bush administration, the United States was widely perceived by Turks as a nation that had declared a covert war against Islam. President Bush's "either you're with us or against us," "axis of evil," and "crusade" discourses served as proof of this, as did the apparent "clash of civilizations" between the Muslim and non–Muslim worlds. The invasion and division of Iraq, the looming threat of a war with Iran, and the likelihood of conflict with Syria were all regarded as a part of the Bush administration's Broader Middle East and North Africa Project, which included a remapping of the region. The map, as outlined by Ralph Peters, a retired U.S. Army colonel, introduced radical border changes to the region, which he believed would bring lasting ethnic peace and reduce tension.[4] The map, Peters claimed, would correct the ills of those drawn by European colonial powers, almost all of which ignored the ethnic and national realities of the area. However, the prospect of radical border change infuriated almost all nations in the region, as the proposed map threatened their territorial integrity and paved the way for future ethnic and religious conflicts as well as Western colonialism. Many viewed the map as a tool to destabilize the nation-states of the Middle East and to facilitate American intervention and control. Thus, it was seen as yet more proof of the Bush administration's unilateral policies and neo-conservative agenda, which had its roots in the Project for the New American Century. The map further eroded America's credibility and popularity in Turkey, and Turks responded with their own redrawn map of the United States, which divided the nation into several ethnic and religious regions.[5]

According to a report distributed by the Pew Research Center in early 2005, global anti–Americanism was at an unprecedented level after the Iraqi War began. In Turkey, where official patriotism had been equated with pro–Americanism since the end of World War II, U.S. approval ratings fell to 12 percent. Turkey, at least based on public opinion polls, emerged as one of the most anti–American countries in the world: 71 percent of Turks saw the U.S. as a potential threat to global peace and security, and more than 60 percent of Turks believed that the major motive of U.S. involvement in the region was to control Middle Eastern oil. Moreover, almost half of Turks thought that the U.S. targeted "unfriendly" Muslim countries in order to protect Israel at all costs (*Trends 2005*, 106–122). Thus in Turkey, President George W. Bush and his administrative agenda represented the source of global evil. The Bush administration failed to appreciate the value of soft power, which as most Turks will admit is longer-lasting and more palatable because it elides militarism and economic domination and plays on social and cultural exchange. Conversely, the Bush administration, which came to symbolize American hard power gone awry, became equated with hypocrisy and warmongering. The credibility of its discourses of democracy, freedom, and human rights evaporated overnight, and the U.S. lost the trust and support of its decades-old, faithful ally. For many Turks, anti–Americanism now meant patriotism.

The Turkish media maintained its suspicious approach towards the Bush administration even when Turkey and the United States seemed to see eye to eye on some issues. There were almost no positive representations of Bush in Turkish newspapers, or in popular-culture outlets such as magazines, comics, television, film, or the Internet. For many, President George W. Bush and Vice President Dick Cheney were the embodiment of evil. A photomontage site portrayed Bush as "President Evil," in reference to a popular computer game and movie, *Resident Evil*.[6] The same site also displayed another picture of Bush, behind whose transparent face loomed a map of Israel. The major Turkish humor magazines (e.g., *Penguen, Leman, Girgir, CafCaf* and *Uykusuz*) consistently placed distorted Bush caricatures on their cover pages in order to convey their deep criticism of the U.S. (e.g., *Penguen*, 2007, no. 7, 230). In one of the cartoons, Bush sarcastically asks his wife if she wants to be "liberated" like the Iraqis (*Penguen*, 2005, no. 7, 125). In another, Bush and Cheney are plotting to exploit the tsunami in Indonesia for potential U.S. military intervention (*Penguen*, 2005, no. 1, 120). In a third cartoon, Bush launches civil war in Iraq by firing off the first shot, wishing Iraqis "a pleasant and competitive civil war" (*Penguen*, 2006, no. 16). In other cartoons, he celebrates his sixtieth birthday by blowing out the flames of burning buildings in Baghdad (*Penguen*, 2006, no. 28), and wishes success to all those fighting in the Middle East (*Penguen*, 2007, no. 25, 245).

Many Turks rejoiced when an Iraqi journalist threw his shoes at President Bush in December 2008. On *Penguen*'s cover, there was a shoe with a speech balloon that played upon Neil Armstrong's immortal words: "One small step for man; one giant leap for mankind" (*Penguen*, 2008, no. 51, 326). Pictures of Abu Ghraib prison were traumatic for Turks and fueled anti–Americanism even further. After the release of the images, *Leman* dedicated one of its cover pages to the torture pictures, printing a cartoon with the caption "The Memorial of the Known Torturer." The cartoon depicted American soldiers erecting the U.S. flag, like in the famous World War II Iwo Jima image, on the naked bodies of Iraqi prisoners (*Leman*, vol. 19). A few weeks later, on another cover page, *Leman* chose to portray American consumer culture as a Trojan horse (*Leman*, vol. 22).

In addition to the Bush caricatures, there was a flood of anti–American novels, movies, and songs which portrayed Bush as "absolute evil," plotting against humanity and especially the Muslim world. Orkun Ucar's and Burak Turna's 2005 novel, *Metal Storm*, which appealed to Turks' subconscious fears, depicted Turkey's hypothetical invasion by American forces. *Metal Storm*, which sold more than half a million copies in a few weeks, triggered seven other sequels, and a flood of anti–American novels and memoirs. Hakanturk's *Turk-Amerikan Savasi* (*Turkish-American War*, 2005); Melih Meric's *Cuval Gunu 4 Temmuz* (*Fourth of July: Hood Day*, 2007); Emir Emre Dogan's *Coni'nin Mehmet Dusmanligi* (*Johnny's Animosity towards Mehmet*, 2007); and Mahir Kaynak's *Basimiza Cuval Gecirenler* (*Those Who Hooded Us*, 2006), all "warned Turks about America's covert military, political and economic goals in the Middle East" (Parlak 376–377). In the 2006 blockbuster film *Kurtlar Vadisi: Irak* (*Valley of the Wolves: Iraq*), which starred American actors Billy Zane and Gary Busey, a covert team of Turkish intelligence operatives travel to Iraq to punish Americans for abuses in the region. At least on the fictional level, the experience proved cathartic: Turks were able to see the "ugly American" being punished for his evil deeds.

## Obama Enters the Scene

According to a poll conducted by the BBC in 2007, 90 percent of Turks still disapproved of Bush's Iraq policy, and 75 percent expressed that the American military presence destabilized the Middle East.[7] The Bush administration's use of hard power in Iraq and Afghanistan had proven too costly and was on the verge of failure. Although the United States could not, and would not, abandon its global interests, it was clear that it could no longer pursue unilateral policies which would alienate the rest of the world. A radical image "makeover" seemed to be the only solution to reversing, or at least decelerating, the erosion of America's image. The U.S. needed a tabula rasa upon which it could restore its reputation as a "friendly" nation, especially within the Muslim world, where it was perceived as the enemy of Islam. Obama, in this sense, emerged as a good alternative to a Republican U.S. president for several reasons. First of all, as a Democrat, he would embody the opposite of what the neoconservative, evangelical Republicans represented. Moreover, his African American background would (at least symbolically) indicate that the U.S. had overcome racial differences and that the "American Dream" was still valid. Furthermore, a president with a Muslim father from Kenya would promote America's image as a country that was not anti–Islam. Last but not least, the looming economic crisis could not be kept at bay any longer, and radical financial measures could be adopted more easily if domestic and global markets saw a positive change in U.S. political leadership. Obama, was, according to Turks, the best choice, especially in terms of American foreign policy: he would, after all, represent a new beginning which would (theoretically) be diametrically opposed to the Bush administration.

Obama became popular in Turkey even before his election to the presidency. He was immediately regarded as an agent of change, a reformer, a guarantor of freedoms, a harbinger of a new era of peace, a promoter of dialogue, an alleged Muslim, proof of mankind's potential for good, a symbol of the American dream, and a miraculous solution to racism. "President Hope's" message of multi-lateralism and a "fresh start" appealed to millions of Turks who had felt intimidated by "President Evil's" message of war, death, exploitation and destruction. Although it was unrealistic to expect such a radical and sudden shift in American foreign policy, marginalized peoples all around the world — and Turks in particular — liked the idea of change inspired by a "superhero" American president whose father was an African Muslim.

By 2008, anti–American and anti–Bush novels focusing on hypothetical Turkish-American wars were slowly beginning to lose their popularity, while books about Obama's life and personal philosophies flew off bookstore shelves. Translations of Obama's three books (*Change We Can Believe In*; *Dreams from*

*My Father*; and *The Audacity of Hope*) were best sellers for several months. In 2009, Turkish authors also rode the coat-tails of these Obama books, writing three substantial books about "President Hope." Ahu Ozyurt's *Obama: Bir Kusursuz Firtina* (*Obama: A Perfect Storm*, 2009), which plays on the title *Metal Storm*, describes why Obama is a revolutionary and historic leader who will set an example for millions. Aytekin Gezici's *Barack Obama: Turkiye Konusmalari* (*Barack Obama: Speeches in Turkey*, 2009) includes a biography of Obama as well as translations of the speeches he gave in Turkey. Necati Ozkan's *Obama'nin Liderlik Sirlari* (*Obama's Leadership Secrets*, 2009) is a self-help book which delves into Obama's extraordinary leadership skills.

Thus it is not surprising that many Turks rejoiced when Barack Obama was elected in November 2008. To celebrate Obama's victory as the forty-fourth American president, peasants in Cavustepe, Van, which is located in eastern Turkey, sacrificed forty-four sheep in his honor. They carried posters with slogans such as "You are a true hero," "You are one of us," and "We love you." Villagers played drums and Turkish clarinets and danced. They even rubbed the blood of the sacrificed sheep on their Obama posters to protect him from the evil eye, and they decorated their homes with images of Obama in much the same way that Turks of the 1960s did with pictures of Kennedy (Parlak, 378).[8] Obama's visit to Turkey on April 6, 2009, was viewed as an opportunity to reinvigorate the long-neglected Turkish-American alliance by helping to reduce the prevailing anti–Americanism in the country. "His choice to come to Turkey, a secular Muslim nation, also suggested that America does not wage war on Islam and Muslims, but on terrorists." While in Turkey, "he reiterated America's support for Turkish membership in the European Union, called on Turkey to normalize its relations with Armenia, and quelled Turkey's concern over an independent Kurdish state in northern Iraq by pledging 'America's support against the terrorist activities of the PKK,'" thus effectively telling Turks what they wanted to hear (Parlak, 379). In his address to the Turkish Parliament, Obama also emphasized Turkey's importance as a critical ally with whom "the United States must stand together — and work together."[9]

Unlike the Bush administration, which failed to understand why the Turkish Parliament voted against participation in the initial Iraqi invasion, Obama praised Turkey's democratic decision-making process as a great achievement. Obama cited the ongoing economic crisis, extremism, the strain on energy supplies, and the proliferation of nuclear weapons as among "the unprecedented set of challenges" that both democracies confront. Moreover, unlike his predecessor's unilateral rhetoric, Obama adopted a multilateral approach based on the respect of mutual interests, as well as the use of transparent dialogue to address local and global challenges: "No one nation can confront these challenges alone, and all nations have a stake in overcoming them. That is why we must listen to one another, and seek common ground. That is why we must build on our mutual interests, and rise above our differences. We are stronger when we act together." Obama also called on Turkey to help settle regional disputes in a peaceful and constructive manner by "supporting negotiations," and he invited both Turkey and Armenia to settle old scores through "a process that works through the past in a way that is honest, open and constructive." He reiterated America's stance that the reunification of Cyprus could occur through "a bizonal and bicommunal federation," and he emphasized Turkey's constructive role as a mediator in "the goal of a lasting peace between Israel and its neighbors."[10]

Obama's visit to Turkey in April 2009 was unprecedented in terms of the warm reaction he received from the Turkish media as well as popular culture outlets. Obama images, quotes, sound bites, and iconography have proliferated through almost every aspect of Turkish popular culture, all within the span of a year. *Garanti*, a Turkish bank, used an Obamaesque actor, Michael Lamar, in its television commercials and print advertisements in order to evoke sentiments of trust which would, ideally, translate into increased investments and optimism about the global financial crisis. In the *Garanti* TV commercial, the normal programming flow is suddenly interrupted with a live broadcast from the White House. In it, "Obama" announces important news about Turkey: "I am sorry. I am truly sorry. I wish *I* could announce such an economic package. Low-interest credit, unemployment [benefits], three times [more bonus points] in supermarkets. All combined in one package. I wish *we* had; but it is a bank in Turkey. It is *Garanti*. I wish *we* had *Garanti* in America."[11] Such explicit pro–Americanism would have been impossible during the Bush presidency — if *Garanti* had attempted such satire with Bush only a year earlier, it would have undoubtedly lost many customers. The commercial was so popular that a newspaper, *Aksam*, published an interview with the "fake Obama."[12] Like *Garanti*, a Turkish underwear clothing brand, *T-Box*, also capitalized on the growing Obama-mania in Turkey by using an iconic poster of the president on billboards in Istanbul. The ad, which plays on words in both Turkish and English, translates as "Your only *hope* is T-Box."[13] Obama's face, and race, have graced everything from cell phones to ice cream and is thus impacting Turkish consumer culture as well: a Chinese cell phone company that sells products in Turkey recently used Obama in its advertisement for knockoff "Blockberry" phones.[14] Meanwhile, a Russian ice cream advertisement that was circulated on Turkish blogs depicted Obama in front of the White House with a caption that read, "The Flavor of the Week: Black in White" or "Chocolate in Vanilla," thus playing on racist political accusations that Obama is an "Oreo": black on the outside and white on the inside.[15]

Contrary to American reports that Obama is proving difficult to caricature, Peter S. Canellos claims that Turks, as with past administrations, seem to be experiencing very little difficulty (Canellos, 2009). What has changed, however, is the way in which the American president is depicted. The Obama photomontages created by popular-culture outlets (on the Internet, in comic books and in humor magazines) differ greatly from those created during the Bush administration, most of which hinted at distrust, hostility, violence and American belligerence. Those concerning Obama are relatively positive and sympathetic. Although Obama is still portrayed as the president of a global imperialistic superpower, his portrayal in political cartoons and on the cover pages of humor magazines suggest a major shift in Turkish attitudes towards the U.S.—one towards change. Obama, above all, is consistently parodied as "one of us." Obama's inoculation against swine flu and his use of a Blackberry cell phone to pray were immediately covered in Turkish newspapers (*Bugun*, July 27, 2009). Moreover, an overwhelming majority of images found on photomontage sites portray Obama dressed like Turkish stereotypes: as a devout Muslim with a prayer hat and beads standing in front of Istanbul's Blue Mosque (no doubt an allusion to his Muslim father and suspicions that he might himself be Muslim, since according to Islam, religion is patrilineal); as a poor shepherd caressing his newborn lamb; as a Black Sea folk dancer; as a singer of hymns about Baghdad; as a contestant on the Turkish version of *Deal or No Deal*; as a soccer player for the popular Turkish team Fenerbahce; as the spokesperson for "Obama-karna," a brand of Turkish pasta; as a peasant from the eastern city of Diyarbakir; as a street vendor selling Turkish kebabs; as a working-class Turk fishing in the Bosphorus; as a patron at "Bar Rock Obama"; or as a guest in a Turkish bath (incidentally, in most of these depictions, Obama is referred to as "Huseyin," not Barack).[16] *Leman* even placed an Uncle Sam–like Obama on its cover page, dressed in religious clothing, pointing his finger to the Turkish people as if chastising them into accomplishing the tasks in his long foreign policy to-do list (*Leman*, 2009, no. 15).

However, not all Turks hailed Obama's visit. Groups in different Turkish cities protested Obama on the grounds that he was in the country to promote America's imperial interests in the region, to demand more Turkish troops for Afghanistan, to pressure Turkey to open its borders with Armenia at the expense of Azerbaijan, to give concessions in Cyprus, to force the Turkish government into recognizing the ecumenical status of the Greek Orthodox Church in Turkey, to prevent further deterioration of Turkish-Israeli relations, and to secure Turkey's support in case of a military intervention in Iran. Many leftist groups labeled Obama a "black Bush," claiming that he was in Turkey to alienate the country from its neighbors and to increase its dependence on the U.S.[17] During a public protest, the Turkish communist party called Obama the new face of the "American Empire."[18] Greenpeace–Turkey used Obama's visit as an opportunity to attract attention to global warming, and several protestors even hung Obama posters from the Bosphorus Bridge asking Obama to "save the climate for peace."[19] Turkish popular culture also reflected the viewpoints of Obama's critics, with humor magazines and photomontage sites leading the way. On one of their cover pages, *Uykusuz* displayed three Turkish politicians dressed like school girls; one of them (Prime Minister Erdogan) is overjoyed because Obama has given him his phone number (*Uykusuz*, 2009, no. 15, 84). A cover from *Penguen* depicts the Obamas in their bed in the White House, with little Erdogan holding his teddy bear, asking if he can sleep with them; a box above the couple states, "Obama came ... said we could solve all our problems ... and returned" (*Penguen*, 2009, no. 15, 342). *Uykusuz* also voiced its concern over Turkey's purchase of $8 billion Patriot missile systems. On another one of its covers, Obama tries to convince Erdogan to buy American missiles, claiming "[Turkey is] surrounded by enemies" (*Uykusuz*, 2009, no. 38, 107). One photomontage site displayed an Obamaesque Turkish political candidate campaigning for mayor in front of a Middle East map dripping with blood.[20] Another depicted Obama pointing at Middle Easterners, asking for their "blood, soul, soil and oil."[21]

The Obama-Erdogan meeting on December 7, 2009, in Washington D.C., was also widely covered by the Turkish media and popular-culture outlets. At the official press conference, Obama expressed pleasure "that America can call Turkey a friend, and I'm pleased that I'm able to call Prime Minister Erdogan personally a friend."[22] Obama's calling Erdogan a friend — and allegedly a brother — became a topic of discussion in the Turkish mass media. All mainstream Turkish newspapers gave the Erdogan-Obama meeting front-page coverage, with many allotting full spreads to the visit. While leftist newspapers were suspicious about the undisclosed demands of the U.S., newspapers on the right (which tend to favor the Erdogan administration) supported the prime minister's contention that the meeting signaled the rising importance of Turkey in the international arena. However, both sides highlighted the "friendship" that has developed between the two leaders. In a political cartoon in *Sabah*, Obama is asking Erdogan, who is dressed like a cowboy, if he would like to add his name to his Facebook friends list (*Sabah*, December 9, 2009, 1). *Hurriyet* depicted the Obama-Erdogan meeting and their close friendship through a cartoon in which Erdogan asks Obama to give him the spare key to the White House ("Tartismali Nobel Obama'nin," *Hurriyet*). *Hurriyet* also referred to Turkey as an "Indispensable Partner," with Erdogan and Obama holding each other's hands ("Hayati Ortak," *Hurriyet*), while another cartoon in *Hurriyet* showed Erdogan writing on his Twitter blog, "Friends, I am now in Obama's room. He is wearing a Mickey Mouse tie" (*Hurriyet*, December 8,

2009, 1). *Posta* once again referred to the troops issue with a political cartoon depicting Uncle Sam as "Uncle Obama," this time telling a Turkish soldier, "I Want You." That Obama welcomed Erdogan with the Muslim greeting "As-Salamu Alaykum," however, was of utmost importance according to *Posta*, as it revealed Obama's sincerity and pledge to engage in dialogue with the Muslim World ("Selamun Aleykum," *Posta*). A photomontage site exploited this "Muslim brotherhood" by manipulating a poster from the popular Turkish movie *Abimm* (*Dear Elder Brother*) to portray Obama and Erdogan as two brothers wrapping their arms around each other.[23]

Obama's selection as the winner of the 2009 Nobel Peace Prize was a great surprise to Turks, many of whom considered the decision to be premature and clearly political. Almost all Turkish newspapers expressed their surprise, if not disapproval. *Cumhuriyet* referred to it as "A Controversial Nobel: Peace Prize Goes to Obama, the Warrior" (*Cumhuriyet*, December 11, 2009, 1). *Aksam* headlined, "He Defended War and Received the Nobel Peace Prize" ("Savasi Savundu, Nobel'i Aldi," *Aksam*). Meanwhile, Turkkaya Ataov stated that the Nobel "War" Prize had been given to the American people to lead them down a peaceful path.[24] *Radikal* critiqued Obama's Nobel speech with the slogan "Wars are necessary for peace" ("Obama Nobel Baris Odulu'nu"). The Turkish humor magazine *Leman* reacted to Obama's Nobel Peace Prize by placing George W. Bush on the cover, complaining that he should have won the prize since he had believed in war all along.[25]

In March 2010, Turkish-American relations became strained when, despite White House objections, the Foreign Affairs Committee of the U.S. House of Representatives passed a resolution which defined the events of 1915 in Anatolia as genocide against the Armenian population. Although the resolution was approved by a one-vote margin, Turkey blamed the Obama administration for not having done enough to prevent the outcome. Turkey's immediate reaction was to recall its ambassador from Washington and summon the U.S. ambassador in Ankara. The Turkish ambassador returned to the U.S. in early April, immediately followed by an Obama-Erdogan meeting whose undisclosed topic might have been Iran. However, relations took another turn for the worse following the May 2010 attack on the Turkish flotilla carrying humanitarian aid to the Gaza Strip. That the Obama administration did not shun the Israeli assault proved America's bias towards Israel, and hence the U.S. government's—and Obama's—unreliability as an ally. Thus, despite the euphoria in the first year of his presidency, favorable perceptions of Obama have been muted by recent events. Consequently in Turkey, just like in many other countries, Obama is no longer regarded as a savior who will change the world but rather as just another American politician with his own agenda.

While Obama has, to some extent, been able to replace the image of the "ugly American" and retains a great deal of popular support especially when compared to George W. Bush, Obama-mania in Turkey is, at least for now, in decline. The Turkish people in general continue to be guarded about the U.S., many refusing to relinquish their suspicion with respect to American motives. Even though President Obama has become a darling of the Turkish media, and was used to sell political ideology as well as everything from ice cream, to banking services, to underwear, the Obama administration's efforts, which also include high-level diplomatic visits by Hillary Clinton, have not been able to dramatically change U.S. ratings in Turkey. In a 2009 Pew Global Attitudes survey, "only fourteen percent of Turks expressed a positive view of the US," which was "the lowest rating among the twenty-five nations included in the poll."[26] Although as a public personality Obama receives high ratings, only one-third of Turks believe that Obama will "do the right thing in world affairs," which suggests that it will be a long haul back to the pro–Americanism of the Cold War years. It seems as though for now Turkey prefers to pursue international policy that prioritizes negotiations with the European Union and peaceful settlement of regional disputes without alienating the United States. Turkish-American relations will improve as long as the U.S. avoids unilateralism and promotes interaction and dialogue through the careful deployment of political diplomacy and smart power. Obama, as the new face of American values, might best serve this purpose.

## Notes

1. See Mustafa Topaloglu, "Obama, Welcome to the Presidency." Music Video. http://www.dailymotion.com/video/x8wwws_mustafa-topaloglu-obama-yep-yeni-or_music (accessed January 5, 2010).

2. Many Turkish political cartoons even depict Obama dressed in a Superman costume. The U.S. comic book industry has also capitalized upon this portrayal of Obama (who is a big Spider-Man fan). For examples, see "The Greatest Comic Book Hero: Barack Obama," http://cizgiromanokurlariplatformu.blogspot.com/2009/04/en-populer-cizgi-roman-kahraman-barack.html (accessed January 11, 2010) and "Barack Obama Shows Up in Spiderman Comic Book," http://www.wcpo.com/content/news/election/story/Barack-Obama-Shows-Up-In-Spiderman-Comic-Book/jUqHjsWr7U-5_6PZaPH7Cw.cspx (accessed January 10, 2010). For an archive of Obama depictions in American comic books, see "The Barack Obama Cartoons and Comics," http://www.cartoonistgroup.com/bysubject/subject.php?p=6&sid=54 (Accessed December 3, 2009).

3. Also see Barack Hussein Obama, "Remarks at the Turkish Grand National Assembly Complex, Ankara, Turkey, April 6, 2009," http://www.whitehouse.gov/the_press_office/Remarks-By-President-Obama-To-The-Turkish-Parliament (accessed December 20, 2009).

4. See Ralph Peters, "Blood Borders: How a Better Middle East Would Look," Armed Forces Journal, June 2006, http://www.armedforcesjournal.com/2006/06/1833899 (accessed January 13, 2010).

5. See "ABD Haritasi," http://www.24haber.com/images/news/abd_haritasi_komedi.jpg (accessed January 18, 2010).

6. See "Bush'u bobilemece," http://www.bobiler.org/monte.asp?m=78652 (accessed January 1, 2010).
7. See "Bush Dibe Vurdu," Hurriyetusa, January 23, 2007 http://www.hurriyetusa.com/haber_detay.asp?id=10670 (accessed January 11, 2010).
8. For an example, see "'You Are a True Hero': Peasant in Van Anointing Obama with Sacrificial Blood," http://galeri.milliyet.com.tr/2008/12/20Yilin_fotograflari__DHA/34.jpg (accessed January 11, 2010).
9. See Barack Hussein Obama, "Remarks at the Turkish Grand National Assembly Complex, Ankara, Turkey, April 6, 2009," http://www.whitehouse.gov/the_press_office/Remarks-By-President-Obama-To-The-Turkish-Parliament (accessed December 10, 2010).
10. Obama, Remarks at the Turkish Grand National Assembly Complex, April 6, 2009. The idea that the U.S. and Turkey can work together as partners to enact meaningful change has also been expressed in the foreign media. One example is Ilhan Tanir, "Obama's Visit May Inspire the 'Change' Turkey Itself Needs," The Daily Star (Beirut), April 3, 2009.
11. See Garanti Bankasi TV commercial. Accessed January 15, 2010: http://www.dailymotion.com/video/x811fp_garanti-ekonomik-canlandyrma-paketi_fun.
12. See "Cakma Obama'yla Konustuk." Aksam, March 29, 2009, http://www.aksam.com.tr/2009/03/30/haber/pazar/148/cakma_obama_yla_konustuk_.html (accessed January 15, 2010).
13. See T-box billboard poster, www.superpoligon.com/img/news/hope_dedik.jpg (accessed January 15, 2010).
14. See Blockberry telephones, http://www.veteknoloji.com/resimler/haberdetay/blockberry-01obama.jpg (accessed January 15, 2010).
15. See ice cream advertisement, http://casualtyofdesign.files.wordpress.com/2009/03/obama-icecream.jpg (accessed January 15, 2010).
16. All these photomontages, and many others, can be found by searching the website www.bobiler.org.
17. See "Obama Protestosu," Aksam, April 6, 2009, http://www.aksam.com.tr/2009/04/06/haber/guncel/2307/obama_protestosu.html (accessed January 15, 2010).
18. See "Istanbul ve Ankara'da Obama Protestosu," April 6, 2009, http://haber.sol.org.tr/mansetler/istanbul-ve-ankarada-obama-protestosu-haberi-12578 (accessed January 15, 2010).
19. See "Greenpeace'den Obama'ya Cagri: 'Orta Dogu'da Baris Icin Once Iklimi Kurtar,'" April 6, 2009, http://www.greenpeace.org/turkey/press/releases (accessed January 15, 2010).
20. http://kafa.bobiler.org/upload/photographs/154633536_.jpg?t=15862 (accessed January 17, 2010).
21. http://kafa.bobiler.org/upload/photographs/172343817y.jpg?t=17170 (accessed January 17, 2010).
22. Remarks by President Obama and Prime Minister Erdogan of Turkey, December 7, 2009, http://turkey.usembassy.gov/statements_120709.html (accessed January 15, 2010).
23. http://www3.bobiler.org/upload/photographs/181381594a.jpg?t=15323 (accessed January 16, 2010).
24. See Turkkaya Ataov, "Nobel 'Savas' Odulu Obama'nin" [Nobel "War" Prize goes to Obama], Turk Solu, December 16, 2009, http://www.turksolu.org/263/ataov263.htm (accessed January 15, 2010).
25. See Leman (Istanbul) No. 2009/43, October 14, 2009, http://www.medyafaresi.com/i.php?p=fl/4a6_60a7c.jpg&w=468&h=603 (accessed January 16, 2010).
26. See Richard Wike and Erin Carriere-Kretschmer, "Negative Views of US Unchanged in Turkey," Pew Global Attitudes Project, http://pewresearch.org/pubs/1429/negative-views-of-america-unchanged-in-turkey (accessed January 20, 2010).

# References

*Aksiyon* (Istanbul) No. 748, April 6, 2009.
"Ben Barack Huseyin Obama." *Turkiye Newsweek* (Istanbul) No. 24, April 12, 2009.
*Cafcaf* (Istanbul) No. 23, May 1, 2009.
Canellos, Peter S. "In a Stroke of Brilliance, Obama Defies Easy Caricature." *Boston Globe*, April 7, 2009, A2.
Clinton, Bill. *Hayatim*. Trans. Ali Cevat Akkoyunlu. Istanbul: Dogan Kitapcilik, 2005.
Dogan, Emir Emre. *Coni'nin Mehmet Dusmanligi*. Istanbul: Baslik Yayinevi, 2007.
Gezici, Aytekin. *Barack Obama: Turkiye Konusmalari*. Istanbul: Karakutu Yayinlari, 2009.
*Girgir* (Istanbul) No. 14, April, 8, 2009.
Hakanturk (Kurtulus Osman). *Turk-Amerikan Savasi*. Istanbul: Akademi TV, 2005.
"Hayati Ortak." *Hurriyet*, December 8, 2009, 1.
"He Is a Muslim." *Posta*, April 7, 2009, 7.
"Huseyin'i Cok Sevdik." *Yenigun*, April 8, 2009, 1.
Kaynak, Mahir. *Basimiza Cuval Gecirenler*. Istanbul: Truva Yayinlari, 2006.
*Kurtlar Vadisi: Irak* (2006). Dirs. Serdar Akar, Sadullah Senturk, perf. Necati Sasmaz, Billy.
*Leman* (Istanbul) Vol. 419, October 20, 1999, 1.
*Leman* (Istanbul) Vol. 19, May 7, 2004.
*Leman* (Istanbul) Vol. 22, May 28, 2004.
*Leman* (Istanbul) No. 909, April 8, 2009.
*Leman* (Istanbul) No. 2009/15, April 8, 2009.
*MediaCat* (Istanbul) No. 17, April 1, 2009.
Meric, Melih. *Cuval Gunu 4 Temmuz*. Istanbul: Basin Kulubu, 2007.
Obama, Barack. *Amerikan Ruyasini Gerceklestirmek Icin Barack Obama'nin Plani* [*Change We Can Believe In*]. Trans. Ozkan Ozdem. Istanbul: Pegasus Yayinlari, 2009.
Obama, Barack. *Babamdan Hayaller* [*Dreams from My Father*]. Trans. Zeynep Arikan and Istem Erdener. Istanbul: Pegasus Yayinlari, 2008.
Obama, Barack. *Umudun Cesareti: Amerikan Ruyasini Yeniden Canlandirmak Uzerine Dusunceler* [*The Audacity of Hope*]. Trans. Enver Gunsel and Munevver Demir Bayhan. Istanbul: Pegasus Yayinlari, 2009.
"Obama Nobel Baris Odulu'nu 'Baris Icin Savasmak Gerek' Diyerek Aldi." *Radikal*, December, 11, 2009.
Ozkan, Necati. *Obama'nin Liderlik Sirlari*. Istanbul: MediaCat Kitaplari, 2009.
Ozyurt, Ahu. *Obama: Bir Kusursuz Firtina*. Istanbul: Alfa Basim Yayim Dagitim, 2009.
Parlak, Zafer. "Perceptions of America: Pro- and Anti-Americanism in Turkish Novels, Comics, Movies, Songs and Newspapers." In *The Theme of Cultural Adaptation in American History, Literature, and Film: Cases When the Discourse Changed*, ed. Laurence Raw, Tanfer Emin Tunc, and Gulriz Buken, 359–381. Lewiston, NY: Edwin Mellen Press, 2009.
*Penguen* (Istanbul) No. 2005/1, 120, January 6, 2005.
*Penguen* (Istanbul) No. 2005/7, 125, March 10, 2005.
*Penguen* (Istanbul) No. 2006/16, April 13, 2006.
*Penguen* (Istanbul) No. 2006/28, July 6, 2006.
*Penguen* (Istanbul) No. 2007/7, 230, February 15, 2007.
*Penguen* (Istanbul) No. 2007/25, 245, June 21, 2007.
*Penguen* (Istanbul) No. 2008/51, 326, December 18, 2008.
*Penguen* (Istanbul) No. 2009/15, 342, April 9, 2009.
*Penguen* (Istanbul) No. 342, April 9, 2009.
"Savasi Savundu, Nobel'i Aldi." *Aksam*, December 11, 2009, 1.
"Secret Muslim." *Hurriyet*, April 8, 2009, 17.
"Selamun Aleykum." *Posta*, December 7, 2009, 1.
"Tartismali Nobel Obama'nin." *Hurriyet*, December 9, 2009, 1.
*Trends 2005*. Washington, D.C.: Pew Research Center, 2005, 106–112.
Tunc, Tanfer Emin. "Technologies of Consumption: The Social Semiotics of Turkish Shopping

Malls." In *Material Culture and Technology in Everyday Life: Ethnographic Approaches*, ed. Phillip Vannini, 131–143. New York: Peter Lang, 2009.

Ucar, Orkun, and Burak Turna. *Metal Firtina*. Istanbul: Timas, 2005.

*Uykusuz* (Istanbul) No. 84, April 8, 2009.

*Uykusuz* (Istanbul) No. 2009/15, 84, April 8, 2009.

*Uykusuz* (Istanbul) No. 2009/38, 107, September 17, 2009.

Zane, Ghassan Massood, and Gary Busey. DVD, Pana Film, 2007.

# France's News Media and Obama's French Popularity
## Interview with Sébastian Compagnon
NICHOLAS A. YANES

Sébastian Compagnon has been a journalist in France for close to a decade. In addition to being formally trained in the field, he possesses a master's degree from the University of Strasbourg; he has written for French papers such as *La République des Pyrénées*, *l'Eclair*, *Sud Ouest*, and *La Dépêche du Midi*. For the 2010/2011 academic year he taught French at the University of Iowa, and after finishing, he returned to working for *La République des Pyrénées*.

When France is discussed in the United States it is often seen as an abstracted liberal state which people on the Left typically lionize and conservatives usually criticize. Due to these deployments of France in U.S. discussions, and the correlation between Obama's popularity and positive press coverage, I've wanted to learn how French media outlets depict the United States for some time. Given that President Obama's popularity transcended national boundaries and became a nearly global phenomena, I felt it would be of value to this project to find out how media outlets responded to Obama's election, and if this has influenced how France's news sources describe the United States.

*Q: Before we discuss how French news media outlets responded to President Obama's election, would you discuss how people in France interact with news sources in contrast to Americans? For instance, much of American news outlets are dominated by stories dealing with celebrities and popular forms of entertainment; can the same be said for French news sources?*

A: Now that I can really compare "media diet" in both countries, I would say that, generally speaking, in Europe, it's easier to find real journalism available in mass media such as TV, radio, websites and newspapers. Of course, "infotainment" exists in France, particularly on TV talk shows. There is a "market" for celebrities' news and gossip, but law in France protects strongly private life. So we know a lot about American stars. Online, the "wall" between news and entertainment is thinner. A popular pure player like *Lepost.fr* does a lot of gossip and trash to generate traffic. It's interesting to underline that *Lepost.fr* owns *Le Monde*, the most serious newspaper in France! It's a little bit like if the *New York Times* would own TMZ.com.

*Q: Excluding stories about President Obama, how do you think French news stories typically depict the United States? There's this mind-set in many Americans that European news outlets depict the U.S. negatively. Could you shed some light on this issue? Do you believe French news outlets have an inherently anti–U.S. agenda?*

A: My opinion is that the way a foreign country is depicted in media is always wrong and stereotyped because we only hear about it because of bad things: wars, crimes, disasters, scandals. In France, we used to say that a journalist's job is not to talk about trains that are on time. So yes, when we hear about the United States in French media it's often about financial crisis, killings, guns, obesity, gangs, drugs. During the George W. Bush era, the U.S. was seen as a country only populated by ignorant cowboys, ultra-conservative people, and a very wealthy but very selfish elite. French media just forgot to focus on the other parts of America: moderate people, open-minded middle class, liberals, academics, artists, et cetera. The question is, why does French media, in a way, "love to hate" the U.S.? I believe that we see U.S. society as what can happen to us if we don't react and resist. In the French media, the word "Americanization" is always used in a negative way. It's synonymous with the uncontrolled power of money, the end of public services, junk food, standardized culture, et cetera. It's really comfortable, in my opinion, because it makes people feel that they are OK and that the problems in the world are "because of the Americans." I wouldn't say that there is an "anti–U.S. agenda" in the media outlets. I have a more "historic" theory. We mustn't forget that American and French models of society see themselves as "universal." So, in a way, French people still think that there is a "competition" between these two countries.

*Q: In regard to the 2008 elections in general, do you believe the 2008 U.S. presidential election received more press coverage in France than previous elections? Were French citizens more interested in the 2008 U.S. presidency, or were they lukewarm about the issue?*

A: Clearly, the press coverage of the 2008 elections was huge in comparison with the preceding ones. I remember that in my very local newspaper, we published a double-deck page about Americans living in France and how they were following the presidential race. On the streets in my town, I saw a car with a sticker "Obama '08: Yes We Can." Like in many countries, the end of the Bush era and the possibility for a black man to be the most powerful state man on earth were very exciting. On BFM TV, a cable news outlet, there was a daily briefing of the campaign. I think it was the first time I saw such interest in American politics in French TV. The other reason for this coverage is, I believe, the quality of the debate. After eight years of neo-conservative discourse, John McCain and Barack Obama produced a very nuanced, responsible and smart discussion. The debates were broadcasted on France 24 (a French television channel), but due to the hours of the live debates (often beginning at 3 A.M. in France), not a lot of people could watch it live.

*Q: Overall, French news outlets seemed to have fairly positive reactions to Obama winning the U.S. presidency. Was there something about Obama that appealed to the citizens of France, or would they have been excited about any liberal replacing President George Bush?*

A: Obviously, two factors were powerful: the end of the Bush presidency and the victory of a young mixed-race man elected by the Americans we love: young, creative people, minorities and non-racist Americans. It appealed to the citizens of France because the question of minorities is still a little "taboo" due to the French regime being "race blind." In France, official ethnic statistics are forbidden by law to avoid "discrimination." Obama was the "good" future French would dream of for their country: a model of a nation where you can be successful even if you're not the "standard" white.

Another factor is the huge disillusion in France just a year after Sarkozy's election in 2007. The country was ready for change, but then Sarkozy came in with a very "bling-bling" style. The first vacations he took were on a yacht lent to him by a millionaire, Vincent Bolloré. We could see photos of our new president with Ray-Ban aviators on the deck. A few months after that, he divorced his wife and then married Carla Bruni, an ex-top model. I think that "grassroots" people, and a lot of conservatives who voted for him, were shocked by this lack of class. Talking about politics, he jumped from one topic to another, announcing six laws at the same time. It seemed very messy and inappropriate to a lot of French. Obama looked, on the contrary, like a wise man, a moderate. Obama was the contrary of Sarkozy. There's a rumor saying that Sarkozy was furious and jealous when Obama won, because he knew he was losing all the attention he had in the world since his election.

*Q: One factor that contributed to Obama's popularity and positive news coverage in the United States was his use of social media. How do you think social media in France affected the way French news outlets represented Obama?*

A: In 2008, social media in France were seen as a "teenager" thing.

Obama's victory and use of social networks changed the perception "serious media" had of these tools. Since 2008, French media try to use much more social media.

But change is still difficult for "old media." They use Facebook, but to generate more traffic, not necessarily to engage more the readers. In politics, Sarkozy's government doesn't use social media. It pretended to do so with the "debate on national identity" online. But contributions against this debate, and all the hidden goals of it, were censored! I believe that social media is more a mind-set revolution than a technological one.

*Q: A significant portion of Obama's news coverage in the U.S. dealt less with his politics, and more with his impact on popular culture. For instance, there are several news stories dealing with Obama appearing in comic books or being mentioned in songs. How do you believe French media outlets dealt with this? In other words, do you feel French news outlets focused more on Obama's politics and policies, or more on his popular appeal?*

A: I think the majority of French don't really know what he represents in popular culture. I remember some rappers using his speech in Philadelphia, "A More Perfect Union," and I received a link by e-mail to watch the "Obama Girl" video on YouTube. I also remember a story in the French cultural weekly *Les Incorruptibles* talking about Obama's background, his favorite records and movies, et cetera. People in France enjoying rap, basketball games and comics were probably aware of this dimension of Obama.

*Q: Despite France's large Muslim population, there have been legal actions taken which can be seen as hostile to the Islamic faith, one example being France's president Nicolas Sarkozy declaring that the Islamic burqa is not welcomed in France. Did any French media outlets cover the false rumors which claimed Obama was secretly a Muslim? If so, did this affect how some may have viewed him?*

A: French media talk a lot about the Tea Party movement, their love to plot "conspiracy theories," et cetera. The controversy about Obama's faith and the one on the mosque in Manhattan were covered and seen as some of the radicalization of politics in the U.S. Meanwhile, in France, Sarkozy pronounced very offensive speeches against "strangers," the Gypsy minority, after a horrible "debate on national identity" and this law against the Islamic veil. Apparently, some politicians don't have a lot of ideas to address serious problems, beginning with jobs and the economy, so they distract by focusing the media's attention with easily stigmatized people. There are more than 5 million Muslims in France. It's the most important Muslim community in the West. About 98 percent are moderate, democratic and don't mix religion with politics. This law against the "burqa" is not democratic, impossible to enforce and would apply to only three thousand women. I think the way

"Islam fear" is used by politics these last months in the West is absolutely irresponsible.

*Q: Obama's election seemed to be a rare moment in which the world was excited about a U.S. presidential election to the point where we could find people mimicking his rhetoric globally. What do you think are some of the long-term effects Obama's election may have had on French news media? Given that his popularity has declined in the U.S. since his election, has his popularity equally diminished in French news outlets?*

A: Obama is a reference for the next political campaigns. Even the mayor of my hometown in France, Pau, wrote "Yes We Can" in English, on her first "greeting cards." The use of social media is having an effect. A French politician, Arnaud Montebourg, from the Socialist Party, was in the U.S. in fall 2010 to study how Democrats use the Internet.

Obama's message of unity is universal, maybe too vague, some would say. I think there is a misunderstanding because some on the left wing believed Obama was a "revolutionary." To me, he is deeply a centrist. He never says "no" or "yes" but "Let's move forward." Sometimes it's very annoying and inefficient and it creates a lot of disillusion. Some columnists in France are very harsh with him. They criticize his "spinelessness" and his "lack of courage." But at the same time, we know in France that the "big mouth" and poseurs don't equal actions.

# Conclusion
## What Happened to Obama-Mania?
### Nicholas Yanes

When I first thought of this project I was visiting my family in Florida during the winter break of the 2008/2009 academic year. With Obama's election a month in the past and his inauguration a month away, all forms of entertainment were featuring references to Obama as a means to not only profit off his popularity, but (for most of these items at least) to continue the process of galvanizing Obama's supporters. Now, a little under two years later, I'm writing my concluding thoughts about this project and where Obama is now in relation to popular culture, and I find myself thinking, "What happened to Obama-mania?" Presidential campaigns have been a source of material for popular entertainment for decades, but the 2008 campaign seemed to energize creators of mass entertainment and their audiences in an unprecedented fashion. Even when acknowledging that popular entertainment has treated elections as source material, Barack Obama still stood out. Part of his early popularity clearly stemmed from the fact that he was first African American to have a real chance of winning his party's nomination and was seen as a complete departure from the previous administration. Nevertheless, a significant portion of Obama's mass popularity grew out his charismatic rhetoric about the problems the United States was facing and how he could set us on a better path. Eventually, his popularity increased so much that many began to view Obama as more a pop icon than a political figure — a criticism that John McCain made in an attack ad comparing Obama to Britney Spears and Paris Hilton, an ad which itself seemed to me more like a parody of a campaign commercial than one that could do serious damage. It was this aspect of Obama's campaign strategy that not only allowed him to galvanize a broad base of supporters, but made him an ideal artifact of contemporary popular culture worth investigating.

## Barack Obama: The "Where's Waldo?" of U.S. Presidents and Popular Culture

At this point, Derrais Carter and I are both in the third year of our PhD programs, and I find myself struggling to articulate my thoughts about Obama in context with popular culture. This is not because of some absurd notion that popular entertainment has shied away from discussing the nation's forty-fourth president, but because I find that trying to think of a single approach to understanding Obama's relationship with popular culture may be ambitious, but in the end, merely a good starting point at best; a sentiment I feel is true even if (as the majority of contemporary scholarship suggest) there can be no unified approach to understanding popular culture. While there may never be a single means of deciphering why Obama resonated with so many aspects of popular culture (which is exemplified by the diversity of topics in this collection), I do view a clear break in the forty-fourth president's popularity with mass entertainment.

After all, Obama has been represented in the television series *The Family Guy* ("Excellence in Broadcasting"); *The Cleveland Show* ("Harder, Better, Faster, Browner"); *Hannah Montana* ("Hannah Montana to the Principal's Office"); *South Park* ("About Last Night..." and "The Coon"), and his inspirational qualities were invoked in *The Office* ("Scott's Tots"). Obama's likeness has also been represented in films such as the Bollywood movie *My Name Is Kahn* (2010), and he has been rendered in Ray Griggs' documentary, *I Want Your Money* (2010). Obama also inspired or has been the subject of several songs. Will.i.am used lines from Obama's New Hampshire presidential primary concession speech to create the song "Yes We Can." Obama was also the subject of "Barack the Magic Negro," a song written by Paul Shanklin and supposedly recorded for Rush Limbaugh's radio show. On a lighter note, Obama was also mentioned in Three 6 Mafia's song, "Lolli Lolli (Pop That Body)." Furthermore, Obama has not only appeared in several comic books, but his presence in one issue of Spider-Man made that publication one of the highest-selling comics of the past decade, its significance thoroughly explored in Robert G. Weiner and Shelley E. Barba's contribution to this collection. Excluding his own authored works, Obama has been the subject of several texts since his political ascendancy. These works include but are not limited to the following: Dinesh D'Souza's *The Roots of Obama's Rage*; Bob Woodward's *Obama's Wars*; Jonathan Alter's *The Promise: President Obama, Year One*; David Remnick's *The Bridge: The Life and Rise of Barack Obama*; David Limbaugh's *Crimes against Liberty: An Indictment of President Barack Obama*; Laura Ingraham's *The Obama Diaries*; Stanley Kurtz's *Radical-in-Chief: Barack Obama and the Untold Story of American Socialism*, and my personal favorite (not because I read it, but because of its title) *Obama Zombies: How the Liberal Machine Brainwashed My Generation* by Jason Mattera. This list of books was compiled merely by typing "Obama" into Amazon.com's search engine and seeing what was found; and while there are several more texts which specifically address Obama in their titles, there are far more books being published that discuss Obama without specifically mentioning him in the title. Additionally, there is even an online video game starring Barack Obama called *Super Obama World*. Styled after the classic *Super Mario Bros.* games, *Super Obama World* is "set in Sarah Palin's home state of Alaska, you control President-elect Barack Obama as you battle pigs and pit bulls with lipstick, hockey moms, Russian soldiers, greedy oil-company executives, and Sarah Palin herself" (*Super Obama World*).

While Obama's appearance in all of these cultural artifacts reflects that the vast majority of the population knows that Barack Obama is the president of the United States, the diverse meanings layered onto Obama (significant examples of these meanings ranging from him being depicted as a savior to him being viewed as the harbinger of communism) points to a significant problem facing popular culture scholars and Obama at the time this is being written — this problem being what is "popular culture" when the media consumed by Americans is so varied and fragmented that no one form of entertainment is regularly enjoyed by the majority of the nation?

## What Happened to American Popular Culture?

At this point a trained academic will assume that I'll begin to cite scholars such as Stuart Hall, Ray B. Browne, Andrew Ross, Marshall McLuhan, Pierre Bourdieu, Umberto Eco, Jean-Francois Lyotard, or Jean Baudrillard to examine Barack Obama and popular culture. Instead, I find it far more useful to look to Stephen Colbert for assistance. On August 22, 2006, Stephen Colbert began his show, *The Colbert Report,* by showing the audience a *scrapbook* from his childhood which he used to document the nation-uniting commercials that touched his heart; one of these commercials being Dunkin' Donuts' "Time to Make the Doughnuts" campaign from the 1980s. Distraught by the lack of advertisement unity, Colbert states,

> It's not just advertising where the center cannot hold — it's all across the pop-culture landscape. There's no one band we all love. There's no one newsmen that we can trust/believe is a subversive. There's not even one computer game where when the nation closes its eyes they still see the shapes falling [a reference to Tetris]. Where is America's cultural cohesiveness? Where's the common experience? ... Well, in order to unify us as a people, tonight I've decided on the commercial that will now

define us as a nation [*The Colbert Report*, "American Pop Culture: It's Crumbelievable — Intro"].

The commercial selected was for Kraft's Crumbles, a cheese product which the commercial claimed was not only good, but "Crumbelievable." This slogan became the focus of his show that night because as Colbert claimed, "That's not just a commercial for cheese that hits the spot when shredded cheese is just too shredded, and a block of cheese is just too blocky. It's also a perfect metaphor for the state of our pop culture, crumbled into little pieces" ("American Pop Culture: It's Crumbelievable — Pop Culture Icons"). So while American popular culture is mostly made up of the same stuff, its *crumbly* nature has allowed for mass-culture artifacts to be created that mostly exist isolated from other popular narratives and items.

Colbert further buttresses this argument in his analysis of cable television's potential effect on families and, in turn, the nation. Addressing the viewer, Colbert claims,

> We have a problem. And if you're watching TV right now — and most of you are — you're a part of the problem, especially if you're watching TV alone. You see, we don't gather around the TV like we used to. There is no one thing we all experience together. For instance, we all remember where we were when Kennedy was shot, but nobody shoots Kennedy anymore ["American Pop Culture: It's Crumbelievable — Cable TV vs. The American Family"].

Colbert makes his point clear when he shows that in the 1950s 62 percent of Americans watched *I Love Lucy*, while in the 1980s the highest-rated show, *The Cosby Show*, was only watched by 51 percent of the country. Fast-forward to 2005, and the nation's most-watched television program, *CSI*, was only watched by "a quarter of the audience." Colbert blames this decline in ratings on the rise of cable television ("American Pop Culture: It's Crumbelievable — Cable TV vs. The American Family"). With hundreds of channels on cable television — each with their own distinct focus — it can no longer be assumed that the majority of the masses will be familiar with the same television shows.

This is where Obama's uniqueness and importance as a cultural iconic stood out for me. Obama did what no other single figure could accomplish in an era of media fragmentation; he managed to gain the attention of the masses in a manner that no media figure or entity had been able to do in 2008. This is in part due to Obama's campaign surpassing Republican efforts to collect data on potential voters to better encourage them to not only vote but to volunteer for the campaign. As Mark Madden wrote for Salon.com,

> The sheer scale of the operation — because of Obama's large network of supporters and heavy emphasis on field organizing — means the data can be sliced in ways that the Bush-Cheney campaign couldn't have dreamed of in 2004. It's most likely also

more advanced than what either side did in the 2006 elections, or, for that matter, what John McCain is doing [in 2008] [Madden, "Barack Obama's Super Marketing Machine"].

Placing Madden's argument in context with presidential candidate Obama's mass-media presence, it becomes clear that what also contributed to Obama's success was not that his campaign could reach millions of people, but that it could relay a consistent narrative about the candidate and his policies. A clear example of this is that Obama's door-to-door volunteers could arm themselves with "printouts from the Obama campaign's web site which provided a side-by-side comparison between Obama's and John McCain's tax proposals for families" to show how the average American would fiscally benefit from Obama's tax plans (Stirland, "Obama's Secret Weapons: Internet, Databases and Psychology"). On top of this, Obama launched a website, *Fight the Smears*, designed to counter attacks against Obama designed to make people think that he was not born an American citizen, that he associates with terrorists, or that he is a Muslim instead of a Christian (*Fight the Smears*). Yet, even the best example of Obama's presidential campaign dominating mass media hints towards the narrative fragmentation surrounding President Obama's first years in office. I am fully aware that Obama was able to galvanize a large portion of the U.S. population with his landmark television special, *American Stories, American Solutions*, which was watched by over 30 million viewers — these viewers being far from a national majority (Moraes, "Obama Enter the League of Must-See TV").

Despite this audience size, how the presidential candidate managed to appear in multiple forms of media and control the narrative about himself and his policies so well is something that I still find astonishing. Obama was referenced in a multitude of cultural artifacts and different forms of entertainment, a significant example of this being that he was one of the first presidential hopefuls to make extensive use of Facebook, Twitter and other forms of social media. Yet his collected and measured personality and statements prevented people from creating a negative stereotype of Obama that could undermine his success. In contrast, the caricatures developed about others involved in the 2008 presidential race not only seemed to take on a life of their own and to seemingly control the media narrative surrounding a candidate, but also clearly impacted how audiences (and the politicians themselves) would think of them as a potential leader.

A perfect illustration of this phenomenon is Tina Fey's *Saturday Night Live* parody of Sarah Palin. Not only did Tina Fey's mockery of Palin force the actress to defend her performance by pointing out that Palin is a tough and rugged individual capable of being the center of a few jokes, but Palin herself even used one of the statements Fey made while humorously channeling

Palin, "I'm going rogue," as the main title for her biography, *Going Rogue: An American Life*. While it appears that Palin has managed to turn this comedic depiction of herself into a tool to increase her popularity, this is something Obama himself never had to significantly deal with during his campaign.

## *When Campaigning Stops and Governing Begins*

Overall, it appears that presidential candidate Obama understood something that President Obama has seemingly forgotten. This being that one cannot simple make a statement and assume that those in control of news outlets will relay the message to the masses consistently and effectively. Nor should one assume that people, even your supporters, will go out of their way to find out what you have done, what you intend to do and how it will affect them. In short, what I am struggling to understand about Obama's changing relationship with popular culture is his failure to realize that even as president he has to continue campaigning to get his message across.

This was highlighted when President Obama made a historic appearance on ABC's *The View* on July 29, 2010, when he became the first sitting U.S. president to appear on a daytime talk show. Early into this episode of *The View*, Joy Behar asked President Obama,

> You've really done a lot I think. You signed two hundred plus laws into being since you're in office. Financial reform has taken place, you got health care, you've put two women on the Supreme Court. I can go on and on about your accomplishments, and yet the right wing, through Fox News and other outlets, they seem to be hijacking the narrative. Where, on your side, is the narrative? Where is your attack dog to come out and tell the American people "Listen, this is what we did?" [*The View*].

Obama responded to this question by humorously saying, "Joy, that's your job." He goes on to say, "The one thing that does frustrate me sometimes is the sense that we shouldn't be campaigning all the time. There is a time to campaign and there is a time to govern, and what we've tried to do over the last twenty months is to govern" (*The View*). Similarly, President Obama has also been critical of the twenty-four-hour news cycle, claiming in an interview with CBS News chief Washington correspondent Bob Schieffer that

> the twenty-four-hour news cycle and cable television and blogs and all this, they focus on the most extreme elements on both sides. They can't get enough of conflict; it's catnip to the media right now. And so the easiest way to get 15 minutes of fame is to be rude to somebody. In that environment I think it makes it more difficult for us to solve the problems that the American people sent us here to solve ["Transcript: Obama on *Face the Nation*"].

The irony of these statements by President Obama is that the surge of popularity that won him the Democratic nomination and inspired the support for his campaign that got him into the White House is in part due to the twenty-four-hour news cycle. This why, in the end, the president's decision to stop working with the twenty-four-hour media is what I feel killed Obama-mania.

We now live in an age of "narrowcasting." Traditional broadcasting outlets, whether they are television or radio companies, aim at appealing to as many people as possible and have been fairly successful at accomplishing this in the past; however, this strategy is evanescing. Though there will always be something that is able to grab the attentions of the vast majority of Americans, most of us — as Stephen Colbert articulated — watch programming that fits our specific interests and gather news from outlets that appeal to our distinct politics. Devices like DVRs and websites like hulu.com not only allow people to watch programs when they want to watch them, but these technologies reinforce the notion that information a person may be interested in can be delivered in a manner that satisfies their need for instant gratification, regardless of whether it is television content that is continuously available online or messages no greater than 140 characters. This is something governmental information cannot do.

Besides the fact that few people care enough to go out of their way to thoroughly learn about proposed federal legislation, this type of information isn't easily adaptable for immediate mass-media consumption. Bills dealing with budgets or even specific laws are so long that they could take hours, if not days, to read, making these legislative documents difficult to immediately understand. And while traditional broadcasters will simply summarize proposed complex bills, people now turn to narrowcasters — those media outlets dedicated to reaching audiences with specific political leanings — to find out if something is compatible with their politics or not. Obama, however, was able to bridge the gulfs separating people by the narrowcasted streams of information they subscribed to during the campaign, creating the Obama-mania that is the subject of this text; and then he turned away from this strategy.

## *Obama's Divorce from Popular Culture*

On the June 12, 2009, episode of *Real Time with Bill Maher*, Bill Maher ended the show criticizing President Obama's continuous television appearances by stating, "Remember during the campaign when John McCain attacked Obama for acting like a celebrity, and we all laughed at the grumpy old shell-shocked fool? Well, it turns out he was right. It's getting to where you can't turn on your TV without seeing Obama" (Maher). Maher later suggested that Obama should adopt some of the characteristics of President George W. Bush so that he can finally begin to push through the policies and changes he campaigned on but had failed to accomplish. Maher finishes this monologue by saying, "I'm glad Obama is president, but the 'audacity of hope' part is over. Right now, I'm hoping for a little more audacity" (Maher). Though Maher isn't wrong, his argument is incomplete.

The reason why Obama failed to maintain the widespread support he had during the election is not because he spent his first year in office appearing on different shows, but because when he did appear on these shows he neglected to use them as a platform to continually maintain and increase his number of supporters. The average person rarely goes out of his or her way to learn what policies the U.S. president is actively working on at that moment, so while it is fantastic that Obama strove to maintain a presence in the popular mind-set, he needed to spend less time discussing his family's pet dog, telling of his daughters' first days of school, or even providing tours of the White House. Instead, he needed to be consistently communicating to the American people what reforms he was working on and why it would benefit the nation. He needed to continue campaigning for his policies, and not idealistically hoping that people would go out of their way to learn about his policies by conducting their own research, following him on Twitter or subscribing to his YouTube channel (which as of the fall of 2011 only has around 200,000 subscribers). Since he avoided communicating to the U.S. population the narrative he felt would justify his decisions, media outlets with politics antithetical to Obama's were able to take control over how and what people learned about Obama's administration by filling the void Obama left behind and bridging the distances between a variety of niche media outlets. As a result of Obama failing to campaign to the U.S. citizenry how his policies would affect them, the average American's perception of the country is out of sync with reality. The most striking example of this is a Bloomberg national poll conducted between October 24 and 26, 2010, which found that though "the Obama administration has cut taxes — largely for the middle class — by $240 billion since taking office on Jan. 20, 2009" (Przybyla & McCormick), more than half of Americans believe their federal taxes have gone up.

In the end, what has turned Obama-mania into "Obama, He Could Do Worse" is that Obama views campaigning and governing as two distinct activities that should only be conducted at certain times. However, separating campaigning and governing has only led to a division that has left President Obama exposed to consistent criticism, consequently diminishing the enthusiastic support he once had. By working on this project, I now have a better understanding of Obama's shifting relationship with popular culture and why the mania surrounding his election has evanesced during his first few years in office. In an era of continuous news cycles and millions of daily blog updates, Obama needs to campaign for his policies, not only to keep the nation informed, but more importantly, to keep his base energized. This is the challenge for President Obama's remaining term and future political leaders. As popular culture has become fragmented (or "crumbled" as Stephen Colbert would describe it), the ability to penetrate the different media outlets will only become increasingly difficult.

# References

"American Pop Culture: It's Crumbelievable!—Cable TV vs. the American Family." *The Colbert Report.* Stephen Colbert. Comedy Central. August 23, 2006. http://www.colbertnation.com/the-colbert-report-videos/73427/august-23-2006/american-pop-culture-it-s-crumbelievable-cable-tv-vs—the-american-family.

"American Pop Culture: It's Crumbelievable!—Intro." *The Colbert Report.* Stephen Colbert. Comedy Central. August 23, 2006. http://www.colbertnation.com/the-colbert-report-videos/182209/august-22-2006/american-pop-culture-it-s-crumbelievable-intro.

"American Pop Culture: It's Crumbelievable!—Pop Culture Icons." *The Colbert Report.* Stephen Colbert. Comedy Central. August 23, 2006. http://www.colbertnation.com/the-colbert-report-videos/73425/august-23-2006/american-pop-culture-it-s-crumbelievable-pop-culture-icons.

"Barack Obama Addresses Iraq, Issues of Race in Campaign." *This Week.* ABC News. June 10, 2007. http://abcnews.go.com/ThisWeek/Video/videoLogin?id=3169647.

*Fight the Smears: Learn the Truth About Barack Obama.* Organizing for America. http://fightthesmears.com (accessed June 21, 2009).

Madden, Mike. "Barack Obama' Super Marketing Machine." *Salon.com.* July 16, 2008. http://www.salon.com/news/feature/2008/07/16/obama_data.

Mooney, Alexander. "McCain Ad Compares Obama to Britney Spears, Paris Hilton." CNN.com. July 30, 2008. http://edition.cnn.com/2008/POLITICS/07/30/mccain.ad/index.html.

Moraes, Lisa de. "Obama Enter the League of Must-See TV." *Washington Post.* October 31, 2008. http://www.washingtonpost.com/wp-dyn/content/article/2008/10/30/AR2008103002536.html.

Przybyla, Heidi, and John McCormick. "Poll: Americans Don't Know Economy Expanded with Tax Cuts." *Bloomberg.* October 29, 2010. http://www.bloomberg.com/news/2010-10-29/poll-shows-americans-don-t-know-economy-expanded-with-tax-cuts.html.

*Real Time with Bill Maher.* Bill Maher. HBO. June 12, 2009. http://www.hbo.com/real-time-with-bill-maher/index.html#/real-time-with-bill-maher/episodes/0/157-episode/article/new-rule.html.

Stirland, Sarah Lai. "Obama's Secret Weapons: Internet, Databases and Psychology." *Wired.* October 29, 2008. http://www.wired.com/threatlevel/2008/10/obamas-secret-w/.

"Super Obama World." *ZenSoft.* http://www.zensoft.com/games_online_sow.html.

"This Week Transcript: Barack Obama—George Stephanopoulos' Exclusive Interview with President-Elect Barack Obama." ABCNews.com. January 11, 2009. http://abcnews.go.com/ThisWeek/Economy/story?id=6618199&page=3.

"Tina Fey on Palin Persona." *The Late Show with David Letterman.* CBS. October 18, 2008. http://www.youtube.com/watch?v=f6iC-LjhUxo&feature=fvsr.

"Transcript: Obama on *Face the Nation*—Complete Text of White House Interview with Bob Schieffer." CBSNews.com. September 20, 2009. http://www.cbsnews.com/stories/2009/09/20/ftn/main5324077.shtml.

*The View.* Television Show. ABC. July 29, 2010.

# Appendix
## A Bibliography of Obama in Comics
### NICHOLAS A. YANES

Comics, comic books, graphic novels, graphic literature, sequential art, or however you want to label it is a medium that has probably featured the most explicit and implicit references to Barack Obama. As a matter of fact, there are so many comic books featuring Obama that there is a Wikipedia page dedicated to Barack Obama in comics. What is fascinating about this Wikipedia entry (currently titled "Barack Obama in Comics) is that no other medium has an entry like this. Whether this is a result of comic book fans being more Internet savvy than music fans, or that there are simply too many references to Obama in web videos and songs to catalogue them anywhere, will be impossible to state, but the Wikipedia entry does reflect that people — whether journalists, comic book creators or fans — were deeply interested in the notion of Obama being featured with some of America's most beloved comic book characters.

Listed here are the comic books that depict Obama or another figure from the 2008 election. While some of these books will be summarized, some of them will simply be listed. The reason for this is twofold. One, some books are part of such a large continuity of stories that summarizing them adequately would lead to the creation of a full research paper. Two, some books came out before anyone even began to notice or care about 2008 presidential campaign figures appearing in comics. This led to these books being undersold at first; this is especially a problem for books that were never popular to being with. Once titles with campaign figures became a collector's item, their values increased to the point where the average consumer (and therefore, the average academic) could no longer afford copies.

## Comic Books Featuring Barack Obama

Bendis, Brian Michael (w), and Olivier Coipel (a). *Siege* #1–4. New York: Marvel Comics (December 2009–May 2010).
    *Siege* is a mini-series that concludes a story arc begun by *Avengers Dissembled*—published between 2004 to 2005 and also written by Bendis. Prior to *Siege*, an event occurred that drove the heroes underground and allowed villains (posing as heroes) to take control over the world's premiere law enforcement agency, S.H.I.E.L.D, which was temporarily named H.A.M.M.E.R. Led by the former Green Goblin, Norman Osborn, *Siege* tells the story of H.A.M.M.E.R. and other villains attacking Asgard, the home to the heroic Thor. This quickly becomes a matter of national security, and portions of this story are narrated by President Obama and his Security Council. The story concludes with the heroes winning and the recently returned Steve Rogers (the original Captain America) being appointed as head of security of the United States and de facto head of the superhero community.

Crowley, Michael, and Dan Goldman. *08: A Graphic Diary of the Campaign Trail*. New York: Three Rivers Press (January 2009).

Diggle, Andy (w), and Roberto De La Torre (a). *Thunderbolts* #128–129. New York: Marvel Comics (March–April 2009).

Espinosa, Rod (w), and Chris Allen (a). *Obama: The Comic Book*. San Antonio, TX: Antarctic Press (November 2008).

Gertler, Nat (w), and Lonny Chant (a). *Licensable BearTM* # 4. About Comics (July 2007).
    This is believed to be the first appearance of Obama in a comic book. Published before Obama became the Democratic Party's presidential candidate and while Hillary Clinton was still ahead in the polls, this issue was created before Senator Obama became the presidential contender that would be elected to the White House. Being that this title is far below the radar of most comic book consumers and that only 1,050 copies were originally printed, this book is probably the most sought-after Obama comic.

Hama, Larry (w), and Christopher Schons (a). *Barack the Barbarian*. Chicago, IL: Devil's Due Publishing (June 2009).

Hutchison, David (w)(a). *President Evil*. San Antonio, TX: Antarctic Press (July 2009).
    Similar to *Barack the Barbarian*, this graphic novel is a satire. Inspired by the movies *Evil Dead*, *Army of Darkness* and zombie films, this story features "Ba-rot" Obama joining forces with his political allies and revivals to battle Zombies; the zombie plague being the end result of the swine flu. The story also features fun twist on other political figures. For instance, John McCain is presented as the hyper muscular John McPain.

Larsen, Erik (w)(a). *Savage Dragon* #137. Berkeley, CA: Image Comics (September 2008).
    Savage Dragon, who is obviously the main character of his series, *Savage Dragon*, is a large, muscular, green male humanoid with a fin on his head. Additionally, he has a history of working as a police officer for the Chicago Police Department and being a bounty hunter. A story arc in 2004 featured him running for president, so it only made sense that the series would touch upon the 2008 election. Issue 137 only features Savage Dragon saying Obama's name after a reporter asks him who he is endorsing for president.

Larsen, Erik (w)(a). *Savage Dragon* #145. Berkeley, CA: Image Comics (February 2009).
    *Savage Dragon* #145 contains a more substantial presentation of President Obama. The issue focuses on Savage Dragon becoming a police officer again and being assigned

with protecting the president while he visits Chicago. Savage Dragon and the president share a page together as Savage Dragon says he'll do his best to protect Obama, and the president expresses faith in Dragon's ability to do so. The issue then shows President Obama giving a speech which is interrupted by an attack from a group of super villains. Though Savage Dragon's and the Secret Service's combined efforts get the president to safety, it is revealed that the attack on the president was a diversion so that other villains could pull off a robbery and not have to face a significant number of police officers.

Liefeld, Rob (w)(a). *Youngblood* #8. Berkeley, CA: Image Comics (February 2009).

*Youngblood* is a series about a superhero team that first appeared in 1987. Due to this title's popularity fluctuating so much over the years, it has been canceled and restarted several times. A new volume of *Youngblood* began in January 2008 and by issue 8 used Obama as a means to boast sales. Similar to "Spidey Meets the President: Marvel Bonus Back Up Feature," the story dealing with Obama is a backup story and has no real connection to the main narrative. Published in February 2009, this minor six-page story features President Obama using his authority to create a new Youngblood team lineup. While the use of Obama in this may have temporarily increased sales, it was short-lived being that no new issues have been published since May 2009.

Lobdell, Scott (w), and Paulo Henrique (a). *The Hardy Boys* #16, "Shhhhhh!" New York: Papercutz (January 2009).

Written by longtime X-Men scribe, Scott Lobdell, this issue reveals that Joe and Frank Hardy's mother—Lana Hardy—is a librarian, and this story finds her introduced to President Obama. This story also includes portions of Obama's 2005 keynote speech to the American Library Association's Annual Conference in 2005. While the main plot of the story is another generic Hardy Boys mystery, the subplot involving Lana Hardy and President Obama emphasizes the importance of libraries.

Mariotte, Jeff (w), Tom Morgan (a), and J. Scott Campbell (c). *Barack Obama: The Comic Book Biography*. San Diego, CA: IDW Publishing (October 2008).

Mariotte, Jeff (w), Tom Morgan (a), and J. Scott Campbell (c). *Presidential Material: Barack Obama*. San Diego, CA: IDW Publishing (October 2008).

Morrison, Grant (w), and Doug Mahnke (a). *Final Crisis* #7. New York: DC Comics (March 2009).

Considered the ultimate crossover story, *Final Crisis* touches upon almost every aspect of DC Comics' seventy-year history. The main plot deals with the villain Darkseid conquering Earth and attempting to destroy reality. To assist Superman, another character gathers alternate Supermen from different realities. It is revealed that on one alternate Earth, Superman is an African American, and his secret identity is President Barack Obama. While Obama/Superman only appeared in a few pages, it is clear that his presence is not only a reflection of Obama jokingly claiming to be Superman during the 2008 annual Alfred E. Smith Memorial Dinner, but it also touches upon the hope and expectations placed on Obama.

Powers, Mark (w)(a). *Drafted: 100 Days*. Chicago, IL: Devil's Due Publishing (June 2009).

An inter-galactic war is being waged, and in the early twenty-first century, humanity is drafted by one side to become soldiers in this battle. While not part of the main narrative, this issue is a standalone story that takes place after the first wave of aliens have been defeated. It follows Senator Obama as he is conscripted to a construction unit to rebuild the recently destroyed city of Chicago.

Serrano, Elliott (w), and Ariel Rey Padilla (a). *Army of Darkness: Ash Saves Obama*. Vancouver, WA: Bluewater Productions (September 2009).

Ward, Chris (w), and Azim Akberali (a). *Political Power: Barack Obama*. Vancouver, WA: Bluewater Productions (September 2009).

Wells, Zeb (w), Todd Nauck (a), and Frank D'Armata (a). "Spidey Meets the President: Marvel Bonus Back Up Feature." Amazing Spider-Man #583. New York: Marvel (March 2009).

> For a thorough analysis of this issue, please see Robert Weiner and Shelley Barba's contribution to this book, "Obama and Spider-Man: A Meta-data Media Analysis of an Unlikely Pairing"

## Comic Books Featuring Others from the 2008 Presidential Election

Bailey, Neal (w), and Ryan Howe (a). *Female Force: Michelle Obama*. Vancouver, WA: Bluewater Productions (April 2009).

Bailey, Neal (w), and Ryan Howe (a). *Female Force: Hillary Clinton*. Vancouver, WA: Bluewater Productions (April 2009).

Bailey, Neal (w), and Ryan Howe (a). *Female Force: Sarah Palin*. Vancouver, WA: Bluewater Productions (April 2009).

> This title is part of Bluewater Productions' desire to produce a line of comics dedicated to significant female political figures. What makes this title interesting is that Neal Bailey, the writer, places in the issue a mini-essay about media bias and clearly states his liberal leanings. Despite Bailey's liberal leanings, this issue provides a decent, but rushed, overview of Palin's career. The sense that this narrative is quickly run through is of no fault of Bailey's, but is due to the reality that it is only thirty-two pages long.

Bailey, Neal (w), and Ryan Howe (a). *Female Force: Hillary Clinton*. Vancouver, WA: Bluewater Productions (April 2009).

Dunn, Joe (w), Fred Perry (w), Brian Denham (w), and Ben Dunn (a). *Sarah Palin vs. the World*. San Antonio, TX: Antarctic Press (January 2011).

> In the process of reducing complicated information and personalities into sound bites, people are often reduced to caricatures. One caricature created during the 2008 elections that has continued to resonate with comic book fans and the public in general is Sarah Palin's. This issue is clearly inspired by the *Scott Pilgrim* manga series by Bryan O'Malley. In this series, which was the source of the movie *Scott Pilgrim vs. the World*, Scott Pilgrim has to combat and defeat the Evil Exes in order to date Ramona, the girl of his dreams. *Sarah Palin vs. the World* follows a similar structure in that she must defeat opponents in order to get her dream job. This comic also mimics *Scott Pilgrim*'s stylistic deployment of video-game iconography. According to Antarctic Press' summary for this book, the opponents range "from career politicos to 'gotcha' media men to secret service agents." More specifically, the story follows Palin as she defeats Levi Johnston, Joe McGinniss (the reporter who moved next door to Palin's home in Alaska so he could conduct research about her for an unauthorized book), and John Boehner, and competes against President Obama in a game of basketball.

Helfer, Andy (w), Stephen Thompson (a), and J. Scott Campbell (c). *Presidential Material: John McCain*. San Diego, CA: IDW Publishing (October 2008).

Maida, Jerome (w), Beniamino Bradi (a), and Deborah Max (c). *Political Power: Al Franken*. Vancouver, WA: Bluewater Comics (June 2010).

While the election of the first African American to the office of the president was truly an historic event, no senatorial election has been so bitterly contested in the past few decades as Al Franken's and Norm Coleman's competing campaigns to become one of Minnesota's senators. This edition of *Political Power* traces Franken's life from his work on *Saturday Night Live* to his eventual entry into politics and the political contest that was eventually decided by the Minnesota Supreme Court.

Mifsud-Gaines, Catherine (w), and Rick Parker (a). *Tales from the Crypt* #8. New York: Papercutz (October 2008).

Written by the daughter of William Gaines, the owner of EC Comics who created the *Tales from the Crypt* series, this issue uses the horror genre to mock the book-banning controversy that surrounded Sarah Palin after she was selected to be John McCain's running mate. Invoking her father's beloved trademark satire, Mifsud-Gaines' story avoids throwing its support behind either candidate by merely focusing on the problem of censorship.

Salamof, Paul (w), and Keith Tucker (a). Bo Obama: The White House Tails. Vancouver, WA: Bluewater Comics (February 2010).

Like most of you, I was overcome by a sense of disbelief when I first heard about this issue. It is, after all, a comic book about the president's dog. However, while this book is mostly an effort to further capitalize on all things associated with Obama, it is a unique tool to get young children interested in history and the White House. Told from Bo's perspective, this comic looks at previous presidential pets and provides an examination of the White House. So is this book ridiculous? Yes, but it can still be used as a tool to get children interested in presidential history.

Wey (w), and Jonathan Rector (a). *Political Power: Joe Biden*. Vancouver, WA: Bluewater Comics (October 2009).

# About the Contributors

Rauf **Arif** is a Fulbright scholar teaching at the University of Iowa. He has a print and broadcast media background and has published in major newspapers in Pakistan. His vivid political observations on U.S.–Pakistan relations have appeared in the local U.S. media. He is pursuing a doctoral degree in the political communication side of mass communication as a basis for working as an analyst in U.S.–Pakistan relations.

Jenny **Banh** is an anthropology Ph.D. candidate at the University of California, Riverside. She received a B.A. in anthropology at University of California, Los Angeles, and her M.A. in cultural studies at Claremont Graduate University. Banh has been an adjunct professor for nine years, mainly in social science and humanities classes, within the local Southern California college system.

Shelley E. **Barba** is a meta-data librarian at Texas Tech University. She often gives presentations at library conferences on the many uses of meta-data in libraries and research ventures and her work has appeared in the *Texas Library Journal*. She lives in Lubbock.

John T. "Jack" **Becker** is an associate librarian at Texas Tech University Libraries. He earned master's degrees in library science and American history. His areas of interest are the history of the west, West Texas, New Mexico, and the Civil War. When President Obama decided to speak to the nation's schoolchildren in 2009, Becker was amazed at the storm of protest this simple act created, whipped up mainly by talk radio programs.

Derrais **Carter** is an American studies doctoral student at the University of Iowa. His research examines 20th-century black masculinity. He is also interested in the history of black popular music, with an emphasis on sampling in hip-hop culture. His previous publications include "This Is What a Feminist Looks Like" in *Men Speak Out: Views on Gender, Sex, and Power* (Taylor & Francis, 2007), and "Blackness, Animation, and the Politics of Black Fatherhood in *The Cleveland Show*," in the *Journal of African American Studies*.

James **Carviou** is a Ph.D. candidate at the University of Iowa in the School of Journalism and Mass Communication and serves on the board for the *Journal of Communication Inquiry*. His research focuses on the influence of popular media in constructing norms of masculinity and its role in fostering identity and perception in mainstream society.

Travis L. **Gosa** is an assistant professor of social science at Cornell University. He received a Ph.D. in sociology from Johns Hopkins University in 2008. His research examines the social worlds of African American youth, new racial politics, music, and digital inequality and he is writing a book on hip hop culture and the black-white achievement gap.

Robert E. **Gutsche**, Jr., is a Ph.D. candidate in mass communications in the School of Journalism and Mass Communication at the University of Iowa. He is now an assistant professor at Florida International University. As a journalist, his work has appeared in the *Chicago Tribune*, the *Washington Post*, the *New York Times*, *Newsday*, the *Wisconsin State Journal*, the *Milwaukee Journal Sentinel*, and other publications. His research focuses on social and cultural meanings of news, the sociology of news work, and visual representations in the news.

Yuya **Kiuchi** received a Ph.D. in American studies from Michigan State University. He is an assistant professor in the Department of Writing, Rhetoric, and American Cultures at Michigan State University. His research interests include post-bellum African American culture and history, use of media for social change and community empowerment, history of memory production and consumption, and identity formation through media use and content production.

Angela **Nelson** is an associate professor in the Department of Popular Culture at Bowling Green State University. She has edited *"This Is How We Flow": Rhythm in Black Cultures* (University of South Carolina Press, 1999) and co-edited *Popular Culture Theory and Methodology* (University of Wisconsin Press, 2006) with Harold E. Hinds, Jr., and Marilyn F. Motz. Her teaching and research focuses on black popular culture, including popular and religious music and representations of African Americans in comic art and television.

Patrick B. **Oray** is a Ph.D. candidate in American studies at the University of Iowa. His intellectual interests include the history of race, ethnicity, and immigration in the U.S., the study of comparative black identities, and the relationship between media and power in the public sphere. He was born in Montreal and raised in Chicago.

Zafer **Parlak** is an assistant professor in the Department of American Culture and Literature, Izmir University, Izmir, Turkey. He received a B.A. from Bogazici University, and M.A. and Ph.D. degrees at Ege University. He also received a B.Ec. from Anatolian University, and an M.Ed. from Beykent University. His areas of interest include U.S. foreign and diplomatic history, Turkish-American relations, and the U.S. Peace Corps in Turkey.

Erika **Schneider** received a Ph.D. in art history from Tyler School of Art at Temple University, an M.A. in art history from Boston University and a B.A. in

French and art history from Mount Holyoke College. She teaches art history survey, modern and contemporary art history as well as museum studies at Framingham State College.

Etse **Sikanku** is a doctoral candidate at the University of Iowa specializing in media representations, new media, and political and international communication. His new media interests cover systematic agenda-setting investigations among online publications and other news mediums. His work has been published in the *International Communications Research Journal* and the *Journal of Black Studies*.

Caroline A. **Streeter** is an associate professor of English and African American studies at UCLA, where she teaches interdisciplinary courses incorporating literature, film and multimedia. She publishes and lectures widely about mixed-race identity in America. Her book *Tragic No More: Gender, Mixed Race, and Celebrity in American Culture* is forthcoming from the University of Massachusetts Press.

Tanfer Emin **Tunc** is an assistant professor in the Department of American Culture and Literature at Hacettepe University, Ankara, Turkey. She received B.A., M.A. and Ph.D. degrees in American history, and an advanced graduate certificate in women's studies from the State University of New York at Stony Brook. She specializes in women's history and literature, gender and sexuality, and American ethnic history/literature.

Justin S. **Vaughn** is an assistant professor of political science at Boise State University. He earned a Ph.D. in political science at Texas A&M University and is a member of the Executive Council of the Presidency Research Section of the American Political Science Association. His research focuses on the role popular culture plays in shaping the presidential image, management theory as applied to the inner workings of the White House, and how presidents strategically utilize bipartisan rhetoric.

Robert G. **Weiner** is an associate humanities librarian at Texas Tech University and librarian for art and sequential art. He is the author of *Marvel Graphic Novels: An Annotated Guide* (2008) and editor of *Captain American and the Struggle of the Superhero* (2009) and *Graphic Novels in Libraries and Archives* (2010, all with McFarland). He teaches a course on the presidents in film and popular culture for the Osher Lifelong Learning Institute at Texas Tech University.

Nicholas A. **Yanes** is a graduate student in the University of Iowa's Department of American Studies. His academic interests are contemporary popular culture and early U.S. culture. He studies comic books, video games, the complicated relationships between corporate interests and mass production, and the development of the military industry. His dissertation examines the roles William Gaines, EC Comics and *MAD* magazine played in shaping audiences in the 20th century.

# Index

Afghanistan 119, 129, 134, 218, 221, 224
African Americans 10, 19, 20, 32, 35, 39, 54, 64–69, 72, 74–77, 88, 90, 129, 139, 145, 171, 173, 175, 176, 180, 186, 252
*American Idol* 135–136
*American Progress* 32–35
"American Stories, American Solutions" 187, 240
Antarctic Press 246, 248
*The Apprentice* 136
Arif, Rauf 3, 133, 251
*Audacity of Hope* 17, 27, 88, 22
*Avengers* 128, 246

Banh, Jenny 2, 63, 251
*Barack the Barbarian* 3, 115, 128–130, 246
Barba, Shelley E. 3, 113, 237, 248, 251
Barely Political 189, 192
Barthes, Roland 29–31, 34–35
baseball 138
*Batman* 118, 124, 128, 129
Becker, John 3, 151, 251
Behar, Joy 241
Benjamin, Walter 64
Berkowitz, Daniel 3, 184
Bluewater Productions 247, 248, 249
Bollore, Vincent 233
*Boston Legal* 2, 63–80
brainiac 137
branding 1, 2, 4, 7, 28, 29, 31, 36, 38–41, 59, 177, 178, 187, 192, 193, 197, 198, 200, 202, 205, 223, 224
Bush, George H.W. 114, 129, 151, 155
Bush, George W. 4, 22, 52, 69, 104, 114, 119, 123, 129, 133, 134, 137, 138, 162, 185, 187, 213–227, 232, 233, 239, 243
Bush, Laura 161, 162

C-SPAN 151
Captain America 114, 121, 129, 246, 253
Carter, Derrais 1, 3, 184, 251
Carter, Jimmy 50, 78, 114, 129

Carviou, James 3–4, 133, 189, 251
CBS 135, 241
celebrity 9, 10, 107, 108, 134, 138, 242, 253
Chappelle, Dave 51–53, 60
Cheney, Dick 219, 220, 239
Chicago, Illinois 10, 20, 21, 23, 34, 39, 49, 90, 143, 161, 173, 197, 246, 247, 252
Chisholm, Shirley 139
Christianity 50, 65, 143, 174, 240
Civil Rights 16, 19, 38, 48, 66, 134, 178
citizens: African American 11, 23, 52, 60, 65, 66, 90, 93; French 4, 232, 233; global 21–24; Japanese 210; Turkish 216; United States 11, 16, 58, 125, 153, 161, 164, 174, 243
*The Cleveland Show* 237, 251
Clinton, Hillary 10, 39, 135, 139, 140, 171, 172, 205, 227, 246, 248
Clinton, William (Bill) 114, 119, 129, 155, 157, 213, 217
CNN 71, 79, 91, 158, 159, 198, 199, 200, 202
Colbert, Stephen 86, 238, 239, 242, 244
*The Colbert Report* 86, 238, 239
collective memory 3, 133, 134, 135, 136, 140, 141, 142, 147
comic book 1, 3, 80, 111, 113–125
Compagnon, Sebastian 4, 231–235
*Conan the Barbarian* 116, 128, 129
Confederacy 169, 170

*The Daily Show* 171, 186
DC Comics 118, 125, 128, 247
*Deep Impact* 46, 56–57, 60
Democratic National Convention 35, 90, 98, 100, 101, 167, 171, 174, 178
Democratic Party 10, 140, 169, 246
Department of Education 151, 152–154, 158
Department of Homeland Security 180
Devil's Due Publishing 129, 246, 247
Dole, Elizabeth 139
*Dreams from My Father* 17, 22

255

Duncan, Arne 153, 154
Dunham, Ann (Obama's mother) 173

*E pluribus unum* 16, 19, 80
EC Comics 249, 253
Edwards, John 144, 146
Erdoğan, Recep Tayyip (prime minister of Turkey) 215, 225, 226
Ettinger, Amber Lee ("Obama Girl") 3, 87, 172, 177, 178, 189–193
exceptionalism 22, 33

Facebook 10, 39, 40, 155, 157, 185, 191, 225, 234, 240
Fairey, Shepard 2, 34, 35, 37, 69, 97–108
*Family Guy* 237
femininity 137, 139
Ferraro, Geraldine 139
food 13, 14, 89, 202, 205, 232
food stamps 52
Ford, Harold, Jr. 168, 178–180
FOX 58, 135
Fox News 66, 168, 180, 241
France 4, 14, 31, 35, 105, 122, 134, 137, 138, 199, 202, 204, 231–235, 253
Freeman, Morgan 2, 45, 46, 47, 56, 57, 58, 60
frontier 33–35, 137, 142, 144
Fukui Prefecture, Japan ("City of Obama") 197, 198, 199, 201–209

Gadaffi, Muammar 17
Gaines, William 249, 253
*Generation X* 128
*G.I. Joe* 128
Gingrich, Newt 17, 161, 191
globalization 1, 9, 13, 14, 17, 21, 22, 217
Goffman, Erving 138–142
Gosa, Travis Lars 2, 85, 252
graffiti 2, 12, 18, 97, 100–105
Gutsche, Robert E., Jr. 3, 133, 184, 252

Hama, Larry 3–4, 128–130
*Hannah Montana* 237
Haysbert, Dennis 2, 45–47, 56, 58–61, 73
*Head of State* 46, 52, 54, 61
health care 12, 66, 72, 74, 78, 80, 89, 152, 157, 187, 241
Hilton, Paris 236
hip hop 2, 4, 14, 38, 53, 69, 85–86, 88–92, 94–95, 103–105
Honolulu, Hawaii 199, 203, 204
"Hope" 12, 37, 39, 88, 93, 99, 102, 133, 200

Howard Stern 192
Huckabee, Michael Dale "Mike" 143, 146
hybridity 19, 34–35, 38, 88

"I Got a Crush on Obama" 87, 172, 178, 189
identity 2, 10, 16–19, 21, 23, 36, 98–99, 133, 171, 180, 192, 206, 213, 247, 252; national 28–29, 31–36, 88, 167, 174–175, 234; racial and ethnic 2, 17–18, 20–21, 23, 88–89, 94, 173–175, 253
IDW Publishing 115, 247, 248
Image Comics 246, 247
Indonesia 16, 17, 21, 24, 173, 220
Internet 1, 10, 12, 13, 39, 40, 66, 87, 92, 100, 113, 115, 123, 135, 138, 152, 163, 164, 168, 172, 177, 178, 208, 219, 224, 235, 240, 245
interracial 3, 167–181
Iowa Caucus 171
Iran 218, 224, 226
Iraq 72, 98, 119, 123, 134, 147, 213, 216, 218–222

Japan 4, 13, 14, 197–210
Jay-Z 63, 70, 86, 89, 90
Jefferson, Thomas 163
*Jersey Shore* 135
Jesus Christ 143
"Jim Crow" 10, 87, 175
John Deere 144
Johnson, Charles 11
*Jon & Kate Plus Eight* 136
Jones, James Earl 2, 46, 48
journalism 17, 136, 138, 184, 231, 251, 252

Kansas 11, 16, 35, 80, 87, 167, 174
Kellner, Douglas 9, 10, 12
Kennedy, Edward 134
Kennedy, John F. (JFK) 11, 39, 55, 107, 108, 114, 129, 134, 148, 185–187, 213, 222, 239
Kennedy, Patrick 134
Kenya 11, 16–18, 20, 21, 23, 35, 80, 87, 167, 173, 180, 197, 203, 209, 217, 221
Kerry, John 104, 137, 138
Kibaki, Mwai 17
Ku Klux Klan (KKK) 68, 87, 93, 169
Kuichi, Yuya 4
Kurtzman, Harvey 129

Leno, Jay 123, 146
*Lepost.fr* 232
Lex Luthor 137

*The Life of Pope John Paul II* 130
Limbaugh, Rush 65, 78–80, 120, 157, 237
Lincoln, Abraham 4, 38, 102, 121, 185, 186
Louis, Joe 170, 171
*Loving v. Virginia* 176
Luo (Kenyan tribe) 16–18, 23

*MADtv* 172
Maher, Bill 242, 243
Marvel Comics 3, 69, 113–115, 117, 118, 119, 121–130, 246–248, 253
masculinity 3, 133–150, 170, 251, 252
McCain, Cindy 146, 147
McCain, John 45, 72, 104, 124, 140, 143, 145–148, 188, 233, 236, 240, 242, 246, 248, 249
Mickey Mouse 225
Middle East 49, 56, 92, 213, 216, 218, 219, 220, 221, 225
Mifsud-Gaines, Catherine 249
miscegenation 168, 176, 179, 180
*Le Monde* 232
"A More Perfect Union" (speech) 20–23, 36, 174, 234
movies 55, 119, 135, 220, 234, 246
MTV 1
Murphy, Eddie 51–53, 60
music 1, 13, 14, 47, 48, 69, 85–96, 105, 128, 172, 189, 214, 227, 245, 251, 252
Muslim 38, 66, 87, 93, 143, 163, 164, 168, 213–230, 234, 240
myth 2, 28–42, 85, 86, 94, 120, 136, 184

NAACP 162
*Nam* 128
NATO 216, 218
Nelson, Angela 1, 9
new media 3, 9, 10, 39, 40, 41, 134, 180, 189, 192, 253
newspapers 1, 3, 4, 12, 16, 19, 66, 77, 101, 120, 121, 152, 159, 161, 169, 199, 208, 213–215, 217, 219, 223–226, 231, 232, 251
*Newsweek* 134, 138, 141–143, 145–147, 177, 179
Nixon, Richard 108, 114, 125, 129, 213
Nobel Peace Prize 4, 226

Obama, Barack 3, 10, 12–14, 45, 47, 59, 64, 65, 71, 72, 77, 78, 80, 98, 108, 115, 117, 116, 118, 119, 124, 128, 135, 151, 152, 160, 164, 175, 198–203, 209, 210, 227, 231, 232, 237, 240–244, 246–248, 251
Obama, Malia 13, 177

Obama, Michelle 13, 23, 77, 115, 147, 160, 177, 181, 248
Obama, Sasha 13, 177
Obama Girls 200, 203
Obama-mania 4, 28, 41, 85, 92, 95, 124, 213–230, 236–244
*The Office* 237
Omizuokuri festival 201
"One-drop rule" 173, 175, 180
*The Onion* 56
Oray, Patrick B. 1, 2, 28–42, 252
O'Reilly, Bill 180

Palin, Sarah 135, 139, 140, 188, 197, 238, 240, 241, 248, 249
Parlak, Zafer 4, 213–230, 252
*People* 134, 138, 141, 144, 147
*Playboy* 179
*Plessy v. Ferguson* 175, 176
post-racialism 2–3, 11, 60, 63–65, 67–72, 74–75, 77, 79–80, 85–95
presidential election 2008, 28, 36, 45, 59, 61, 71, 85, 87, 115, 133, 134, 135, 138–140, 143, 147, 187, 188, 190, 191, 202, 209, 232, 245, 246, 248
Pryor, Richard 49–51, 53, 61

radio, talk radio 39, 53, 78, 91, 152–154, 157, 158, 161, 163, 164, 231, 237, 242, 251
Ramos, Jorge 171
Reagan, Ronald 49, 106, 114, 129, 151, 164, 213
reality television 136, 178
Relles, Ben 3, 4, 189–193
*Resident Evil* 219
Romney, Willard Mitt 145
Roosevelt, Franklin Delano (FDR) 114, 163, 164, 185
Russert, Tim 171, 172
Ryan, Nolan 138

Sarkozy, Nicolas 233, 234
*Saturday Night Live* (*SNL*) 114, 128, 130, 135, 172, 186, 240, 249
*Savage Dragon* 115, 246, 247
Scarlett O'Hara 170
September 11th, 2001 (9/11; 9–11) 93, 94, 138, 151, 162, 164, 168, 174, 218
Sikanku, Etse 1, 2, 16
slavery 10, 11, 20, 32, 36, 65, 87, 90, 92, 169, 170, 175
social media 185, 233, 234, 235, 240
social networking 9, 10, 39, 40, 154, 156, 157, 185, 191, 192, 234

The South  78, 161, 169, 170, 178
*South Park*  237
Southern (United States)  4, 50, 167, 170, 175, 179, 180, 251
Spears, Britney  236
Spider-Man  113–127, 129, 227, 237, 248
Stephanopoulos, George  171
Superman  114, 118, 125, 129, 137, 145, 227, 247
Supreme Court of the United States (SCOTUS)  59, 76, 155, 168, 175, 241, 249
*Survivor*  135, 136

Tea Party  5, 130, 163, 234
*Teen Mom*  135
television  1, 2, 12–14, 19, 39, 45, 47, 56, 59–61, 63, 64, 66, 69, 70, 73, 108, 113–115, 135, 136, 138, 146, 168, 169, 172, 178, 179, 184, 190, 198–200, 202, 204, 214, 215, 219, 223, 231, 233, 237, 239–242, 252
Texas  33, 56, 154–163, 202, 251, 253
*Time*  78, 134, 138, 141, 142, 144–146
TMZ.com  232
Tokyo  201, 203, 204, 208, 210
Tunc, Tanfer Emin  4, 213–230, 253
Turkey (Country)  4, 213–230, 252, 253
Turner, Frederick Jackson  34
*24* (TV Show)  45, 46, 56, 58–60, 73
Twitter  88, 92, 185, 191, 225, 240, 243

"ugly American"  214, 220, 227
Uncle Tom  90, 170

United States  1–5, 9–12, 16–17, 19, 22, 26, 28, 33, 35–36, 38, 47–49, 54, 63–67, 72, 74–76, 79, 86, 88, 125, 128, 135, 138, 141, 155, 157, 161–163, 167, 173–175, 198, 213–219, 221–222, 227, 231–233, 236, 238
University of Iowa  184, 231, 251, 252, 253

Vaughn, Justin S.  2, 45
Vietnam  128, 145, 213
*The View*  186, 241
viral  40, 87, 135, 162, 178, 180

Weiner, Robert  3 113–127, 237, 248, 253
Wells-Barnett, Ida B.  167, 169, 170, 180
White House  50, 55, 58, 89, 114, 124–125, 134, 138, 151, 153–154, 156–159, 210, 223, 225–227, 242, 243, 246, 249, 253
*Wife Swap*  136
*The Wizard of Oz*  174
Wolverine  128
*Wonder Woman*  122, 128
Wood, Wally  128
Wright, Rev. Jeremiah  20, 35, 38, 143

Yanes, Nicholas  1–4, 16–27, 128–130, 184–188, 231–235, 236–244, 253
YouTube  3, 10, 39, 40, 66, 88, 172, 178, 190–193, 234, 243

www.ingramcontent.com/pod-product-compliance
Ingram Content Group UK Ltd.
Pitfield, Milton Keynes, MK11 3LW, UK
UKHW041933140426
5217IPUK00014B/447